The
Renaissance

Other Books in the Turning Points Series:

Turning | Points
IN WORLD HISTORY

The Renaissance

Stephen P. Thompson, *Book Editor*

David L. Bender, *Publisher*
Bruno Leone, *Executive Editor*
Bonnie Szumski, *Editorial Director*
David M. Haugen, *Managing Editor*

Greenhaven Press, Inc., San Diego, California

Library of Congress Cataloging-in-Publication Data

The Renaissance / Stephen P. Thompson, book editor.
    p.   cm. — (Turning points in world history)
    Collection of previously published essays, articles, etc.
    Includes bibliographical references (p.   ) and index.
    ISBN 0-7377-0219-2 (alk. paper). — ISBN 0-7377-0218-4
(pbk. : alk. paper)
    1. Middle Ages—History. 2. Renaissance. I. Thompson,
Stephen P., 1953–   . II. Series: Turning points in world history
(Greenhaven Press)
DB200.R45 2000
940.1—dc21   99-34765
                                                                      CIP

Cover photo: Palazzo Cucale, Mantua, Italy/SuperStock

Printed in the U.S.A.

Contents

Chapter 3: Renaissance Discoveries and Transformations

ment stressed individual conscience and the reading of the Bible, and it deemphasized the authority of the church.

The Renaissance and Reformation shared a common historical viewpoint which saw values and ideals originating in the ancient world as superior to those of the present day. Humanists and reformers agreed that these ideals needed to be re-taught and re-established in Europe; important Reformers never abandoned these humanist perspectives and values.

Chapter 4: Achievements and Developments of the Later Renaissance

Though it shared the Italian focus on the ideas of ancient Greece and Rome, the Northern Renaissance was shaped by such additional forces as the printing press, the Reformation, and the more religious and satirical tone of Northern humanism, represented by such figures as Erasmus and Thomas More.

French and English literary achievement came of age during the sixteenth century, heavily influenced by both classical models and the writings of the Italian Renaissance. The essays of the Frenchman Montaigne, the poetry of the Englishmen Sidney and Spenser, and plays of Marlowe and Shakespeare are highlights of the Northern Renaissance.

Renaissance humanism did not encourage scientific endeavor, but the intellectual movement Neoplatonism and innovations in perspective and proportion by Renaissance artists contributed greatly to the new science. Three of the greatest Renaissance scientists, Copernicus, Kepler, and Galileo, were all influenced by these intellectual trends.

Chapter 5: The Significance of the Renaissance

Foreword

Certain past events stand out as pivotal, as having effects and outcomes that change the course of history. These events are often referred to as turning points. Historian Louis L. Snyder provides this useful definition:

> A turning point in history is an event, happening, or stage which thrusts the course of historical development into a different direction. By definition a turning point is a great event, but it is even more—a great event with the explosive impact of altering the trend of man's life on the planet.

History's turning points have taken many forms. Some were single, brief, and shattering events with immediate and obvious impact. The invasion of Britain by William the Conqueror in 1066, for example, swiftly transformed that land's political and social institutions and paved the way for the rise of the modern English nation. By contrast, other single events were deemed of minor significance when they occurred, only later recognized as turning points. The assassination of a little-known European nobleman, Archduke Franz Ferdinand, on June 28, 1914, in the Bosnian town of Sarajevo was such an event; only after it touched off a chain reaction of political-military crises that escalated into the global conflict known as World War I did the murder's true significance become evident.

Other crucial turning points occurred not in terms of a few hours, days, months, or even years, but instead as evolutionary developments spanning decades or even centuries. One of the most pivotal turning points in human history, for instance—the development of agriculture, which replaced nomadic hunter-gatherer societies with more permanent settlements—occurred over the course of many generations. Still other great turning points were neither events nor developments, but rather revolutionary new inventions and innovations that significantly altered social customs and ideas, military tactics, home life, the spread of knowledge, and the human condition in general. The developments of writing, gunpowder, the printing press, antibiotics, the electric light, atomic energy, television, and the computer, the last two of which have recently ushered in the world-altering information age, represent only some of these innovative turning points.

Each anthology in the Greenhaven Turning Points in World History series presents a group of essays chosen for their accessibility. The anthology's structure also enhances this accessibility. First, an introductory essay provides a general overview of the principal events and figures involved, placing the topic in its historical context. The essays that follow explore various aspects in more detail, some targeting political trends and consequences, others social, literary, cultural, and/or technological ramifications, and still others pivotal leaders and other influential figures. To aid the reader in choosing the material of immediate interest or need, each essay is introduced by a concise summary of the contributing writer's main themes and insights.

In addition, each volume contains extensive research tools, including a collection of excerpts from primary source documents pertaining to the historical events and figures under discussion. In the anthology on the French Revolution, for example, readers can examine the works of Rousseau, Voltaire, and other writers and thinkers whose championing of human rights helped fuel the French people's growing desire for liberty; the French *Declaration of the Rights of Man and Citizen*, presented to King Louis XVI by the French National Assembly on October 2, 1789; and eyewitness accounts of the attack on the royal palace and the horrors of the Reign of Terror. To guide students interested in pursuing further research on the subject, each volume features an extensive bibliography, which for easy access has been divided into separate sections by topic. Finally, a comprehensive index allows readers to scan and locate content efficiently. Each of the anthologies in the Greenhaven Turning Points in World History series provides students with a complete, detailed, and enlightening examination of a crucial historical watershed.

Introduction:
Living Up to the Past

The European phenomenon known as the Renaissance is perhaps best characterized as an intellectual and educational movement that originated in Italy in the later decades of the 1300s. It spread throughout Europe over the next two and a half centuries, culminating in the English Renaissance, which flourished into the early 1600s. The Italian humanists of the late fourteenth and early fifteenth centuries believed that the life of their society would be tremendously enhanced by a return to the values and ideals of ancient Rome and Greece. But the idea of refashioning one's society, its political and educational institutions, on the model of societies long since declined, presented vast uncertainties as well as possibilities. As British scholar Margaret Aston writes:

> The idea of Renaissance was itself dualistic, implying sleep and awakening, going down as well as coming up, darkness before light, losing before finding. It was necessary to excavate before it was possible to build anew, and to see again in a new light implied new eyes, or at least better vision. There was a great sense of exhilaration, and at the same time a nervousness in the challenge of living up to the past. "Now indeed, may every thoughtful spirit thank God that it has been permitted to him to be born in this new age." The words of the Florentine humanist Matteo Palmieri, in his book *On Civic Life*, written in the 1430s, were echoed by many others, inside and outside Italy.[1]

This optimistic view of human potential and the human capacity to reestablish the greatness of the classical past fostered a cultural climate in Italy conducive to such creative innovations as the poetry of Petrarch, the philosophy of Ficino, the art of Leonardo and Michelangelo, and much, much more.

Late Medieval Society

How did the Renaissance emerge from late medieval society? Europe in the early fourteenth century was profoundly pessimistic, judging by the focus on suffering and death in its artwork and writings. But perhaps its dark view of the human condition was understandable. Throughout the fourteenth century, Europe experienced horrible years of famine; northern Italy alone experienced three particularly severe famines between 1352 and 1375. In addition, this century saw the worst manifestations of the plague, such as the devastating outbreak of 1347. According to the best scholarly estimates, in just three years this advent of the plague killed between 25 and 30 percent of all Europeans. This precipitous decline in population profoundly affected the economic structure and everyday life of society, causing a shortage of workers and a severe economic depression. The psychological effect must have been devastating as well.

During these same years, however, the city-states of Italy, such as Venice and Florence, began to emerge as autonomous, prosperous political units, flourishing on the basis of industry and trade. Because Italy was located in the center of Mediterranean trade routes, these city-states emerged as centers of European trade and banking during the fourteenth century. As their profits increased, the wealthier merchants of Florence and other cities became patrons of the arts and culture. As Italian artists sought to compete in the greatness of their creations, they began to turn more and more to the classical monuments and architecture around them for inspiration. In addition, the demands of commerce called for educated businesspeople who could not only read and write, but also understand and write increasingly complex trade agreements and legal documents. Thus, educational reform in the Italian cities had a practical dimension, for it enabled the expanding core of Italian lawyers to both communicate effectively and understand the precedents of Roman law. To meet this perceived need, there arose a group of educators and scholars, called the humanists, who grounded their new educational system in the legacy of laws and literature of ancient Rome. And, in an age before the creation of public libraries, they began to actively research and collect the best ancient texts they could find for their purposes.

Renaissance Humanism

The ideas we associate most fundamentally with the Renaissance, then, emerged in Italy during the second half of the fourteenth century. In alliance with the agenda of commercial interests, scholars such as Francesco Petrarch (1304–1374) began to promote the recovery of ancient texts as a way of restoring the legacy of Italians, the greatness of their past civilization. From the great Roman statesman and philosopher Cicero, Petrarch borrowed the idea of the liberal arts, or *studia humanitatis*, which focused on grammar, rhetoric, poetry, history, and moral philosophy. The humanists emphasized rhetoric and eloquence in place of the logic that had come to dominate the scholastic philosophy in medieval universities. In the decades after Petrarch's death, Italian humanists continued to advance his agenda, especially the ability to read, write, and speak classical Latin as the centerpiece of the new educational model.

Many of these humanist scholars came to believe that their revival of classical values and standards would lead to a new golden age of culture for the Italian city-states. As noted British scholar Peter Burke suggests:

> To understand the significance of the revival of classical form in architecture, say, or in the drama, or the enthusiasm for the discovery and editing of ancient manuscripts, we need to view them as portions of a far more ambitious enterprise. It was nothing less than the restoration to life of ancient Rome. . . . Like the ancients, many humanists believed in a cyclical interpretation of history, according to which one age could be a kind of recurrence or re-run of an earlier one. Some of them thought that they and their fellow-citizens could become "new Romans," in the sense of speaking like Romans, writing like them, and emulating their achievements, from the Colosseum and the *Aenied* to the Roman Empire itself.[2]

A New View of History

The leading premises of the Renaissance were based on this radical new perspective about history, the idea that ancient Rome and Greece were profoundly accomplished cultures that had flourished and then declined. Further, the centuries since the decline of Rome constituted a dark age for learning, a time when all the wisdom and lessons of the ancient world were forgotten. And, in the humanist view, the present age constituted a new era in which classical wisdom and glory could be revived. This radical view was, of course, rather exaggerated, for important legacies of the ancient world were still very much in evidence, such as the extensive philosophical reliance on the Greek philosopher Aristotle in medieval universities. The project of the Italian humanists, though, was to recover the lost wisdom, art, and culture of the ancient world, to emulate it, and to reconstruct their present culture along classical lines.

The power of this open and optimistic worldview was undeniable, and it exerted influence over Europe for several centuries. As scholar Donald R. Kelley says:

> To Petrarch and his followers, nothing that was human (and little that was divine) was foreign. Curiosity, nostalgia, and an attitude of tolerance would lead to a deeper understanding of the past and a willingness to extend such understanding beyond the boundaries of Christendom. What resulted was a transformation not only of knowledge but also of values and assumptions about the human condition.[3]

Through their research, the Italian humanists established important principles about the study of ancient languages, a science that was called philology, and later modern linguistics. They also succeeded in recovering a treasure trove of classical literature, including important forgotten works by the Roman statesman Cicero and by the Greek philosopher Plato.

Perhaps the most important contribution of Italian humanism to the larger culture of Europe was its promotion of the study of the language of ancient Rome, Latin, as the center of the new educational paradigm. This principle was adopted by northern humanists as well, leading to more extensive cultural unification and cross-currents than had been known before, lasting over several centuries. In fact, the most notable continuity between the Renaissance in early fifteenth-century Italy and the Renaissance two hundred years later in England is the prominence of the classical Latin language in the political and educational spheres of both societies. For example, the influential treatise *The Courtier* by Castiglione was translated from Italian into English in 1561 and went through two more editions by the time of Queen Elizabeth's death in 1603. But during that same period in England, the translation of *The Courtier* from Italian into Latin went through five editions. In other words, *The Courtier* was read more often by educated English readers in Latin than in English. This shows how pervasive the knowledge of classical Latin was in the sixteenth century and how it served as a common language among educated Europeans. As late as the 1640s, the English poet John Milton served the government as Latin secretary, a cabinet-level post, since all diplomatic correspondence between European governments took place in Latin.

The High Renaissance in Italy

When looking at the artistic achievements of the High Renaissance period in Italy—roughly 1490 to 1525—it is easy to conclude that the Renaissance was a time of great genius. The art produced during these years by Leonardo da Vinci, Raphael, and Michelangelo is still familiar in the modern world. When people use the somewhat archaic expression "Renaissance man" to mean someone who is accomplished in a variety of endeavors, they often have in mind such figures as Leonardo and Michelangelo. Both men aspired to know their subjects better than anyone who had gone before. Leonardo's passions included engineering, painting, sculpture, writing, designing, and the imaginative inventing found in his notebooks. Michelangelo was an architect, engineer, painter, sculptor, and passionate poet. Both artists were compulsive, driven personalities, fragmented by their diverse interests and their passion to create, but both are a testament to the power of creative genius unleashed by the Renaissance.

An Expansion of Horizons

A number of important innovations and discoveries in the fifteenth and sixteenth centuries made it impossible for Europeans to live as their ancestors had lived. The most important of these occurred near the end of the Italian Renaissance and just before the achievements of the northern Renaissance. Foremost among these transformations was Christopher Columbus's discovery of the New World, along with subsequent voyages of discovery by a host of Europeans. The idea that the geography of the planet was not what it had been assumed to be for centuries was both humbling and exhilarating in its sense of new possibilities. A second radical innovation during these years was the invention of the movable type printing press around 1450. Decade by decade this printing press spread across Europe, churning out edition after edition of the Bible, classical texts, almanacs, and later, just about anything people would buy. Within the fifty years following Johannes Gutenberg's invention, there were fifty-one printing presses in Germany and seventy-three in Italy. Both classical humanists and Protestant reformers hailed the printing press as essentially an endorsement from heaven. The leading French humanist Guillaume Budé virtually equated the Renaissance movement with the "miracle" of printing: "The invention of printing is the restitution and perpetuation of antiquity."[4] The limits and boundaries of education were exploded, for books became much cheaper and much more widely available than ever before.

The beginnings of scientific thought that would later become the Scientific Revolution began to gain acceptance during the later Renaissance. Also called the Copernican Revolution, the theory of a sun-centered universe was initiated by Copernicus and furthered by such figures as Kepler and Galileo. Again, if such ancient truths as the belief that the earth was the center of the universe could be shown to be inaccurate, what other new visions and revisions of accepted truth were possible? A fourth source of radical change in the heart of the Renaissance period was the Protestant Reformation, which called into question many of the traditions and assumptions of the Catholic Church, as well as the proper relationship of Christians to the authority of the church.

The Reformation of the Church

Medieval Christians lived in the shadow of the church. From the cradle to the grave, from infant baptism to extreme unction, from event to event on the church calendar, the lives of ordinary Christians were profoundly shaped by the rituals and traditions of the medieval Catholic Church.

The Reformation originated in Germany in 1517 and spread into northern Europe over the next forty years. The movement began as a protest, led by German professor Martin Luther, against abuses in the Roman Catholic Church, but it soon was identified by the various Protestant churches that separated from Rome, developing their own doctrine and church procedures, many of which led to an emphasis on the individual believer's conscience over the authority of the church itself. By 1600 Protestantism dominated in England along with most of Germany and the Scandinavian countries. After being torn by war between the two factions, France reverted to Catholicism, while Spain and Italy remained Catholic throughout the period. The Reformation was immensely influential on the lives and beliefs of ordinary Christians throughout Europe.

The Reformation was itself influenced in the beginning by the work of the great Renaissance humanists, such as the Dutch scholar Erasmus, who strove to recover the actual meaning of ancient texts—including the Bible—and to make accurate translations of them. One humanist slogan was *ad fontes*, that is, back to the original sources. Protestants embraced this overall project and expanded it to include a return to the original rituals, sacraments, and traditions of the first Christians, as distinct from the layers of tradition grown up around the Roman Catholic Church. Protestants also endorsed the fundamental emphasis of Renaissance humanism on the reform of educational systems to include study of the ancient languages, as well as the humanist effort to expand educational opportunity. Further, the Protestants pushed for the translation of the Bible into the vernacular languages of each European country. Martin Luther's oft-stated desire was that even the lowly ploughboy should be able to read the Bible for himself in his own language. This Protestant emphasis on education and vernacular languages contributed mightily to the greatness of the later literary Renaissance in northern Europe, especially in France and England during the sixteenth and early seventeenth centuries.

The Darker Side of the Renaissance

Although the arts and sciences flourished during the Renaissance, life was still brutish and short for most people. Poverty was widespread in every European country. Outbreaks of the plague continued to haunt Europe from the fourteenth through the seventeenth centuries, decimating large areas, including half the population of some cities. Wealthier people tended to leave the cities for the countryside during outbreaks of the plague. For those who had no country home, the responses were less than rational. As scholar De Lamar Jensen observes:

> Every known method of prevention was employed to combat the disease, from ringing bells, shooting firearms, and playing loud music, to burning goat horns, absorbing the poisons with live birds and spiders, and wearing strange amulets made of "unicorn horn" or exotic stones, or hazelnut shells filled with mercury, or the head of a toad held next to the body. The omnipresence of this dreaded pestilence brought an awareness of death to Renaissance life and provided a grim paradox to the age of "rebirth."[5]

The failure to combat the plague, which was spread by rats, starkly reveals the weaknesses in Renaissance science, the failure to grasp the basics of sanitation, and the widespread prevalence of superstition in the face of the unknown.

Another irrational Renaissance response to the unknown was the widespread persecution of witches throughout Europe during the latter half of the Renaissance. Scholars estimate that during the sixteenth and seventeenth centuries thousands of people—the vast majority of them women—

were executed for the crime of witchcraft. Modern scholars still wrestle with explanations for this phenomenon. Some have pointed to the intellectual climate as the key factor. One popular book, the *Malleus malefaciarium*, or *The Witches' Hammer*, written by two Dominican monks in 1486, presents a web of superstition and misogynistic prejudices as fact, claiming that the root cause of witchcraft is "carnal lust" in women. Scholars have also examined the role of famine, economic upheaval, war, and transience as factors in the persecution of witches, arguing that accusations of witchcraft were a kind of "scapegoating," a way of assigning blame for uncontrollable misfortune. Certainly stereotypical prejudices about women played a role in this as well. It is part of the paradox of the Renaissance that an age capable of such artistic and cultural accomplishments, with its emphasis on the value of the individual, was also capable of such sustained superstition and cruelty.

Renaissance Aspiration

The optimistic Renaissance attitude about human potential and creativity can be summed up in the concept of aspiration, which is the desire to go beyond what has been known before, what has been done before, to go beyond in all human endeavors. It began as an attempt to imitate and emulate the great works of Greece and Rome, but it evolved into the attempt to surpass even the ancients. The British poet and playwright Ben Jonson had this in mind about Shakespeare when he wrote that Shakespeare's only equals in tragedy were the greatest Greek and Roman tragedians, and that in writing comedies, he surpassed "all that insolent Greece or haughty Rome sent forth, or since did from their ashes come."[6] High praise indeed from a rival playwright!

The explorers searching the seas, the scientists searching the heavens, the scholars searching ancient cultures, and the religious reformers searching for authentic models unadulterated by tradition—all were involved in the quest for what had been previously hidden and unknown. If a whole new continent had existed all these centuries unknown to Europeans, what other secrets and mysteries could be uncovered?

Writers began to imagine the world in whole new ways. In his *Utopia*, for example, Thomas More wrote of a society with radically different political institutions and social arrangements than those prevailing in sixteenth-century Europe. He dared to depict a society that was not dependent on the seemingly timeless institutions of kingship and the Catholic Church, but rather founded on human reason, a society reminiscent of Plato's ideal in *The Republic*.

But it was often recognized that aspiration, the attitude that human beings can uncover all mysteries and solve all problems, bordered on hubris, or excessive pride, and that unchecked aspiration for anything had its attendant dangers. After all, Renaissance writers were quite familiar with the story of the fall of Lucifer, who aspired to power, and the story of Adam and Eve, who aspired to the forbidden knowledge of good and evil. The story of Icarus, who made waxen wings to fly to the heavens but crashed when he flew too close to the sun, was a well-known classical version of the dangers of aspiration.

The Renaissance play *Doctor Faustus* by Christopher Marlowe dramatizes vividly the dangers of unbridled Renaissance aspiration, in this case the search for the power of secret knowledge. The character of Faustus achieves advanced scholarly degrees in medicine, law, theology, and philosophy, but remains unsatisfied. His profound academic knowledge has made him skeptical of conventional religion. "Come, I think hell's a fable," he says at one point. He turns to magic, selling his soul for the promise of hidden knowledge. In Marlowe's version of the story, Faustus suffers from self-deception and gains only illusory powers, powers on the level of a parlor magician. For his bargain, Faustus achieves only lasting damnation, for the Renaissance world depicted in the play is still governed fundamentally by the Christian scheme of salvation.

The Renaissance in Northern Europe

The Renaissance reached northern Europe relatively late. One obvious reason for this was the Hundred Years' War between England and France, which preoccupied those countries from 1337 to 1453. Overlapping this conflict was the civil war in England called the Wars of the Roses, which finally concluded in 1485, the same year as the establishment of the first printing press in England. In addition, no scholars stepped forward to reform the English educational system until around 1500. This reform effort, in combination with the new availability of the writings of the Renaissance Italian humanists, comprised the early stages of the Renaissance in England.

Adding further to the development of the northern Renaissance was the establishment of the important Aldine Press in Switzerland in the 1480s. In its first twenty-five years of operation, this press made widely available 126 editions of classical texts that had previously existed only in manuscript form, including all the major Greek authors. Thus the great Latin and Greek texts became available for study in the universities of northern Europe to an extent undreamed of in the early stages of the Italian Renaissance. The educational system in England was not fully reformed to focus on classical languages until the mid–sixteenth century. But once the new system was in place, such pupils as the shoemaker's son, Kit Marlowe, the bricklayer's son, Ben Jonson, and the glove-maker's son, Will Shakespeare, could attain a deep and wide-ranging familiarity with classical culture unknown before that time.

The educational curriculum at Shakespeare's grammar school in Stratford provides a window into the long-lasting, powerful ideal of a classical education. Shakespeare's main years of education were the decade of the 1570s, from ages six to sixteen. During those ten years, Shakespeare, along with all the other middle-class sons of Stratford, studied ten hours a day, six days a week, under their university-educated teacher. The vast majority of each day's study was Latin grammar and literature; in fact, in the upper forms the boys were required to speak only Latin, and were censured for speaking English in the classroom.[7] There are suggestions in Shakespeare's plays that such a system was a dreary and unsatisfying way to go through boyhood. Yet the evidence of Shakespeare's classical education is everywhere in his plays, from his early borrowings from the Roman playwrights Plautus and Seneca, to the inspiration of the poetry of the Roman poet Ovid, to his reliance on the historian and philosopher Plutarch in the creation of his plays *Julius Caesar*, *Antony and Cleopatra*, and others.

Thus, the later Renaissance in northern Europe, especially in England, was immersed in the study of the classics, yet it was influenced by other intellectual forces as well. The northern Renaissance shared with the Italian Renaissance a passionate love of classical Greece and Rome; in this regard, Plato and Cicero were just as influential in England and France as they were in Italy. The northern Renaissance, though, was shaped by additional factors such as the availability of the full range of great Italian Renaissance writers, from Petrarch and Pico to Castiglione and Machiavelli. The northern Renaissance also took shape during and after the Reformation, a movement that forged a new kind of self-consciousness among many Europeans. The questions and issues raised by the Reformation challenged many northern Europeans to take a hard look at their faith, to try to decide what they personally believed. The reading public in newly Protestant countries had an insatiable desire to understand the implications of their new faith. Thus more than half of all books printed in England during the sixteenth century were on religious topics.

During Shakespeare's lifetime, from 1564 to 1616, for example, the most popular writers in England were three Protestant writers: Henry Smith, William Perkins, and the French Protestant leader John Calvin. The works of these writers were widely read and discussed, demonstrating the concern of English Protestants with issues of salvation and Christian values now that Protestant principles and churches had supplanted Catholicism in England. The comfortable coexistence of Renaissance and Reformation culture in England may be illustrated by the endeavors of the famous British translator Arthur Golding, who provided England with the best translations of the Roman writers Ovid and Seneca, among others. Golding also translated the complete sermons of Calvin into English, an undertaking that took more years than all of his classical translations together.

But perhaps the most important legacy of the Reformation on English literature may be the emphasis on the introspective conscience and the corresponding sense of individual personality achieved in much of northern European literature. Certainly introspection was central to the extremely influential love poetry of Petrarch, and it was also the hallmark of the great French essayist Montaigne. Yet the English experience took the interior consciousness of dramatic character to new depths, as in the tormented anguish of Faustus, the guilty conscience of Macbeth, and the haunted soliloquies of Hamlet. In this regard, English Renaissance writers provided some of the most lasting achievements of the Renaissance, works of literature that are both enjoyed and studied to this day.

Notes

1. Margaret Aston, *The Panorama of the Renaissance*. New York: Henry N. Abrams, 1996, p. 11.

2. Peter Burke, *The Renaissance*. 2nd ed., New York: St. Martin's, 1997, pp. 16–17.

3. Donald R. Kelley, *Renaissance Humanism*. Boston: Twayne, 1991, p. 28.

4. Quoted in Kelley, *Renaissance Humanism*, p. 32.

5. De Lamar Jensen, *Renaissance Europe*. Lexington, MA: D.C. Heath, 1981, p. 95.

6. Ben Jonson, "To the Memory of . . . William Shakespeare," in *Ben Jonson and the Cavalier Poets*, ed. Hugh Maclean. New York: W.W. Norton, 1974, pp. 86–87.

7. Cf. Samuel Schoenbaum, *William Shakespeare: A Compact Documentary Life*. New York: Oxford University Press, 1977, pp. 62–72.

Chapter 1

The Origins of the Renaissance

Turning|Points

IN WORLD HISTORY

Culture and Education in the Italian City-States

John R. Hale

According to scholar John R. Hale, the origins of the Renaissance may in part be traced to the rise of the Italian
city-states, whose prosperity and political independence
stimulated a range of cultural endeavors. Thriving busi-
nesses required educated workers to carry out complicated legal and business transactions; this in turn stimulated the educational system which drew on the lessons
and wisdom of ancient Rome and Greece.

The important development that we call the Renaissance actually began in Italy in the waning years of the Middle Ages,
about 1300 A.D. Giotto, the most revolutionary painter of
his day, was then 33; Dante, author of the *Divine Comedy*, 35.
By the middle of the 14th Century, the Renaissance had become a distinct and recognizable cultural movement. Over
the course of the next 200 years—until the sack of Rome [in
1527] by the soldiers of Charles V, ruler of the Germanic
empire beyond the Alps—the world as Dante and Giotto
saw it was transformed. Men and nature were treated not as
generalizations of themselves, but as individual beings and
things, interesting for their own sake. . . .

A New Age

It was Renaissance Italians who invented the term "Dark
Ages." They looked back on the barbarian invasion of Rome
[in 410 A.D.] as the drawing down of a coarse blind, and on
the intervening 10 centuries as a period of trance. It was, to
them, both a joy and a duty to force the blind up again, to

breathe life into the literature, the monuments and the values that had made Rome great.

To this task they brought a growing spirit of confidence, strengthened by the existence of men of genius in every branch of art and learning. There were poets and scholars like Petrarch and Boccaccio, sculptors like Donatello, architects like Brunelleschi, painters like Masaccio—to pick out only a few. No wonder Matteo Palmieri, writing in the mid-15th Century, could joyfully exhort his fellow man to "thank God that it has been permitted to him to be born in this new age, so full of hope and promise, which already rejoices in a greater array of nobly-gifted souls than the world has seen in the thousand years that have preceded it." No wonder the Renaissance architect Antonio Filarete could characterize the Middle Ages as a crude era, one in which "learning was lacking in Italy, people became vulgar in speech and ignorant of Latin," and observe that it was only 50 or 60 years before his own time "that men's minds were sharpened and awakened."

The learning that Filarete was referring to was a secular learning. In contrast to the largely theological studies of the Middle Ages, it was based on an avid study of classical authors. To go forward it was necessary to go back; to advance from the Middle Ages it was necessary to return to antiquity and relearn the lessons which had enabled Rome to produce her great civilization. Medieval scholars had known about men like Virgil, Ovid and Cicero, Aristotle and Plato; but not until the 14th Century, and then only in Italy, was an attempt made to see the whole classical world as a culture in its own right. The study of this culture came to be called humanism. And humanists were concerned not only with discovering and editing Greek and Roman books, but with sorting out those elements in ancient thought which could help men live better, more responsible lives. They turned to Rome not only for instruction about law, politics and the arts, but even for moral guidance.

The Italian City-States

The key to understanding this fascination with antiquity lies in the economic and political life of the Italian states—"Ital-

ian states" rather than "Italy" because the dissolution of the
Roman Empire had also dissolved the peninsula's political
unity. Northern Italy became part of the old Empire's young
successor, the German-centered, German-governed Holy
Roman Empire. Central Italy was dominated by the political
power of the papacy. A branch of the French dynastic house
of Anjou ruled southern Italy as the Kingdom of Naples. But
even these divisions were not cohesive within themselves. In
the north, the city-states of Venice and Milan went their
own way, independent of the Germanic emperors. In the
center, important towns like Bologna were largely free from
papal influence. And from the late 13th Century onward
there was constant rivalry between the Kingdom of Naples
and various Sicilian cities and towns controlled by the Spanish house of Aragon.

Until the beginning of the 14th Century, none of these
individual political units was sufficiently autonomous or
prosperous to produce a vigorous culture of its own. Then,
in the comparatively brief period of a few decades, autonomy
was achieved in a series of crises. . . .

By this time the larger Italian cities were thrivingly prosperous. Italy as a whole had the immense advantage of being
situated right in the heart of the greatest trading area in the
medieval and Renaissance world, the Mediterranean basin.
Coastal towns like Genoa and Venice had unique opportunities, and took them. In addition, many of the goods imported by sea were redistributed by land, bringing prosperity to towns like Florence, whose location made it a hub for
such traffic, or like Milan, which became a way station for
transalpine export into the heart of Europe.

This precocious economic development produced a
power structure that was peculiarly Italian. Instead of being
centered in the great landed estate, as elsewhere in Europe,
power was centered in the town. Beginning in the 12th Century, the feudal lords of the Italian countryside had been
forced to become citizens of the nearest town. Only by
doing so could they share in its prosperity and retain some
semblance of political influence over its government. By the
late 13th Century this urbanization of power was complete.

Florence had risen to such an impressive combination of wealth and social coherence that it could challenge a Pope. When Boniface VIII demanded that the Florentine government reverse a sentence that displeased him, Florence replied that he had no business interfering in "the policies and decisions of the Florentine commune."

Investing in Culture

By the 14th Century, through the accumulating profits of trade and industry, Italian cities had become lavish patrons of the arts. Florence, for example, had begun to build its vast cathedral, Santa Maria del Fiore. Not even a period of depression, aggravated by the Black Death—the terrible plague that devastated Europe in the middle of the 14th Century—failed to stem the flow of patronage. When profits fell, Italian merchants and bankers learned to become more efficient in their business methods. It was Italians who pioneered much of what later became standard capitalist practice: partnership agreements, holding companies, marine insurance, credit transfers, double-entry bookkeeping. And, as the depression deepened, Italian businessmen invested in culture for its permanence of value, much as anxious businessmen buy fashionable art today.

Wealth, however, cannot buy culture, it can only buy its works. Culture is nourished by money, but its nucleus is a wider exposure to learning. During the Renaissance, to get rich and to stay rich required a relatively high standard of education. First and foremost, this education was utilitarian: a man could not be successful in commerce and industry without knowing how to read and write and being skillful at figures. But the ways of the Renaissance world required something further. More business meant more partnership agreements, more complicated wills, more conveyancing—in short, more law. Legal studies boomed steadily throughout the Renaissance, attracting the largest enrollment at universities, and causing professors of law to be paid among the highest of academic salaries. And as the city-states grew, the business of government became more complicated, creating a demand for a well-educated secretariat at home and for diplomats who could speak with persuasion and eloquence abroad.

The Study of Ancient Culture

There was, then, a steadily increasing pressure for a more practical kind of education than the one provided by the theological studies of the Middle Ages. Professional skills were needed—also worldly attitudes. The humanistic program of studies took shape to provide them. This program involved the reading of ancient authors and the study of such subjects as grammar, rhetoric, history and moral philosophy. By the 15th Century such a course was officially known as *studia humanitatis*, or "humanities," and the men who pursued this knowledge came to be known as humanists.

Humanism means something different today, but in the Renaissance it stood for a view of life that, while devoutly accepting the existence of God, shared many of the intellectual attitudes of the ancient pagan world. It was interested in esthetics, saw the usefulness of a knowledge of history, and was convinced that man's chief duty was to enjoy his life soberly and serve his community actively. Thus humanism restored to balance the scales which the Middle Ages had tilted with a concern for eternity. It stressed earthly fulfillment rather than preparation for paradise. It had its spiritual side, but it reflected a society that was more interested in worldly matters—a society that was practical, canny, self-conscious and ambitious.

But humanism could not become a real movement, involving a whole society, until that society had a positive need to learn about the classical past—until it saw in the wisdom of Rome an answer to its own problems. The classical revival was preceded not only by modifications in the small world of medieval university curricula, but by an irrational yearning for change that spread through the whole medieval world. The Middle Ages may look static, but in fact they were characterized by considerable dissatisfaction. Men sensed that things were not going as they should—in either church or state—and longed for some sort of regeneration, some sort of revival. Rome, once the secular as well as the spiritual capital of the world, became the focus of these aspirations. Men yearned for the rebirth, the renaissance, of Rome's past glories.

Paradoxically, the first activists in this movement arose within a profession that normally opposes change: the law. To meet the demands of a more complex society and a more involved economy, lawyers began to re-examine the great codes of ancient Roman law, the *Digest* and the *Codex*. Instead of simply relying on abstracts prepared by medieval commentators, they began to pay attention to what had been in the minds of the actual compilers of these great legacies. And in the course of relating their problems to decisions handed down in antiquity, they had to imagine the conditions of life in ancient Rome. This led them to other classical works and, inevitably, from reading for business to reading for pleasure. Thus a highly conservative profession became a hotbed of pioneers intent upon carrying out humanist reform.

By the end of the 13th Century, lawyers in the northern Italian cities, especially in Padua and Verona, were displaying a lively interest in the poetry, as well as the history and law, of ancient Rome. They were searching in libraries for forgotten manuscripts and reading them with scholarly zest. Like their humanist successors, they were concerned with establishing the correct words of a text and attributing them to the right author. This desire to rub the patina from medieval glosses, and bring up the original, bright and clear, gave the Renaissance a firsthand knowledge of what the ancients had actually said, and enabled it to speak with them directly, across the centuries.

Discovery of Ancestors

It is difficult to imagine the excitement that attended this unearthing of new and purer texts, this tuning in on voices that spoke with such joy and conviction about the noblest, most triumphant age that Italy has ever known. Above all, since most of the ancient writers studied were Roman, it was an intensely personal excitement. The Italian humanists were discovering their own ancestors, finding buried treasure in their own house. To Petrarch, Cicero was not just a dusty sage, but a real person to whom he could write a letter—and did. To Machiavelli, banished from political life, living in squalor and inactivity on a small farm outside Florence, nothing was sweeter than to lock himself away in his study; there he could forget the humiliating present and "converse" with the great Roman figures of the past, learning how they coped with the crises of their world, applying their solutions to the crises of his own.

This desire to imitate and learn from the long-dead Romans led men of the Renaissance to study principally the historians, men like Livy and Tacitus. But the writings of such men as Quintilian and Cicero were almost as important. Their theories on education, on the qualities of character and mind that best suited a man to meet the challenges of the Roman world, were thought to be equally applicable to the world of the 14th and 15th Centuries. One Roman quality particularly stressed was that of all-round competence, which became the hallmark of Renaissance man. It was from these Roman theorists also that the Renaissance adopted the belief that a man's learning should be put at the disposal of others, that he should live an active civic life rather than revel privately in the delights of scholarship. . . .

Discovery of the Self

In the Middle Ages to praise man was to praise God, for man was a creation of God. But Renaissance writers praised man himself as a creator. They played down the sinfulness he was born with and emphasized his ability to think and act for himself, to produce works of art, to guide the destiny of others. They freed man from his pegged place in the medieval hierarchy, halfway between matter and spirit, and allowed him to roam at will, through all the levels of being, sometimes identifying himself with the brutes, sometimes with the angels. He was seen as the ruler of nature—the lord, although not the Lord, of creation.

This new vision of man sprang from a heightened awareness of self. Medieval men had been preoccupied with searching their souls, but Renaissance men were much more intrigued with exploring, and indeed parading, their own personalities. Petrarch is a perfect example. Although his se-

rious interests centered on his work in discovering and editing ancient texts, Petrarch was also interested in himself. In
his letters, designed for posterity as well as his friends, he left
a record of his reactions to love affairs and friendship, to
mountains and the flowers in his garden. They are an intellectual and emotional self-portrait, the first since antiquity.

It was in this same spirit of self-interest that men began to
call attention to themselves as unique and individual beings.
Composers began to sign their music. Around 1340 a self-
confident Florentine banker had the audacity to have his
portrait painted for his tomb, and in 1453 Piero de' Medici
commissioned a portrait bust of himself. One of Michelangelo's greatest sculptures, the Julius monument for St.
Peter's in Rome, celebrated a single Pope—on the Pope's orders. Another of Michelangelo's designs, the chapel for the
Church of San Lorenzo in Florence, was commissioned by
the Medici to memorialize two members of their family. And
an interest in one man as an individual prompted Boccaccio,
in his life of Dante, to attempt to describe a man's personality instead of merely rattling off a string of edifying anec-
dotes about his accomplishments.

Limitations of Latin

But humanism was not an unmixed blessing. While the rediscovery of the culture of ancient Rome speeded Renaissance man in the direction he wanted to go, it also imposed
its own itinerary. In some ways it was not a good one. Take,
for example, language. A man can best explain himself and
his world in his own language, the vernacular. Dante, Petrarch and Boccaccio were all intensely and successfully personal writers in the common tongue of their day—but they
were prestigious exceptions. Almost everyone else was influenced by Rome; it became fashionable to write in Latin. Not
until late in the 15th Century, when the powerful Lorenzo
de' Medici chose to compose poems in the dialect of the
Tuscan common man, did the vernacular begin to gain re-
spectability. Then, through the works of men like Machiavelli and Castiglione, literature assumed its primary function of helping a society to understand itself.

The influence of the past was strengthened by the fact that the Renaissance had no conception of evolutionary progress. Men did not believe, as modern men do (with misgivings), that society can steadily improve itself by inventing new ways to exploit natural resources and organize economies and governments. Their impulse was to rediscover, not invent. They sought to improve man's condition not by looking forward to the frontiers of knowledge, but by looking back to its reservoirs. It seemed to the Renaissance that the ancients had done nearly everything about as well as it could be done. Change was possible; indeed, each new generation of painters was praised because it was "more modern" than the last. But "more modern," to the Renaissance, really meant closer to the precepts laid down by Rome.

The Roots of Renaissance Humanism

Isabel Rivers

The intellectual movement that came to be known as humanism was the driving force behind many of the enduring scholarly and literary achievements of the Renaissance. Isabel Rivers, lecturer in English at the University of Leicester, traces the origins of Renaissance humanism in the competing educational and philosophical writings of ancient Rome and Greece, especially in the very influential writings of the Roman Cicero. Led by the Italian scholar Petrarch, Italian humanists began to turn away from the medieval techniques of logical disputation derived from Aristotle and toward Cicero and Plato's more rhetorical approach to wisdom. Later, through the scholar Erasmus, humanist educational and civic ideals took root in northern Europe as well.

The word 'humanism', used first in the nineteenth century, has acquired such a wide range of potential meanings and is often applied so carelessly that it has lost much of its original force. Its broad current meaning is a view of life which displaces God and puts man at the centre. The expression 'Renaissance humanism' needs to be used much more precisely if it is to have any value. Although 'humanism' was not a word current during the Renaissance, 'humanist' was. 'Humanist' is an anglicisation of the Italian *umanista*, meaning a Latin teacher, which in turn ultimately derives from Cicero's use of the word *humanitas*. The Latin *humanitas* has a double meaning: first, mankind in a general sense (hence our word 'humanity'), second, as a translation of the Greek *paideia*, culture or liberal education which fully develops a man (this sense survives in the modern term 'humanities'). Renaissance humanism was primarily an educational movement which began in Italy in the early fourteenth century and reached England at the end of the fifteenth. A humanist was a classical scholar with two complementary aims: to recover the moral values of classical life, and to imitate the language and style of the classics as a means to that end. He hoped to unite wisdom *(sapientia)* and eloquence *(eloquentia)*.

The Importance of Cicero

Cicero [106–43 BC] was the hero of the humanists for a variety of reasons. As politician, orator and moralist he combined action and contemplation, public and private life, and hence was himself a model of the complete man. His literary style was for the humanists the embodiment of eloquence. His philosophical works, especially *Of Duties* (probably the most widely read classical work in the Renaissance), gave the humanists their ethics, while his rhetorical works, especially *On the Orator*, gave them their educational theory and in effect defined their role. Two rival systems of education coexisted in classical and Hellenistic Greece: the philosophical, going back to Plato, which provided a specialised and difficult intellectual training in mathematics, logic and metaphysics, and the rhetorical, going back to Isocrates, which was primarily literary in emphasis, taught the art of declamation, and prepared men for political life. In the Hellenistic world the emphasis was on rhetorical training, often conceived very narrowly. This was the kind of education that the Romans borrowed from the Greeks: it provided men with the skills necessary for success in public life, whether politics or the law courts. Cicero, who had experience of both kinds of Greek education, tried to bring them closer together and to transmit both traditions to Rome. In his philosophical works, such as *Tusculan Disputations, On the Nature of the Gods*, and *Of Duties*, Cicero paraphrased and popularised Greek moral philosophy and theology, while in his rhetorical works, such as *On the Orator* and *The Orator*, he adapted Greek rhetorical methods for Romans, at the same time attempting to widen the meaning of oratory. Cicero believed that the two kinds of education could not be separated without damage to both. Philosophy without oratory is sterile, while oratory without philosophy is dangerous. Eloquence and wisdom belong together. Yet in spite of this belief Cicero belongs ultimately in the camp of the rhetoricians. He has little interest in logical argument or philosophical problems for their own sake. For Cicero philosophy really means ethics, defining how men should behave, while oratory means persuading men to behave in the ways defined by ethics. The orator must himself be a good man. (This formulation was elaborated by Quintilian in *The Education of an Orator*, and was repeatedly taken up in the Renaissance.) This belief in the moral and utilitarian function of education and in the social and political obligations of the man of letters makes Cicero the heir of Isocrates and of the rhetorical tradition and the father of humanism.

The Medieval Emphasis on Logic

In the medieval period the conflict between philosophy and rhetoric continued, now one and now the other dominating the educational system. The trivium (grammar, rhetoric and logic), the first part of the medieval system of the seven liberal arts, perpetuated both the classical literary and rhetorical tradition and the philosophical tradition that was temporarily to overthrow it in the thirteenth century. In France in the ninth and again in the early twelfth centuries we find the elements of humanism: the copying and reading of Latin poetry, philosophy and oratory. John of Salisbury, who studied at Chartres in the mid–twelfth century, had an enormous knowledge of available Latin literature. Yet this humanism was displaced late in the twelfth century and in the thirteenth by the increasing importance of the study of logic. In the thirteenth-century universities the arts course was a preliminary to the queen of the sciences, theology. In the intellectual system known as scholasticism which dominated medieval education, theology was joined with the more technical and abstract branches of philosophy—logic, epistemology and metaphysics. The principal classical author studied was Aristotle (the complete corpus of whose works was made available in translation via Arabic and directly from Greek by the end of the thirteenth century), but Aristotle the logician was given primacy over Aristotle the political theorist and rhetorician. To the schoolmen (as the later humanists disparagingly called the scholastic theologians) Aristotle was 'the Philosopher'; when the humanists attacked Aristotle it was the scholastic application of his work that they had in mind. Following a three-fold method of question, argument and conclusion (as exemplified in what was to be the most influential of scholastic works in succeeding centuries, the *Summa Theologiae* of Thomas Aquinas), scholastic writing ignored the rhetorical techniques of persuasion in favour of logical disputation.

It was against this abstract, rigorous and technical educational system, combining philosophy and theology, that the humanists rebelled. The beginnings of Renaissance humanism have been detected in Italy in the late thirteenth century, but the chief spokesman for the new attitudes was Petrarch in the mid–fourteenth century. Although Petrarch had much less access to classical literature than later humanists, and although he could not read Greek, nevertheless he established the principles and prepared the way for the development of humanism. The international language of learning in the West throughout the Middle Ages was Latin; it was a living, growing language, which had developed a sophisticated philosophical vocabulary. Petrarch repudiated medieval, scholastic Latin, and demanded a return to classical Latin, the language of Virgil and Horace in poetry and Cicero in prose, a language unable to accommodate medieval philosophy. For Petrarch medieval Europe had lost the values with the language and literature of the classical world, and he led the humanist attempt to revive them. The first step was to recover the texts of classical authors and to reintroduce the study of Greek in the West. Although humanists tended to exaggerate the extent to which classical literature was 'lost' during the medieval period (for if medieval monks had not copied classical manuscripts they would not have survived), nevertheless many important works ignored for hundreds of years were put into circulation again—for example, Aristotle's *Poetics* (available in Latin in the thirteenth century but not taught), Livy, Tacitus and the complete text of Quintilian. Knowledge of Greek established itself slowly during the fifteenth century, and reached its height with Ficino's translation of Plato and Plotinus into Latin. The invention of

The Admiration of Cicero

As Petrarch apologetically observes in the following passage, he is not the first Christian scholar to be enthralled by the "genius and eloquence" of the Roman writer Cicero. The potential conflict expressed here between Christian values and classical values is a recurring theme throughout the Renaissance period. Most Renaissance humanists found a way to harmonize or reconcile these often conflicting sources of value, as Petrarch does here.

I do not deny that I am delighted with Cicero's genius and eloquence, seeing that even Jerome—to omit countless others—was so fascinated by him that he could not free his own style from that of Cicero. . . .

If to admire Cicero means to be a Ciceronian, I am a Ciceronian. I admire him so much that I wonder at people who do not admire him. This may appear a new confession of my ignorance, but this is how I feel, such is my amazement. However, when we come to think or speak of religion, that is, of supreme truth and true happiness, and of eternal salvation, then I am certainly not a Ciceronian, or a Platonist, but a Christian. I even feel sure that Cicero himself would have been a Christian if he had been able to see Christ and to comprehend His doctrine. Of Plato, Augustine does not in the least doubt that he would have become a Christian if he had come to life again in Augustine's time or had foreseen the future while he lived. Augustine relates also that in his time most of the Platonists had become Christians and he himself can be supposed to belong to their number.

Petrarch, *On his Own Ignorance and That of Many Others*, in *The Renaissance Philosophy of Man*, ed. Cassirer, Kristeller, and Randall. Chicago: University of Chicago Press, 1948, pp. 114–15.

printing towards the end of the fifteenth century greatly helped the humanists in their task of disseminating classical literature, and some printers, for example Aldus Manutius of Venice, were themselves classical scholars. By the early sixteenth century the major Latin and Greek works of oratory, history, political and moral philosophy and poetry had been put into print by the humanists. Whereas scholasticism had developed in universities and had been the province of ecclesiastics, humanism was fostered by courts and princes. Logic, the art of disputation, had been the weapon of the schoolmen; rhetoric, the art of persuasion, was the weapon of the new class of humanist administrators. Learning, the humanists believed, must not be divorced from public life; the humanist regarded himself as a public servant. In this sense humanism can be regarded as a secularisation of learning.

But humanism was not at all an unchristian movement, although humanists (with important exceptions, such as the Florentine Neoplatonists) were on the whole indifferent to theology. Early Christian Fathers such as Jerome and Augustine had been ambivalent in their attitude to classical letters and the rhetorical tradition: in his famous Epistle 22 Jerome recounts the dream in which he is accused at the Judgement of being a Ciceronian, not a Christian, yet in Epistle 70 he defends the Christian use of classical learning with the biblical example of the taking of a captive wife (Deut. 21:10–13). Most humanists, beginning with Petrarch, attempted to harmonise classical ethics with the practical Christianity of the gospels. This Christian humanism flourished particularly in northern Europe, and the Dutch humanist Erasmus was its chief exponent. Erasmus, who was fond of referring to the schoolmen as 'barbarians', attacked scholasticism for its intellectualism, its method and its (to him) bad Latin. Christianity was for him a matter of conduct not of speculation, and he believed the pagan moralists, especially Cicero, to be closer to Christ than the scholastic theologians. The *philosophia Christi* (philosophy of Christ) that he taught was supported by the classics and the early Fathers, especially Jerome. Erasmus' radical act was to apply to the Scriptures the critical textual and philological methods the Italian humanists had been applying to classical literature. In 1516 he published the first edition of the New Testament in Greek, with a Latin translation that corrected the errors in the Vulgate. Erasmus saw himself above all as an educator in the Ciceronian sense: the pursuit of *bonae litterae*—'good letters', otherwise known as 'the new learning' (the study of classical Latin and Greek, with Hebrew in addition)—would lead to the practice of the philosophy of Christ.

The Spread of Christian Humanism

Erasmus, together with the younger Spanish humanist Vives, was the formative influence in the development of English humanism. Englishmen had travelled to Italy in the fifteenth century and taken an interest in Italian humanist scholarship, but the first important generation of English humanists was that of Colet and More in the early years of the reign of Henry VIII. Indeed the beginnings of English humanism can be dated from 1497 when Colet (who had studied in Italy and come under the influence of Ficino and Pico) began to lecture on St Paul's Epistles, applying the new critical methods without reference to scholastic commentaries. Erasmus, who formed the chief link between Italian and northern humanism by maintaining an enormous correspondence with fellow humanists and working in different humanist centres throughout Europe, paid three visits to England, the most important being from 1509 to 1514 on the accession of Henry VIII. Erasmus influenced three aspects of English humanism, educational, religious and political. Colet's foundation of the first English humanist school, St Paul's, in 1510 was the direct result of Erasmus' educational principles: dedicated to the child Jesus, the school aimed to lead its pupils through good letters to the good life. Erasmus' attacks on scholastic theology, monasticism and abuses in the church helped prepare the way for the English Reformation, though Erasmus himself was not a Protestant reformer. In addition, Erasmus helped to strengthen the orientation of English humanists towards the court and public life. Humanists, who had many enemies in the universities, looked to the courts for patronage; the accession of three new princes in the early sixteenth century, Henry VIII in 1509, Francis I of France in 1515, and the Emperor Charles V in 1518 seemed at first like a golden age for the new learning. In 1516 Erasmus was appointed a councillor to Charles, and addressed to him *The Education of a Christian Prince*, a handbook of political and moral behaviour which belongs in an old tradition of 'princes' mirrors' going back to Isocrates' *To Nicocles*. The English work following this tradition most closely is Sir Thomas Elyot's *Book named the Governor*. The humanists were anxious to educate a new generation of courtiers and politicians who would in turn mould their princes according to the humanist pattern. This idealism was to be severely tested in the course of the century. One of the important questions raised in Sir Thomas More's *Utopia* (1516) is whether the man of letters has any obligation to serve the prince, who is unlikely to follow his advice. . . .

Humanism's Central Concepts

Although humanism did not imply adherence to any particular philosophical or ethical system, nevertheless we can distinguish certain key concepts. The first is imitation. Humanist educators taught their pupils to imitate closely the style and language of classical authors—the method is described in Ascham's *The Schoolmaster*. At its worst this was an absurd and stultifying exercise (satirised in Erasmus' *Ciceronianus*), divorcing style and content; at its best imitation meant taking as a pattern not only the style but also the attitudes and conduct of the chosen model. The second concept is pragmatism. The humanists disapproved of abstract, theoretical knowledge; they valued knowledge as it could be used to promote the good life. They believed optimistically that education makes men better; Vives, Bacon and Milton all express in different ways the view that education removes the consequences of the fall and restores man, a rational and fully developed creature, to his Creator. The humanists valued highly those classical ethical works, such as Aristotle's *Nicomachean Ethics* and Cicero's *Of Duties*, that represent man as a political being who perfects himself in society (Elyot's *Governor*, borrowing from *Of Duties* I, provided the earliest English account of the four classical cardinal virtues, justice, prudence, temperance and fortitude). The third key-concept of the humanists is duty. Plato's portrait of the education of the philosopher-king in *The Republic* V–VII tantalised the humanists: on the one hand it was an unattainable ideal, on the other hand it was an ideal that must be attempted. Hence the fascination of the relationship between philosophers or men of letters and rulers: Plato and Dionysius, Aristotle and Alexander, Plutarch and Trajan (though the last was not historical). Erasmus' relationship with Charles V and More's with Henry VIII were consciously in this tradition. Yet the humanist obligation to public service implied the acquiescence of the prince in his moral education, and princes were not so pliable. More's execution by Henry VIII in 1535 for refusing to compromise his 'good counsel' epitomises the tragic tensions inherent in humanism. Because of this tension the humanists felt strongly the temptation of the retired, contemplative life, of Horace's *otium* (leisure) as against Cicero's *negotium* (business); the garden often seemed a more fitting symbolic setting for the pursuit of wisdom than the court.

Although the humanists were above all concerned with classical literature, and although the international language of scholarship remained Latin (paradoxically, humanist insistence on Latin purity helped to render it a dead language), nevertheless humanist educational methods and attitudes had a profound effect on vernacular literature. One of the significant humanist achievements was to make the major works of classical literature available in English translation by the early seventeenth century: Shakespeare is the most obvious beneficiary.

The Humanist Break with the Middle Ages

Charles G. Nauert Jr.

In the following essay, Renaissance scholar Charles G. Nauert Jr., professor of history at the University of Missouri-Columbia, assesses the motives and achievements of the Italian humanist movement in the earliest stages of the Renaissance. He contends that the most important achievement of this movement was its radical new view of world history, a view which designated the centuries after the fall of the Roman Empire as the "Dark Ages." Italian humanists, led by Petrarch, sought to restore the wisdom and cultured civilization of ancient Rome and Greece as a way of improving the values and institutions of their own time. Nauert also describes the stages of Italian humanism as it evolved.

The movement [humanists] created came to be called humanism (though not till the nineteenth century). Although in the loose and intellectually slipshod usage of the nineteenth and twentieth centuries, the modern connotations of the words *humanism*, *humanist*, and *humanistic* (implying a philosophy of life that is nonreligious or even antireligious and this-worldly) have been read back into Renaissance humanism, the humanists were in no sense the purveyors of a distinctive philosophy of life: they were not as a group any more antireligious or this-worldly than their counterparts in the Middle Ages or than other groups (scholastic philosophers for example) in their own centuries.

It is even misleading, though perhaps not quite so false, to say that humanism laid greater emphasis on man and on human dignity than had medieval intellectual traditions. The humanists were simply those who rediscovered, popularized, and explained the culture of ancient Greece and Rome, chiefly as they found it expressed in Roman and Greek literature. From the time of Cicero at least, the study of grammar, rhetoric, poetry, ethics, and history had been known as the *litterae humaniores* (today we still call them "the humanities") because the Romans regarded them as the studies most necessary for an educated man. . . .

By the late thirteenth century, among the Italian merchants, lawyers, notaries, and *dictatores* [professional letter writers] there developed an interest in poetry, in history, and in broad problems of personal and social ethics. For the first time in the generation just preceding the career of Dante (1265–1321), a native Italian literature emerged. In the same period, literacy—at least in Italian and often also in Latin—became a common attainment. In one direction, these developments led to the founding of a vernacular literature, of which Dante was the first great figure.

But in another direction, the interests of these groups of lawyers and notaries, with their consciousness of Italy's Roman origins, and with their practical daily contact with the Latin language, led directly to an interest in Roman literature. To some extent, the motive was still utilitarian: careful, thoughtful study of Latin grammar and rhetoric was practical for men who lived by their skill with words. To an increasing extent, however, the growing attention to Latin literature was aesthetic. Many of the individuals of the late thirteenth and early fourteenth centuries who popularized the study of Latin language and literature had some connection with the legal or notarial professions. Even Francesco Petrarca, or Petrarch (1304–74), the first really important Italian humanist, was educated in the law though he managed to make his living from poetry. . . .

Even in the work of Dante, a lively interest in the Latin classics was evident, though the approach to classical elements was still medieval. But the classical influence on sophisticated Italians tended to increase in the fourteenth century, and the second and third of the great founders of the vernacular literary tradition, Petrarch and his friend Giovanni Boccaccio (1313–75), were not only humanists but the two principal creators of humanism as a cultural tradition. Both men were masters of Italian language, yet each of them regarded his Latin writings, chiefly on classical themes, as the truly important part of his life's work. After the death of Petrarch and Boccaccio, the growth of enthusiasm for classical studies and for the Latin language continued at so rapid a pace that Italian vernacular literature stagnated. For a century after 1375, most Italians who had something important and serious to write wrote it in Latin.

The Humanist and World History

The truly important point about Renaissance humanism is not its enthusiasm for the classics but its new conception of history, which was the source of the overpowering new interest in the classics. As we have already seen, interest in ancient Greek and Roman culture was always present in the Middle Ages, and at some times and places, notably in France during the twelfth century, a lively study of ancient books arose and had a major impact on thought and literature. Although some important works of Latin literature were little known during the Middle Ages and became widely known only during the Renaissance, the "rediscovery" of Roman literature consisted more in a new outlook on the ancient texts than in the literal findings of books previously unknown. There were some significant new finds, but it is hard to regard this filling out of the corpus of Latin literature as truly decisive in cultural history, considering how much was already well known. . . .

Humanism involved more than demands for minor adjustments in the university curriculum. The humanists were claiming that their mission in life was nothing less than the restoration of "true" civilization in place of the "barbarous" civilization that prevailed in their own time. Such a notion implied definite ideas of historical value, implying above all the worthlessness of the whole medieval heritage—of everything, including the Gothic cathedrals and the scholastic theological books.

These ideas of history were radically new, and as much as any set of ideas can be attributed to any one person, they were the creation of Petrarch himself. During his long and active literary career, Petrarch became convinced that ancient Greek and Roman civilization had reached the highest level ever attained by any society. But this great civilization declined during the fourth, fifth, and subsequent centuries, simultaneously with the power of the Roman empire which had protected it. Europe was flooded by Germanic barbarians whose dominance completed the almost total loss of ancient art and literature. For a thousand years thereafter, European society lived through a "Dark Age"—a term by which Petrarch meant an age that had lost the light of ancient civilization and had achieved nothing of value on its own. This worthless, barbarous civilization, characterized by Gothic architecture and scholastic thought, survived down to his own time. In his terminology, it was "modern."

Historical Discontinuity

Whereas medieval thinkers had regarded their own age as a mere extension of Roman times, Petrarch drew a sharp distinction between two separate historical periods, an "ancient" period characterized by light, by high civilization, and also by the domination of the whole world by the Italians; and a "modern" period characterized by crude barbarism, by cultural darkness, and by the degrading disunity and weakness of the Italians. At least in germ, Petrarch's thought also contained the idea of a third major period in the history of civilization, a future age of cultural revival (rebirth, or "renaissance") in which there would be a rediscovery of the sources of Greek and Roman cultural power, so that a new civilization would grow up, not identical with the ancient but inspired and guided by its best elements.

There is some evidence that Petrarch himself realized that once this new historical age had developed, it would be called "modern," and that the Dark Age lying between the old and the new ages of high civilization would seem a sort of middle period, an unhappy gap in the growth of civilization. Although Petrarch himself never used the exact phrase

"Middle Ages" for that worthless age, his followers within a generation did. Indeed, not only the term "Middle Ages" but also the whole concept of distinct cultural periods in history, and the conventional and still useful division of history into ancient, medieval, and modern periods, was the invention of Petrarch and his followers, the humanists.

The modern student of history is often irritated by the wrong-headedness and unfairness of this attack on medieval civilization. We know, and even Petrarch, Boccaccio, and their followers should have known, that the Middle Ages had already attained a high level of culture. The negative attitude of the humanists toward medieval civilization was not a scientific and scholarly judgment. It can be understood only in terms of the severe breakdown in late medieval civilization. Not in a social or a political sense but certainly in a cultural sense, the Renaissance humanists were rebels against the heritage of the immediate past. The idea of medieval barbarism and Renaissance rediscovery of true civilization is indeed false concerning the Middle Ages, but it is very profoundly true concerning the Renaissance. The denigration of the Middle Ages and the rhapsodic idealization of Antiquity were devices through which a new age of creative thinkers defined their goals and justified their abandonment of prevailing traditions.

What the humanist rebels against medieval culture found in the Latin classics was not primarily new factual knowledge about the classical past, but a new appreciation of classical civilization as a whole. Classical Antiquity gave them a yardstick by which they could measure their own age and find it wanting, thus justifying their hostility to medieval tradition. In a more positive sense, it gave them new inspiration, confidence that a better civilization, a more wholesome society, and even a stronger Italy could be created. It also offered practical guidance in the achievement of these goals. This conviction that current problems could best be solved by conscious imitation of the ancients was a powerful force throughout Renaissance civilization. It was not confined to idealistic poets like Petrarch, but was still powerful a century and a half later in the thought of the hard-bitten and politi-

cally experienced Machiavelli, who thought that the founder-
ing Italian society of the early sixteenth century could be
saved only if it reconstructed on the Roman model everything from its basic political institutions to its manner of re-
cruiting and arming troops.

Moral Reform

In the opinion of Renaissance humanists from Petrarch to
Machiavelli and beyond, the true secret of Rome's greatness
was not some trick of military organization or even of con-
stitutional structure, but its success over a long period in
producing great leaders who were truly devoted to the welfare of their city. The moral grandeur that made the best and
ablest men of Rome dedicate their lives to public service
rather than to amassing private fortunes or seeking private
enjoyment was the key to Rome's mastery of the whole
world. As the Roman ruling classes became corrupted by the
desire for personal advantage in the late Republic and the
Empire, both the physical power and the culture of Rome
declined. The spirit that made Rome great might today be
called patriotism, but the men of the Renaissance commonly
called it *virtù*. For this term the modern English word *virtue*,
with its connotations of strait-laced adherence to a negative
and puritanical moral code governing mainly individual and
private acts, is a poor equivalent. The Italian *virtù* implied
"strength of character" and "public-spiritedness." It dealt
more with one's ethics in public life than with private life. In
order to undo the political, moral, and cultural degeneracy
that humanists saw in their own society and regarded as typically medieval, what was needed was a recovery of this sense
of "virtue" or public spirit—in other words, a moral reform,
in the broadest sense of the word *moral*.

This emphasis on the need for a moral reorientation explains many aspects of Italian humanism that otherwise fit
into no rational pattern. For example, the humanists attacked scholastic education and scholarship, dismissing these
flippantly as mere trifling. They did so because they believed
that scholasticism, with its cold, orderly rationalism and its
apparently deliberate avoidance of literary artifice, was too

narrowly intellectual, too concerned with abstract speculation about metaphysical, logical, and scientific matters, to
stimulate the kind of emotional commitment to a life of
virtue (that is, devotion to public service) which they felt
necessary for the recovery of ancient greatness. In a similar
vein, the constant stress on character formation, on the reading of Roman texts on ethics, politics, and history, and even
the stress on Christian piety that marks the educational reforms of the Renaissance, are closely linked with this desire
to regenerate the morals of society and to graduate young
men whose outstanding trait would not be their deft mastery
of logical disputation but their wholehearted devotion to the
general welfare.

The Need for Eloquence

Finally, the constant harping of humanists on the need for an
elegant and eloquent literary style and their apparently su-
perficial dismissal of brilliant scholastic thinkers because they
wrote inelegant and nonclassical Latin are directly related to
their emphasis on moral regeneration. Eloquent form and
the deliberate, artistic application of stylistic devices in speaking and writing were very important to the humanists. But
this stress on eloquence, on effective use of rhetorical devices
learned from ancient Roman examples, was no mere accidental peculiarity of the humanists. In order to make men virtuous, they argued, more is needed than subtle, logical argu-
mentation. Men are not purely intellectual beings, and hence
their behavior will not be revolutionized by something so
coldly rational as a scholastic disquisition on virtue and political obligation. The real springs of human action are more
emotional than rational. Thus the man who is being educated
for a career of public service and leadership must himself be
personally committed to the common good by nonrational as
well as rational influences, and he must be taught to use the
oratorical and literary devices that will allow him to appeal to
the emotions of the people and carry them along with him.
The growing conviction that humanistic study of Latin literature did in fact make men more effective at persuading their
fellow citizens is precisely why in the closing fourteenth cen-

tury more and more heads of Florentine families, men who themselves were more interested in political power and wealth than in intellectual matters, sought a humanistic education for their sons.

The humanists' professional skills as masters of rhetoric (the art of eloquence) were intended to be instrumental in bringing about a moral regeneration. In their opinion, humanistic studies—grammar, rhetoric, ethics, and history (which they regarded chiefly as a source of concrete illustrations of moral principles)—were to be preferred above all others mainly because they were eminently practical, dealing as they did with the study of man in his social and moral setting and with the arts of modifying human behavior through oratory and writing. The humanists from the time of Petrarch onward challenged the scholastic assumption that the main purpose of man is to understand the world of God and the world of nature. Rather, they believed, the main purpose of man is to understand and control himself and the whole complex web of relationships that bind him to other men. Thus their deliberate preference for rhetoric over philosophy, for eloquence over truth, does not mean that as a class they were "mere" rhetoricians, spineless time-servers who sold their skills to the highest bidder. Their devotion to rhetoric springs partly from their view of man as a being who is not just a disembodied intellect but much more a creature of passion and partly from their conception of themselves as moral reformers struggling to regenerate society and of moral reform itself as the key to solving the many problems of their age. . . .

The Cult of Fame

The humanists' ideal of regenerating the world, and opening up a whole new age of human history through "the recovery of classical antiquity" (that is, through the use of classical eloquence to recreate in modern times a sense of public morality comparable to that of Rome at her best) is linked to another humanistic trait that has elicited much attention and some amusement: their constant concern about their own fame among future generations. The humanists did seek fame. Men like Petrarch may have had some qualms about this desire, but usually they concluded, as he did, that desire for fame was a noble motive, that it had been one of the sources of patriotism and self-sacrifice among the heroes of Antiquity. The notion of fame was inseparable from the humanists' conception of themselves as the men who were initiating simultaneously a new age in history and a profound moral regeneration of modern society. In all modesty, Petrarch could hardly say, "With me there begins a third age in the history of human civilization." And yet in a very real sense, that is what he must have believed, and it was to that goal that he and his followers devoted their most serious efforts. Such men did value themselves highly, but only because they valued their purposes highly. . . .

Greek Studies

Interest in Latin literature naturally led to efforts to gain a deeper understanding by studying the Greek literature that Roman authors frequently cited. Since late Roman times, very few Western Europeans had been able to read Greek. Largely from the Arab world, medieval Christendom had become well acquainted with the works of Aristotle, which had been made available in Latin translations by the early thirteenth century. But neither the Arabs nor medieval Latin Christians showed much interest in any branches of Greek literature other than medical, scientific, and philosophical works, and in the latter field they knew little but the Aristotelian tradition. Greek lyric and epic poetry, drama, history, and rhetorical works, together with philosophical writings in the Platonic, Epicurean, and Stoic traditions, remained largely unknown except for the frequent mention of them in Latin authors. The first major humanist, Petrarch, realized the necessity of learning Greek if he were to gain a deeper understanding of Latin literature, but his attempts were in vain. Petrarch's disciple Boccaccio was a bit more successful, but none of the early humanists really mastered Greek. . . .

Thus at the end of the fourteenth century, what was new was not the opportunity to learn classical Greek but the desire. That desire was the result of the humanistic determination to master the whole cultural tradition of Antiquity and to apply it to the reform and regeneration of Western society and culture. When the first great teacher of Greek in the West, Chrysoloras, lectured for a time at Paris, in the midst of an intellectual world still unaffected by the Renaissance, his activity aroused no interest comparable to the enthusiasm that had greeted him among the humanists of Venice and Florence. The medieval mind was still closed to the influence of any part of ancient Greek culture except Aristotle. But the Italian intellectuals of the fifteenth century were eagerly open to that influence, precisely because of their quest for a cultural rebirth. . . .

Stages of Humanism

Italian Renaissance humanism, like any intellectual movement extending over a long period, passed through a number of stages of development. In its very earliest form, as in the thought of Petrarch, it was largely an intellectual's flight from harsh political and social problems. Petrarch himself was the son of a Florentine political exile, and he grew up at the papal court at Avignon, without the kind of close ties to the world of business and politics that he no doubt would have developed if his family had stayed in Florence. He was a professional man of letters, a poet, fortunate enough to secure ecclesiastical appointments that assured him a modest income without any significant duties. He viewed the hurly-burly of political bickering and the materialistic process of buying and selling as something beneath a man devoted to truth and beauty.

Although his program for regenerating society obviously had implications in the area of political life and devotion to public service, he regarded active involvement in politics as unworthy of a wise man. No doubt unrealistically, he thought that renewed contact with the great works of classical literature would somehow inspire men to achieve a personal moral reform and that in this way society would be improved through humanistic studies. Improved education and the sympathetic support of powerful persons in the Church hierarchy and in secular government were the only concrete ways he proposed to foster the cultural and moral renewal. Though not a monk, Petrarch retained from medieval monasticism the ideal of withdrawal from the temptations and distractions of everyday life and of devotion to a life of contemplating eternal truth and beauty.

This ideal of scholarly aloofness from the active world was very different from the Roman ideal of the citizen's devotion to public service. When Petrarch realized that his ideal Roman hero, Cicero, was eager to abandon his philosophical studies and go rushing into the political struggle for the late Republic, he was shocked that so wise a man should have been so eager for political power. Petrarch's attitude suggests that despite a lifetime of loving study of ancient Rome, he had never grasped the Roman ideal of civic obligation. In the late fourteenth century, some of Petrarch's younger followers at Florence were criticized for a similar rejection of their own civic duties.

The Rise of Civic Humanism

By the end of the fourteenth or the beginning of the fifteenth century, however, prominent Florentine families were increasingly likely to select humanistic educations for their sons, not in order to turn them into poets but in order to make them more effective at discharging their obligation to provide leadership for the Republic. Thus humanism entered a new "civic" phase in which its practical usefulness to those destined to political leadership was emphasized. The classical education of ancient Roman times had emphasized training in oratory (in a very broad sense, involving a total education and not just study of elocution) as the proper preparation for a career of public service. Now this alliance between humanistic study and the life of active public service reemerged. The alliance appears to have been encouraged by the political crisis of the early fifteenth century, when the aggressive Giangaleazzo Visconti, duke of Milan, threatened the independence of Florence. The skills of the humanist as diplomat, political propagandist, and civil servant suddenly appeared very useful for the defense of the Republic. . . .

In reality, humanism also flourished at despotic courts, but it is true that there was a remarkable affinity between Renaissance republicanism and the flourishing of humanistic culture. The civic humanism of figures like Bruni was consciously the ideology of republican governments in Florence and later in Venice. This turning of humanism toward support of active involvement in republican politics, in business, and in direction of the family set the tone for much humanism in the early fifteenth century and was certainly compatible with the whole Renaissance thrust toward regeneration of society. By its affirmation of the active life, the life of politics, business, and family responsibility, humanism became a secularizing (but not necessarily antireligious) ideology running counter to the contemplative, ivory-tower mood of Petrarchan humanists. To men like Bruni, a scholar who turned his back on politics, business, and the family was socially irresponsible. . . .

Decline of the Civic Ideal

The humanist emphasis on active political involvement was not very important in the thought of Lorenzo Valla, who was not a Florentine by birth. Concentration on the task of editing and expounding classical texts and on the study of style and literary form, while inseparable from humanism at every stage, nevertheless provided an alternative direction. Humanism in the later fifteenth century showed tendencies to becomes less "civic" and more academic than in the earlier part of the century. This tendency developed even in Florence, where after 1434 the Medici family held an ever more overt control of the republic. By the time of Lorenzo the Magnificent (in power 1469–92), the republican tone of society gave way to a courtly spirit. Though the political machinery of the republic continued to function, independent political action and too strident a proclamation of republican political ideals increasingly seemed pointless, if not even dangerous. Humanists and artists accordingly tended to glorify the Medicean leadership more and the republic less; and both art and literature assumed a nonpolitical, even a courtly tone.

Chapter 2

Political and Social Contexts of the Renaissance

Turning Points
IN WORLD HISTORY

The Merchant and Economic Expansion in the Renaissance

Eugene F. Rice Jr.

The late Middle Ages saw a period of scarcity, famine, plague, and reduced population in Europe. During the heart of the Renaissance period, however, Europe experienced profound economic changes and growth, as well as population growth and much expanded international trade. Eugene F. Rice Jr., former professor at Columbia University, describes in this essay the rise of the powerful merchant-capitalist in these changing social and economic conditions. Many of these merchants became patrons of the new culture of the Renaissance, and they sought access into the ranks of the nobility throughout the period.

Over two centuries of medieval economic expansion had ended by the beginning of the fourteenth century. The years between 1310 and the 1340's were a period of scarcity and often of famine. The Black Death—which reached Constantinople and the eastern Mediterranean littoral in 1347; Italy, Spain, and France in 1348; Switzerland, Austria, Germany, and Low Countries, and England in 1349; and Scandinavia and Poland in 1350—transformed this subsistence crisis into demographic catastrophe. Fragmentary evidence makes any estimates of the losses impressionistic. The most reliable suggest a reduction of from 12 to 60 per cent in the population, depending on the region, with a global loss for the period between 1348 and 1377 of about 40 per cent. Until far into the fifteenth century, population stagnated at a level well below that of 1347. In response to the fall in population, both prices and the volume of commerce and of industrial and agricul-

Excerpted from *The Foundations of Early Modern Europe, 1460–1559*, 1st ed., by Eugene F. Rice Jr. Copyright ©1970 by W.W. Norton and Company, Inc. Reprinted by permission of W.W. Norton and Company, Inc.

tural production also declined or remained stationary. The long depression ended between 1460 and 1500. During the lifetimes of Luther, Copernicus, and Michelangelo, Europeans enjoyed a remarkable prosperity, a resurgence of industrial, commercial, financial, and demographic growth.

A Century of Prosperity

In the first half of the sixteenth century, population growth was large, generalized, and rapid. In most parts of Europe, population continued to increase, probably less rapidly and less uniformly in the second half of the century, until about 1620. The populations of Sicily and the kingdom of Naples doubled. Rome housed 50,000 people in 1526, 100,000 at the end of the century. In villages in the agricultural region south of Paris, the number of inhabitants doubled, tripled, even quadrupled between the end of the fifteenth century and the middle of the sixteenth. Changes in the rural population of the county of Hainaut, one of the seventeen provinces of the Netherlands, show a similar pattern. From 1365 to about 1470, the population declined. Between 1470 and 1540–1541 it swung sharply upward. Antwerp expanded from 20,000 about 1440, to 50,000 about 1500, to 100,000 about 1560. Calculations of the total population of the Empire are wildly approximate, but studies of particular areas confirm a strong upward trend. Similar evidence of demographic vitality, though with important regional variations, can be found in Spain, Portugal, and Switzerland; elsewhere in the Netherlands and France; and in Scandinavia, Poland, and Russia.

A buoyant expansion of industrial production paralleled this growth in population. The quantities of iron, copper, and silver extracted from Europe's mines quadrupled. Very probably the output of the metallurgical industries expanded as rapidly as mining itself. Wholly new enterprises contributed to industrial prosperity. The production of printed books, for example, already so remarkable before 1500, soared in the sixteenth century, and its progress stimulated older industries like papermaking and the manufacture of spectacles. An increasing urban population encouraged building. Much of Rome as we know it today, to take a single instance, was built in the sixteenth century: fifty-four churches, including St. Peter's, sixty palaces, many villas outside the city, hundreds of buildings to house ordinary citizens, and scores of hotels for pilgrims. Thirty new streets were laid out; most of the old streets were paved; almost a hundred miles of ancient aqueducts were rebuilt to bring in drinking water.

The pattern of growth in textile manufacture, Europe's greatest industry ever since the thirteenth century, was more complex. The preeminence of Italy in the manufacture of woolens faded. Florence, which had produced about 100,000 bolts of cloth a year in the late fourteenth century, produced only 30,000 in 1500; but the decline in woolens was probably more than offset, in value if not in volume, by increases in silk production. The old woolen industry of the Netherlands, centered at Ypres, Ghent, and Bruges, was also in decline; but again the progress of a new industry, the manufacture of lighter, cheaper woolen fabrics, made up for the losses in the old. In the meantime, England, which in the Middle Ages had exported raw wool rather than cloth, superseded Italy and the Netherlands to become Europe's chief producer of heavy woolens of the best quality. In 1503–1509 England exported an average of 81,835 bolts of cloth a year and only 5,000 sacks of wool. By 1540–1548 her average yearly exports totaled 122,254 bolts.

These are only examples. They could be multiplied. Everywhere the evidence is the same; industry was booming, and depending on the commodity, production rose from two to five times what it had been before.

The increases in population and production, and the opening of new trade routes, made it profitable for European merchants to exchange a larger volume of goods over greater distances than they had in earlier centuries. Portuguese merchants pushed east from Malacca to the centers of clove and nutmeg cultivation in the Moluccas, and then north to China and Japan. In the West, Seville was becoming the capital of an emerging Atlantic economy. European trade became literally worldwide in 1565 when Spanish galleons began regularly to link Manila and the Mexican port of Acapulco. Chinese junks visited Manila every year and traded spices, silks, and porcelains for Mexican silver, a traffic reproducing in miniature the exchange forming the basis of intercontinental commerce in the sixteenth century: American silver for eastern spices.

The Expansion of European Trade and Banking

But the romance of intercontinental trade should not obscure the fundamental and more important exchanges of food, raw materials, and manufactured goods among the different regions of Europe itself. England exported its woolens to northern Europe, not to the East. Indians did not drink Portuguese wine; Englishmen did. Spanish wool went to the Netherlands and Italy; Hungarian copper to Germany and France. The market for Venetian goblets and mirrors, Ferrarese ceramics, Flemish tapestries, Neapolitan silks, the products of the metallurgical industries of Nuremberg and Milan, was overwhelmingly European. And the heaviest volume of trade—economically and in tonnage far more weighty than the domestic trade in luxuries or any extra-European trade—involved the prosaic exchange, by way of Antwerp, Europe's commercial nerve center in the first half of the sixteenth century, of the cereals and forest products of the Baltic for the salt, wine, fish, vegetable oils, fruits, and dyestuffs of France and Spain and of southern and Mediterranean Europe in general. Commercial expansion abroad rested on the vigorous multiplication of commercial exchanges at home.

Bankers too enlarged their field of operations. In the Middle Ages banking had been almost exclusively an Italian monopoly. During the several decades before and after 1500, Frenchmen, Englishmen, and Germans joined Italians in consolidating the position of exchange banking in the economies of France and England, while financiers of many nationalities established banking houses in areas that had had few or none before—in Portugal, in Castile, and above all, in Germany. The organized money market widened, and in most of the great commercial centers, merchant-bankers built exchanges, . . . where they bought and sold bills of exchange and speculated on currency rates. In 1531 the new Antwerp bourse was opened "to the merchants of every nation and language." The proud inhabitants boasted of its size and beauty and of the thousand merchants who crowded its daily sessions, so colorful in dress and so various in tongue that the bourse seemed a miniature world, a microcosm, bringing together everything to be found in the large one, the macrocosm.

In 1460 the most impressive business organization in Europe was the Medici Bank of Florence. By 1545, the Fugger Company of Augsburg was the largest firm. The Medici Bank (the firm was called a *banco*, but its activities were commercial and industrial as well as financial) had eight branch offices, the Fuggers, twenty-five. The Medici owned three modest textile firms. The Fuggers owned silver mines in the Tyrol and gold mines in Silesia, mined mercury in Spain, and controlled the larger part of copper production in Hungary. The Medici Bank got into financial difficulties—one among several more important reasons for its decline—when its agent at Bruges made a risky loan to the duke of Burgundy. At the time of the imperial election of 1519, Jakob Fugger loaned Charles, the Habsburg candidate, the colossal sum of 543,000 florins with which to bribe the electors, and he got it back with interest. Finally, the capital of the Medici Bank in 1451 was 90,000 florins; that of the Fuggers in 1547 was over ten times as great. The larger scale of economic activity in the sixteenth century is clear.

The Merchant

The key figure in the expanding economy of Europe between 1460 and 1560 was the merchant. He belonged to an exclusive business elite. The merchant aristocracy of Venice numbered about 1,500 out of a total population of 100,000. In Florence in the same period very probably no more than 2 per cent of the inhabitants were engaged in international trade and banking or held positions of capitalist command in industry. The proportion was not larger elsewhere. In Lyons and Augsburg, Genoa and Seville, London and Antwerp, as

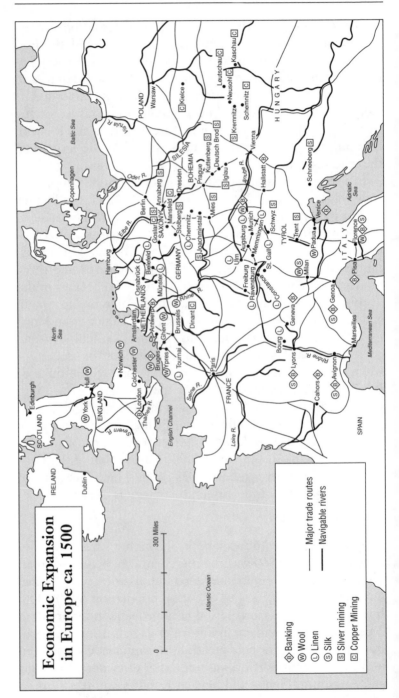

Economic Expansion in Europe ca. 1500

Major trade routes
Navigable rivers

Ⓑ Banking
Ⓦ Wool
Ⓛ Linen
Ⓢ Silk
Ⓢ Silver mining
Ⓒ Copper Mining

300 Miles

in Florence and Venice, most men were shopkeepers, artisans, or wage workers. The merchant's dynamism, economic power, and influence, however, were out of all proportion to his numbers.

Furthermore, the diverse enterprises of the merchant illustrate many characteristics of the economic life of the age. In the high Middle Ages the merchant was usually an itinerant trader who moved his goods in person along the trade routes of the continent. By the early years of the sixteenth century he had been, by and large, a sedentary businessman for many generations. Under improved conditions of transportation, with the greater security for goods and persons enforced by the larger states, with cities like Bruges replacing fairs as centers of international exchange, with the beginning of marine insurance and reasonably rational and enforced codes of commercial law, the merchant became a man in an office. Here a mounting pile of ledgers, with their neat rows of assets and liabilities (recorded in Arabic rather than Roman numerals), informed him at a glance of the conditions of his affairs. From the office he conducted a continuous correspondence with his fellow merchants and with subordinates abroad (his factors), who kept him informed about the state of the market and about the many and varied circumstances, often political or military, affecting the supply and prices of the commodities and currencies he dealt in. Through the factors, who functioned as commission agents, he bought and sold. (Sales were not concluded, as they are today, on the basis of samples. Goods themselves had to be forwarded on speculation to the distant agent for sale, if possible, to local retailers—a system, clearly, that demanded of the merchant the nicest combination of flair and calculation.) He borrowed money and transferred it from place to place by a sophisticated system of bills of exchange. His firm was usually a family partnership, but he often pooled his capital with that of affluent associates for particular ventures: to handle large purchases or loans, to spread the risk in a difficult enterprise, to hire ships and ensure their armed protection. The sixteenth-century merchant was the resident motor of a complex economic machine.

A further characteristic of the early modern merchant, as of his medieval predecessor, was the extreme diversity of his enterprises. For although enough risk had been eliminated from international trade to enable the merchant to stay at home, conditions remained extremely hazardous by modern standards. The merchant therefore sought safety by putting his money into a large variety of separate ventures. Like all merchants until well into the eighteenth century, Renaissance traders dealt in as many commodities as possible, in many different parts of the world, investing only a fraction of their capital in each. Antonio, in Shakespeare's *Merchant of Venice*, expressed a common prudence:

> Believe me, no: I thank my fortune for it,
> My ventures are not in one bottom trusted,
> Nor to one place; nor is my whole estate
> Upon the fortune of this present year:
> Therefore my merchandise makes me not sad.

Even as large a firm as the Medici refused to specialize and dealt in commodities as various as raw wool, woolen cloth, silks, alum, dyestuffs, spices, olive oil, citrus fruits, raw cotton, gold thread, and much else besides.

But in diversifying his business the typical merchant went far beyond simply trading in numerous commodities. The very concept of "merchant" was very different in the sixteenth century from what it is today. We tend to separate industrial, commercial, and financial enterprises and to understand by "merchant" solely a man engaged in trade, commonly retail trade. Few Renaissance merchants engaged in retail trade; that was left to shopkeepers. A merchant occasionally restricted himself to buying and selling on the international market, but such specialization was rare. More often he was also a money changer, and sometimes he was an international banker; he was involved in the economics and problems of transportation; he was an insurance broker; he was an industrialist, large or small; he invested in both urban and rural real estate. In its medieval and early modern usage the word "merchant" implied all of these activities, singly or in combination. The Medici, for example, were merchants.

In addition to their purely commercial business they conducted all manner of banking operations, manufactured woolen cloth and silk, and for a time managed the papal alum mines at Tolfa. . . .

Social Climbing into Nobility

Grown rich in commerce, banking, and industry, the sixteenth-century merchant-capitalist was a man of individuality and ambitious resource. His life was motivated by a rational search for profit. He operated, however, in a society whose ideals were overwhelmingly religious and aristocratic. He could justify his way of life only in opposition to a traditional clerical distrust and a traditional aristocratic disdain. Any elite develops values that reflect its mode of life and legitimize its interests and ambitions. A gradual secularization of the economic ethic of the churches and the creation of a bourgeois morality performed this value-making function for the merchant class. The process began in Italy about 1400, the work of liberal scholastic theologians and civic humanists; it was continued in northern Europe by bourgeois publicists, Calvinist divines, and the Jesuit order. . . .

A popular genre of humanist ethical literature in the Renaissance was the treatise *De vera nobilitate* (*of true nobility*) which put true nobility in virtue and personal merit rather than in birth and taught that virtue is acquired, not inherited. The popularity of such works should probably be explained by their usefulness in legitimizing bourgeois pretensions. The idea of virtue, moreover, was itself given a positive middle-class content. In Italy in the fifteenth century, and north of the Alps in the sixteenth, there emerged clearly for the first time the attitudes which we lump together as "bourgeois morality," attitudes which contrasted sharply with aristocratic values. A noble, insofar as he could be precisely defined at all in the sixteenth century, was "a man who lived nobly." Fundamentally, to live nobly meant to fight and not to work. Above all, the noble was thought to derogate from his nobility (this was generally true in northern continental Europe, much less so in Italy and in England) if he engaged in trade. In contrast, bourgeois morality attributed positive value to productive work. The great sin became idleness rather than dishonor. Again, nobility obliged the aristocrat to maintain a certain standard of expenditure and consumption. If his income was insufficient, he borrowed. The bourgeois, however, practiced a willing thrift and was persuaded that he should spend less than he earned. He was willing to live ascetically so that his enterprise might prosper. By insisting that spiritual athletes live in the world rather than in monasteries, Protestantism reinforced this tendency and gave the individual new incentives to plan his life rationally in the pursuit of a worldly success, which was increasingly taken to be the sign of spiritual health. The noble might squander wealth in the idle enjoyment of what it could buy. The bourgeois found his identity in a very different ideal: constant productive activity and the reinvestment of its fruits.

Merchants were pleased to know that true nobility consisted in personal merit and that willing thrift could be a moral imperative—as long as they were merchants. In practice, however, bourgeois virtue rarely resisted the attraction of aristocratic status; and the ambition of most merchants was to exchange the social ambiguities of trade for the universally recognized prestige of nobility. The sixteenth-century merchant class was therefore extremely fluid, with trade and industry serving as the chief means by which men moved up in the social hierarchy. The kind of social mobility which had been assured by the Church during the Middle Ages (when the son of a peasant might reasonably hope to be pope) in the Renaissance was assured by mercantile enterprise. To be a noble, craftsman, or peasant was a largely hereditary condition; but few bourgeois fortunes remained invested in trade or industry for more than two or three generations. Normally, the grandson of a successful merchant abandoned the risky enterprises in which the family had made its money and invested more safely. He put his money into land, urban real estate, and government bonds. He bought a seigneury, a title and a government office. He gave his sons a humanistic education. By imitating aristocratic manners and investments, by intermarriage, simply by living "nobly," the bourgeois family displaced or merged with the older nobility.

The phenomenon was universal. In Venice in the sixteenth century the ruling class as a whole was gradually transformed from a purely mercantile oligarchy into an aristocracy whose wealth was in land and government bonds. By the early seventeenth century, the Fuggers were settled on their Swabian estates as imperial counts. In England, men of talent and modest origins made fortunes as clothiers or in the wholesale trade of woolen cloth. Their sons held administrative offices and began to buy up land in their home counties. The grandsons settled on these estates and founded gentry families. The pattern was similar in France. In one case, typical of many, a merchant in a small provincial town bought an office for his son in the royal financial administration. The son made a fortune in government finance and bought land and titles. His sons made brilliant careers in the magistracy and in the Church. In 1600, the family hired a genealogist, who traced their origins to a twelfth-century feudal baron. Success in trade and industry, in short, was the elevator which lifted the most enterprising members of lower social groups into the aristocracy. The process might take several generations; but great merchants, constantly recruited from below, ultimately gravitated to the land. Here they assumed the privileges and authority of nobles.

The Prince and the Courtier During the Italian Renaissance

E.R. Chamberlin

The Renaissance period generally saw the strengthening of monarchy throughout Europe. As scholar E.R. Chamberlin observes, some of the most powerful of these Renaissance princes emerged in the city-states of early Renaissance Italy. The rise of the house of Medici in Florence is a prominent example of the way these princes shaped and controlled their societies. The Italian writers Machiavelli and Castiglione both provide influential commentaries on the prerogatives and manners of the Renaissance prince and his court.

At the peak of Renaissance society stood the prince, the single, powerful man who, by a combination of political skill and hereditary authority, virtually ruled absolute over his state. It seems a curious contradiction that this period, which stressed, above all, the freedom of the individual, should have accepted the concept of the single ruler. There was good reason for it. In Italy, where the prince achieved his most brilliant and characteristic form, he was born of the fierce and endless tumults between factions in the cities. Despairing of ever finding peace except under the rule of one man, cities deserted the republican ideal, placing power freely in the hands of a leading citizen. Theoretically, that power was merely lent, not given, but once having enjoyed it few men intended to yield it back. Elsewhere in Europe, similar causes were at work in every country which did not possess a strong, central monarchy. . . .

Theoretically, the term 'prince' could be applied to all

Excerpted from *Everyday Life in Renaissance Times*, by E.R. Chamberlin. Copyright © E.R. Chamberlin 1965. Reprinted by permission of the publisher, B.T. Batsford Ltd.

who held power, whether over thousands or millions, and it is in this sense that Machiavelli and other political writers used the term. Those princes who contributed most to the new society, however, tended to be smaller rather than larger rulers, exerting a social influence out of proportion to their power until their courts were edged off the European stage by the development of the huge, modern nations. Federigo da Montefeltro, whose court at Urbino set a standard in civilised behaviour for 300 years, ruled perhaps 150,000 souls; those over whom the Medici exercised direct control probably did not exceed a quarter of a million. Even the powerful dukes of Burgundy maintained their independence only through the disordered condition of France. In earlier centuries, much of the energies of these princes would have been expended in war, for military victory meant both glory and survival; the Renaissance prince needed less the virtues of courage and military genius than to be versed in the subtle skills of finance and politics, for war now was in the hands of the professionals. His fame depended less upon battle honours than upon the culture of his court, the extent to which he patronised the arts and showed himself capable of conversing with the learned.

The most brilliant of the Renaissance princes were those early members of the house of Medici which dominated Florence for nearly three hundred years. Rarely can a single family have so influenced an entire continent. It was largely through their munificence and taste that there was gathered in the small city of Florence, during the late fifteenth and early sixteenth centuries the band of men who created the Renaissance. The Medici rule in Florence was tempestuous: three times they were thrown out of the city; three times they returned, creating an ever-closer grip upon the constitution. They took much—but they gave more. The ancient republican history of the city came to an end under them but, under them too, the city became the engine-house of the Renaissance. They poured their enormous wealth into the patronage of the arts and sciences. They spent the better part of four million pounds in less than half a century, not merely in adorning their palaces with works of art but also in endowing seats of learning. Cosimo de' Medici, called 'Pater patriae' [father of his country] by a grateful city, displayed the fantastic generosity of the family to the full in 1439 when the Council of Florence met in the city. He made himself the personal host of the scores of dignitaries attending it, among them the Pope, the Emperor of the East and the Patriarch of Constantinople. The conference was an attempt to achieve a working unity between the Church of Rome and the Eastern Church. It failed, but during the five months that it was in Florence it contributed something possibly even greater to Europe. Some of the most learned people of the world were gathered within the confines of the city between March and July of 1439, and outside the deliberations of the Council they found a ready audience in the Florentines, ever hungry for new ideas. Predominant among these scholars were the Greeks whose language provided the key to the sciences which had so long been lost to Europe. Through their influence Cosimo founded the Platonic Academy which his successors cherished.

In 1444 Cosimo began the construction of the first of the Medici palaces. His fellow-citizens protested, thinking it both unfitting and ominous that a so-called private citizen should build upon such a scale. They tried to unseat him but he weathered that particular storm although others were to follow. Later, when the Medici became overlords in law as they were in fact, and took the title of Duke, they built an enormous palace on the far side of the Arno—a sprawling, arrogant building which proclaimed the superior status of the family. But Cosimo's palace, where the Renaissance can be said to have been born, appears more as a private house in its exterior for it fits into the line of the street. It was the first of the Renaissance palaces, providing the model for scores to come. Medici rule was still far from absolute and the palace still had to discharge the function of a castle where the family could shelter from the rage of their fellows. The ground storey therefore appears solid, almost forbidding, but the upper stories are elegant. The great street door gave on to a little court, graceful and airy, and here were placed the statues of *David* and *Judith* which Donatello had been commissioned to produce while the palace was being constructed. The *David* was a work of a kind which had not been seen in Europe for over a thousand years, for it was executed in the round and, like the palace in which it stood, created a precedent for others to follow. . . .

In 1469 Lorenzo de' Medici became head of the family and of the State. He was only twenty years old at the time and, although bred to responsibility, was vividly aware of the burden he had to bear. 'The second day after my father's death, the principal men of the city and of the State came to our house to condole with us on our loss, and to encourage me to take on the care of the city and of the State as my father and grandfather had done. This proposal being against the instincts of my immature age, and considering that the burden and danger were great, I consented to it unwillingly.' His reason for acceptance was the sound, practical reason of finance which the Medici never quite abandoned. 'I did so in order to protect our friends and property for it fares ill in Florence with any who possesses wealth without any share in the government.' The Florentines thereby gained a leader who combined in his person all the qualities of the rich and diverse period. Financier and poet, statesman and scholar, economist and strategist—it seemed that there was no activity in which he could not excel if he so desired. The consummate political and military skill with which he steered Florence through the dangerous shoals of Italian politics ultimately left no trace, for Florence, with all Italy, became subject to foreigners. It was the manner in which he cherished and directed the new-born arts and learning which left its mark upon Europe. His patronage made heavy inroads even upon the great Medici fortune, but he looked upon himself as a custodian, rather than an owner, of wealth. 'Some would perhaps think it more desirable to have a part of it in their purse but I conceive it to have been spent to the great advantage of the public and am therefore perfectly satisfied.' The vast library which he amassed became the first true public library in Europe for it was freely available to all. Agents were engaged not only in Europe but in the East with the express purpose of discovering ancient manuscripts. One scholar brought back 200 Greek works, eighty of which had never before been known in Europe. The names of the innumerable artists he encouraged would be a catalogue of the creators of the Renaissance. Botticelli, five years his senior, had shared his childhood home and later worked for him; Leonardo da Vinci owed his appointment to the Milanese court to him; he gave the 15-year-old Michelangelo a home in his palace with a monthly allowance; Verrocchio, Ghirlandajo, Filippino Lippi—so the list could be extended until it included every talented man working in Florence during the brief years of Lorenzo's life. He died at the age of forty-three, but, though no other Medici could equal the versatility of 'Il Magnifico', yet they continued his work. One of them became pope as Leo X and infused into the most powerful court in Europe some

---

Transformed in the Likeness of Antiquity

In the following excerpt from a 1513 letter to a friend, the Italian philosopher Machiavelli expresses a reverent attitude towards the classical writers he "converses" with each night. For many Renaissance readers, the effect of classical thought and expression was profound, and other leading thinkers also felt their lives transformed through their encounters with the "great men of antiquity."

But when evening comes I return home and go into my library. At the door I take off my muddy everyday clothes. I dress myself as though I were about to appear before a royal court as a Florentine envoy. Then decently attired I enter the antique courts of the great men of antiquity. They receive me with friendship; from them I derive the nourishment which alone is mine and for which I was born. Without false shame I talk with them and ask them the causes of their actions; and their humanity is so great they answer me. For four long and happy hours I lose myself in them. I forget all my troubles; I am not afraid of poverty or death. I transform myself entirely in their likeness.

Niccolo Machiavelli, quoted in Eugene F. Rice Jr., *The Foundations of Early Modern Europe*, 1970, p. 66.

of the ideals which Lorenzo had cherished.

Renaissance society, having perforce accepted the single ruler, did not thereby accept him as a natural phenomenon to be endured or adored. His office was analysed, as it had never been before, in an attempt to explain its growth and function, to prepare a blue-print of a piece of political machinery which was to drive Europe for nearly three hundred years. The machinery was 'political' in the fullest sense, for it governed in some degree every aspect of the lives of men gathered together in communities, decreeing how they should be judged, how they should earn their bread, refresh their minds and bodies, protect themselves from enemies within and without the State. Two books appeared in the early years of the sixteenth century which placed the prince and his court under the microscope, *The Prince* by Niccolo Machiavelli and *The Courtier* by Baldassare Castiglione. They appeared within four years of each other, in 1528 and 1532, respectively, but both had been written, quite independently, many years before—testimony to the fact that the phenomenon of the prince was beginning to engage European attention. Machiavelli's intention was to dissect the mechanics of statecraft in terms of its effectiveness. Morality was irrelevant: if a strategy worked, it was good; if it failed, it was bad. There have been few writers so grossly misjudged as this Florentine republican who produced the classic textbook for the practice of tyranny. It is as though a doctor, having diagnosed a disease, were to be accused of inventing it. Machiavelli was well aware of the construction likely to be placed upon his work and went out of his way to stress that this was the picture of things as they were—that, given that the prince was necessary in civil life, then it was best that he should learn how to conduct himself in the most perilous craft in the world. He should indeed be a wise and virtuous man, but 'the manner in which men now live is so different from the manner in which they should live that he who deviates from the common course of practice and endeavours to act as duty dictates, necessarily ensures his own destruction'. Every man has a price, every seemingly disinterested action can be shown to be rooted in self-interest. A prince should keep his word—but few successful men actually do so. Is it better for a prince to be loved or feared? It depends, Machiavelli replies; circumstances alter cases but, on the whole, it is safer to be feared, for most men are fickle and timid and will abandon in the hour of need those who have favoured them and have no other call upon them than the claims of gratitude. A prince as a commander of troops should always be feared, never worrying about a reputation for cruelty, for this was the only possible way to keep cruel men in order. It was a jaundiced view of the world; none knew better than Machiavelli that men could, and did, die for no other price than love of their country. But such love presupposed freedom; where there was no longer freedom the only incentives were self-interest or fear.

Machiavelli's prince was the first among men but was still a man; the Latin mind declined to invest him with that tinge of divinity which, in the north, came to infuse the idea. In Burgundy, the concept of the duke as being the personification of the State, and therefore as being something greater than a common man, was erected into a principle and a ritual. All the trappings of adoration, more commonly reserved for the worship of God, were his. Religious texts which spoke of the Trinity were freely applied to his comings and goings. After certain festivities in Arras, le Clerc wrote: 'If God were to descend from heaven I doubt if they could do him greater honour than was made to the duke.' Another remarked of the enthusiasm shown in the streets, 'It seemed as though they had God himself by the feet'. The most precious metals were considered only just good enough to touch his sacred flesh, be viewed by his holy eyes. The attendance at table upon him echoed the ritual of the Holy Mass; his very cup-bearer was seen as the priest who, in another church, elevated the chalice. Even as at the altar, the napkin with which the duke dried his hands was kissed as it was passed from courtier to courtier. The torches which lit his way to table were kissed, as were the handles of the knives placed before him. Such adulation would have astonished the Italians. Lorenzo de' Medici, popular and competent though he was, came under heavy and sustained criticisms for his pretensions: 'He did not want to be equalled or imitated even in verses or games or exercises and turned angrily on any one who did so.' No one would have dared even attempt to be the equal of a duke of Burgundy. The excess was to bring its reaction: a king of England lost his head through too much devotion to the Divine Right and the monarchy of France ultimately collapsed in bloody ruin.

Machiavelli's *Prince* was a cold exercise in logic; Castiglione's *Courtier* was a warm, living portrait of the ideal man. 'I do not wonder that you were able to depict the perfect courtier', a friend wrote to him, 'for you had only to hold a mirror before you and set down what you saw there.' The graceful compliment was essentially true for Castiglione possessed most of the qualities he praised: piety, loyalty, courage, an easy learning and wit. Indeed, his life was almost a demonstration of Machiavelli's opinion that a virtuous man was at a disadvantage. As envoy between Pope Clement VII and the Emperor Charles V during the perilous days which culminated in the Sack of Rome in 1527, he was deluded by both, failed in his mission and died a discredited man. The Emperor, who so sorely tried him, said sadly, 'I tell you, one of the finest gentlemen in the world is dead'. Castiglione would have been proud of the epitaph and history, too, remembers him, not as diplomat but as gentleman.

The Courtier was the outcome of four brief years spent at the little court of Urbino. Afterwards, Castiglione was to mix with the truly great and powerful. As representative of the duke at the Papal Court, he came into intimate contact with Raphael, Michelangelo, Bembo; later he was Apostolic Nuncio to the Emperor's court. But always he looked back with nostalgia to the little court set among the hills of the northern Marches. He left Urbino in 1508, but for twenty years thereafter he lovingly polished and repolished his account of a civilised society, creating a monument to his own Golden Age. The duchy of Urbino owed its foundation to Federigo da Montefeltro, a professional soldier who yet managed to create a court in which the new humanist values were dazzlingly embodied. Piero della Francesca's portrait of him shows a man in whom strength is combined with tolerance, who would be surprised by nothing, expected nothing and was well able to defend his own rights. . . . He was a man who made a fortune from soldiering, played off his enemies one against the other and so kept inviolate the 400-odd hill villages and towns which acknowledged him as prince. But he was also a man who, in childhood, had been schooled by Vittorino da Feltre, the greatest humanist teacher in Europe, who infused in his pupils the new view of man. The great library at Urbino was Federigo's work. 'He alone had a mind to do what had not been done for a thousand years and more; that is, to create the finest library since ancient times.' Not for him was the common product of the new printing press; he employed thirty or forty scribes so that all his books should be 'written with the pen, not one printed, that it might not be disgraced thereby'.

In 1450 he began the construction of the palace which Castiglione knew and which attracted travellers on the Grand Tour long after the brief life of the duchy had passed. 'It seemed not a palace but a city in the form of a palace', Castiglione affirmed, 'and [he] furnished it not only with what is customary such as silver vases, wall hangings of the richest cloth of gold, silk and other like things but for ornament he added countless ancient statues of marble and bronze, rare paintings . . .' In this twofold role, admirer of ancient art and patron of modern painters, Federigo was essentially of the Renaissance. He died in 1482 and the dukedom passed to his son, Guidobaldo, who maintained the intellectual atmosphere of the court although he proved himself unable to hold back the militant world outside. It was his court which Castiglione described in the process of building up the portrait of the courtier. It is the picture of a group of brilliant minds, familiar with each other and therefore at ease, who have turned aside briefly from the cares of state and seek refreshment in conversation. There are feasts and entertainments of wide variety; during the day the members go about their business but each evening they meet again, under the presidency of the duchess (for the duke is grievously afflicted by gout and retires early). They talk into the small hours, pursuing each topic informally but with sobriety and order—and merriment too—fashioning between themselves the perfect man. So vividly did the memory stay with Castiglione that he could describe the end of one of these sessions with the poignancy of a paradise lost. . . .

After Castiglione's day, the image of the courtier suffered a decline, becoming either the image of a fop or an intriguing social climber; even the Italian feminine of the word—*'la cortegiana'* or courtesan—became a synonym for a high-class harlot. But for Castiglione, the courtier was the cream of civilised society. He did not have to be nobly born; admittedly, he usually was, for only those born into the upper classes had the leisure or the opportunities to practice the arts, but this recognition that 'courtesy' was a quality of mind, and not of class, went far to explain the wide influence of the book. The courtier must be able to acquit himself in all manly exercises—wrestling, running, riding, but should be equally at home with literature, able to speak several languages, play musical instruments, write elegant verse. But everything should be done with a casual air so that his conversation, though sensible, was sprightly; he was even enjoined to study the form and nature of jokes. In love, he was to be discreet and honourable; in war, courageous but magnanimous. Above all, he was to be a man of his word, loyal to his prince, generous to his servants. He was altogether far removed from that other ideal man, the knight, with his fantastic code of personal honour. In modern language, Castiglione's courtier would be described as a well-educated, 'decent' man, with a strong code of personal morals but tolerant of the weakness of others. It was an ideal by which most men probably measured their lapses, for the standard demanded was high. But that the book filled a void is well shown by the speed with which it entered other languages and how long it maintained its influence. It was translated into French in 1537, into Spanish in 1540, into English in 1561, and, 200 years after Urbino ceased to exist as a state, Samuel Johnson gave his benediction to the book which enshrined its memory. 'The best book that ever was written upon good breeding, Il Cortegiano, by Castiglione, grew up at the little court of Urbino and you should read it.'

Influential Women of the Renaissance

Margaret L. King

During the Renaissance, educational opportunities for women expanded, at least for members of the upper classes. Political power, on the other hand, fell to women only through royal succession, and it was held only with great difficulty. Margaret L. King, professor of history at City University of New York–Brooklyn, traces here the career achievements of the prominent female rulers of the Renaissance, including Catherine de' Medici and Queen Elizabeth, and she assesses their impact and influence on the long Renaissance debate about gender roles.

On the stake that supported the burning corpse of the peasant Joan of Arc, who had donned armor and rallied a king, a placard bore the names that the people of the Renaissance gave to the women they hated: heretic, liar, sorceress. The mystery of that hatred has preoccupied the many tellers of the tale of the life of this patron saint of France. Their answers cannot be recounted here, but without simplifying too much they can be summed up in this way: she was hated because she did what men did, and triumphantly. The men who planted stakes over the face of Europe would not tolerate such a transgression of the order they imagined to be natural. In the age of emblems, Joan of Arc is an emblem of the Renaissance women who attempted to partake in the civilization of the Renaissance: not as bearers of children or worshippers of God, but as forgers of its cultural forms. These women did not share her fate, but a few of them understood it.

Foremost among these women, in the records that that

age has left us, are those who had no choice about the role they played. Like Joan, they bore arms, or wielded powers still more formidable. They were the queens and female rulers who ruled as the surrogates of their absent husbands, dead fathers, and immature sons. Extraordinary in their personal strengths and achievements, they have left no residue: their capital passed through the male line of descent and not to female heirs—at least not in the centuries of which we speak. But as women who held command, even if briefly and without issue, they deserve our attention.

In Italy later in the same century that Joan illumined with her strength, Caterina Sforza posed a more traditional but still boldly independent figure. The illegitimate granddaughter of Francesco Sforza, who was in turn the illegitimate usurper of the dynasty of the Visconti in Milan, Caterina was propelled into the political maelstrom of quattrocento Italy by her marriage to Girolamo Riario, nephew of Pope Sixtus IV. After her husband's assassination in 1488, she fiercely defended her family's interests and the cities of Imola and Forlì. Greatly outnumbered by her besiegers, she defended Forlì against the enemy who held her six children hostage. Twelve years later, she again commanded the defense of those same walls, was defeated, possibly raped, and was brought captive to Rome by Cesare Borgia.

Powerful Female Rulers

While Sforza, like Joan of Arc, assumed a military role, she secured no power; few women, even of the most exalted noble and royal families, ever did. Two major exceptions were the Italian-born Catherine de' Medici, who as the widow of France's King Henri II was the regent for his successors, François II and Charles IX, and Elizabeth, daughter of the Tudor kings of England. Both molded a Renaissance identity for a female sovereign that expressed the ambiguity of their roles. The former adopted for herself the emblem of Artemisia (the type of armed-and-chaste maiden to be considered at greater length below), who was known for her dutiful remembrance of her predeceased husband, Mausolus. Wielding this device, Catherine de' Medici could both act assertively and demonstrate piety to the male rulers between whom she transmitted power. The more independent and bolder Elizabeth was a master builder of her public image and presented herself to her subjects in a variety of feminine identities: Astraea, Deborah, Diana. At the same time, to win support in moments of crisis for the unprecedented phenomenon of a female monarch, she projected androgynous images of her role (man-woman, queen-king, mother-son), and haughtily referred to herself as "prince," with the body of a woman and the heart of a king. She defied the identification of her sex with instability and incompetence. In 1601, the elderly Elizabeth asked Parliament in her Golden Speech: "Shall I ascribe anything to myself and my sexly weakness? I were not worthy to live then"; "my sex," she said a few weeks before her death, "cannot diminish my prestige." Had she married, she might have borne an heir. But had she married, she would have fallen under the influence of a male consort. Instead, a complete dyad in herself, she took no husband and declared herself married to England. Her heroic virginity, more in the pattern of the great saints than of a modern woman, set her apart from the other women of her realm who continued to marry and dwell within the family. Her sexual nature was exceptional, just as her kingly authority was anomalous. In and of herself, she insisted on her right to rule, and was the only woman to hold sovereign power during the Renaissance.

Much of the culture of the late sixteenth-century Tudor court revolved around this manlike virgin whose name still identifies it: Elizabethan. Subtly, the poets, playwrights, and scholars of the age commented on the prodigy among them. Foremost among these commentators was William Shakespeare; in the androgynous heroines of his comedies can be found versions of the monarch, sharp-witted and exalted beyond nature. These female characters, played by boys dressed as women who often dressed as boys to create beings of thoroughly confused sexuality, charmed and entranced like the queen herself. The Shakespearean genius also understood how deeply the phenomenon of a queen-king violated the natural order. In the seemingly lighthearted "Midsummer Night's Dream" he spoke about the abnormality of a political order ruled by a woman when the Amazon Hippolyta was wedded at the last to the lawful male wielder of power. Like Joan of Arc, Elizabeth was perceived (and perceived herself) as an Amazon, and deep in the consciousness of the age she dominated was the discomfiture caused by an armed maiden, a rational female, an emotional force unlimited by natural order.

The Argument over Female Rulers

The phenomenon of enthroned women like Catherine and Elizabeth provoked controversy about the legitimacy of female rule. No one was more outspoken than the Presbyterian John Knox, who charged in his *First Blast of the Trumpet Against the Monstrous Regiment of Women* of 1558 that "it is more than a monster in nature that a woman shall reign and have empire above man." "To promote a woman to bear rule, above any realm, nation, or city, is repugnant to nature, contumely to God, . . . and, finally, it is the subversion of good order, of all equity and justice." When a woman rules, the blind lead the sighted, the sick the robust, "the foolish, mad and frenetic" the discreet and sober. "For their sight in civil regiment is but blindness, their counsel foolishment, and judgment frenzy." Woman's attempt to rule is an act of treason: "For that woman reigneth above man, she hath obteined it by treason and conspiracy committed against God. . . . [Men] must study to repress her inordinate pride and tyranny to the uttermost of their power." God could occasionally choose a woman to rule, John Aylmer wrote a year later, refuting Knox; but most women were "fond, folish, wanton flibbergibbes, tatlers, triflers, wavering witles, without counsell, feable, careless, rashe proude," and so on.

Most defenders of female rule in the sixteenth century could not transcend the problem of gender. While Knox was driven to fury by the accession of Mary Tudor to power, the behavior of her successor Elizabeth the Great enraged the French Catholic political theorist Jean Bodin. In the sixth book of his *Six Books of the Republic*, Bodin explored thoroughly the emotional dimension of female rule. A woman's sexual nature would surely, he claimed, interfere with her effectiveness as ruler. As Giovanni Correr, the Venetian ambassador to France, said of another Queen Mary, the unfortunate monarch of Scotland, "to govern states is not the business of women." Other Venetian ambassadors to the court of Elizabeth's successors were more impressed: that queen by her exceptional wisdom and skill had "advanced the female condition itself," and "overcome the distinction of sexes." Male observers thus viewed the sex of the female monarch as an impediment to rule or considered it obliterated, overlooking it altogether, as though the woman was no woman. Spenser simply made his monarch an exception to the otherwise universal rule of female subordination: "vertuous women" know, he wrote, that they are born "to base humilitie," unless God intervenes to raise them "to lawful soveraintie" (*Faerie Queene* 5.5.25).

Although this problem was agonizing for the few women who ruled, there were only a handful who had to face it: it was rare for a woman to inherit power as did these English queens. It required, in fact, the timely death of all power-eligible males. Most women in the ruling classes did not rule, but only shared some of the prerogatives of sovereignty. In the vibrant artistic and intellectual climate of the Renaissance, particularly in Italy, this meant that they exercised the power of patronage. Women who did not rule or direct with their armies the forces of destruction could wield their authority and wealth to shape thought and culture.

Women as Patrons of Art and Culture

Wherever courts existed as centers of wealth, artistic activity, and discourse, opportunities abounded for intelligent women to perform in the role of patroness of the arts and culture. In France, Anne of Brittany, Queen of Charles VIII, commissioned the translation of Boccaccio's *Concerning Famous Women (De claris mulieribus)*, and filled her court with educated women and discussions of platonic love. The same king's sister-in-law Louise of Savoy tutored the future king François I and his sister, Marguerite, according to the principles of Italian humanism. The latter—Marguerite d'Angoulême, later of Navarre—was the director of cultural matters at her brother's royal court and the protector of a circle of learned men. Influenced by the evangelism of Lefèvre d'Etaples and Guillaume Budé, guided in matters of spirit by the bishop Guillaume Briçonnet, she was at the center of currents of proto-reform. An original thinker herself, her collection of stories, the *Heptaméron*, raised questions about the troubled roles of women in a man's world. From this court circle of active patronesses and educators there derived other women of some power and influence: among them the Calvinist Jeanne d'Albret, Marguerite's daughter and the mother of the future king Henry IV, a valiant fighter for her family and religion; and Renée, the heir of Louis XII who was bypassed in favor of her male cousin François I and made wife instead to the Duke of Ferrara, who chose as a companion for her own daughter the adolescent Italian humanist Olimpia Morata.

In Spain the formidable Isabella guided religious reform and intellectual life, while in England, her learned daughter Catherine of Aragon, King Henry VIII's first queen, was surrounded by the leading humanists of the era. It was for her that Erasmus wrote his *Institution of Christian Matrimony (Christiani matrimonii institutio)* and Juan Luis Vives his *Instruction of a Christian Woman (Institutio foeminae christianae)* and other works. She sought Vives as a tutor for her own daughter, the future queen Mary Tudor. A generation earlier, the proto-figure of the royal patroness and learned woman in England was Margaret Beaufort, Countess of Richmond, already noted as the mother of that country's first Tudor monarch. At the courts of Edward IV and Richard III, she had surrounded herself with minstrels and learned men, supported the art of printing (then in its early stages), endowed professorships of divinity at Oxford and Cambridge (where she founded two colleges), supervised the education of her son and grandchildren, and herself translated from the Latin the devotional *The Mirror of Gold of the Sinful Soul.*

Cultivated Women in Italy

In Italy, where courts and cities and talented men clustered, opportunities abounded for the cultivated woman to help shape the culture of the Renaissance. Notable among such patronesses was Isabella d'Este, daughter of the rulers of Ferrara, sister of Beatrice, who was to play a similar but paler role in Milan, and of Alfonso, Ferrante, Ippolito, and Sigismondo, whom she was to rival in fame. Trained by Battista Guarini, the pedagogue son of the great humanist Guarino Veronese, she had mastered Greek and Latin, the signs of serious scholarship, alongside such skills as lute-playing, dance, and witty conversation. Married to the ruler of Mantua, she presided at that court over festivities and performances, artists, musicians and scholars, libraries filled with elegant volumes; she lived surrounded everywhere by statues, ornate boxes, clocks, marbles, lutes, dishes, gowns, playing cards decorated with paintings, jewels, and gold. Ariosto, Bernardo da Bibbiena, and Gian Giorgio Trissino were among those she favored. She studied maps and astrology and had frequent chats with the ducal librarian, Pellegrino Prisciano. Her *Studiolo* and *Grotta*, brilliantly ornamented rooms in the ducal palace, were her glorious monuments. For these and other projects, she designed the allegorical schemes, consulting with her humanist advisers. Ruling briefly when her husband was taken captive during the wars that shook Italy after the invasion of the forces of France, Spain, and Empire, she was repaid with anger for her bold assumption of authority. Her great capacity was left to express itself in patronage.

Also dislodged from the limited tenure of sovereignty was the wealthy Venetian noblewoman Caterina Cornaro. Born to an ancient Venetian noble family with interests in the eastern Mediterranean—her own mother was from a Greek royal family—Cornaro was married in 1472, at age eighteen, to the King of Cyprus, James II. Her city was concerned with her royal marriage from the start: the island of Cyprus was strategically important, and the Serenissima was jealous of its citizens' involvement in consequential foreign affairs. Venetian concern was justified, for Cornaro became queen of Cyprus a year later, after her husband's sudden death, and held unstable sway, racked by conspiracies, for sixteen years. When Cornaro was tempted by a marriage into the Neapolitan royal house, Venice exerted its authority mightily to force her to abdicate the Cypriot throne. A Neapolitan connection would have meant the alienation of Cyprus from Venetian control. The legate dispatched to the island and charged to persuade her to step down was none other than her brother. He came with offers of an annual salary of 8,000 ducats and a small fiefdom on the Venetian terra firma: she would win fame for herself, he promised, and be known forever as Queen of Cyprus, if she donated her husband's island to her *patria*. Thus compensated by fame and wealth, Cornaro left her rich island kingdom for the miniature one at Asolo. In that court she reigned as queen over a coterie of *letterati:* not the least of them Pietro Bembo, who memorialized the activities over which Cornaro presided in the Arcadian dialogue *Gli Asolani*. Published in 1505 by Aldo Manuzio in Venice, ten years after the conversations that sparked Bembo's imagination had taken place, it circulated in twenty-two editions, Italian as well as Spanish and French. Perhaps more significantly, it influenced the even more famous and complex dialogue of Baldassare Castiglione, commemorating a court presided over by another patroness of letters.

The Qualities of Courtly Ladies

Cornaro's court as described by Bembo prefigures the one in Urbino which Castiglione described. There two women— the Duchess, Elisabetta Gonzaga, and her companion, Emilia Pia—guided and inspired the discussions of proper behavior for both sexes that made up the age's principal handbook of aristocratic values, circulated in some hundred editions and translated into all the major vernaculars: *The Book of the Courtier (Il libro del cortigiano)*. For both sexes, that behavior is sharply defined by the phenomenon of the court: men were not to be too boisterous; women were to be occasions of beauty and delight. No court "however great, can have adornment or splendor or gaiety in it without ladies"; in the same way, no courtier can "be graceful or pleasing or brave, or do any gallant deed of chivalry, unless he is moved by the society and by the love and charm of ladies." "Who learns to dance gracefully for any reason except to please women? Who devotes himself to the sweetness of music for any other reason? Who attempts to compose verses . . . unless to express sentiments inspired by women?"

The virtues that women had to possess to inspire these male achievements were manifold. The courtly lady shares some virtues possessed also by the gentleman—she should be well born, naturally graceful, well mannered, clever, prudent, and capable—but also others which are distinctively hers. If married, she should be a good manager of her husband's "property and house and children," and possess "all qualities that are requisite in a good mother." Beauty is a necessity for her, though not for her male counterpart: "for truly that woman lacks much who lacks beauty." Above all, she must be charming: "she will be able to entertain graciously every kind of man with agreeable and comely conversation suited to the time and place and to the station of the person with whom she speaks, joining to serene and modest manners, and to that comeliness that ought to inform all her actions, a quick vivacity of spirit whereby she will show herself a stranger to all boorishness; but with such a kind manner as to cause her to be thought no less chaste, prudent, and gentle than she is agreeable, witty, and discreet." The qualities the court lady possesses are distinct from those of the courtier she is set to amuse: "above all . . . in her ways, manners, words, gestures, and bearing, a woman ought to be very unlike a man; for just as he must show a certain solid and sturdy manliness, so it is seemly for a woman to have a soft and delicate tenderness, with an air of womanly sweetness in her every movement, which, in her going and staying, and in whatever she says, shall always make her appear the woman without any resemblance to a man." Unlike the queen who bears the power and the glory of the males who otherwise occupy her throne, according to Giuliano de' Medici, Castiglione's spokesman by no means hostile to the female sex, the aristocratic lady must be taught to be something other than a man. The same was true of her humbler counterpart in the bourgeois or artisan classes.

Everyday Life in Renaissance Europe

William Manchester

Although the Renaissance was an age of glorious artistic and literary achievements, most Europeans lacked access to high culture and consequently drew no benefit from the revolution in arts and letters. The mundane lifestyle of Renaissance townsfolk remained predominantly unaltered. In the following essay, author William Manchester provides vivid descriptions of small-town commerce and life, along with an assessment of the predominantly rural and primitive lifestyle of the poorer segments of Renaissance society.

What was the world [of the Renaissance] like—and to them it was the *only* world, round which the sun orbited each day—when ruled by such men? Imagination alone can reconstruct it. If a modem European could be transported back five centuries through a kind of time warp, and suspended high above earth in one of those balloons which fascinated Jules Verne, he would scarcely recognize his own continent. Where, he would wonder, looking down, are all the people? Westward from Russia to the Atlantic, Europe was covered by the same trackless forest primeval the Romans had confronted fifteen hundred years earlier, when, according to Tacitus's *De Germania*, Julius Caesar interviewed men who had spent two months walking from Poland to Gaul [France] without once glimpsing sunlight. One reason the lands east of the Rhine and north of the Danube had proved unconquerable to legions commanded by Caesar and over seventy other Roman consuls was that, unlike the other territories he subdued, they lacked roads.

But there *were* people there in A.D. 1500. Beneath the deciduous canopy, most of them toiling from sunup to sundown, dwelt nearly 73 million people, and although that was less than a tenth of the continent's modern population, there were enough Europeans to establish patterns and precedents still viable today. Twenty million of them lived in what was known as the Holy Roman Empire—which, in the hoary classroom witticism, was neither holy, nor Roman, nor an empire. It was in fact central Europe: Germany and her bordering territories. There were 15 million souls in France, Europe's most populous country. Thirteen million lived in Italy, where the population was densest, 8 million in Spain, and a mere 4.5 million—the number of Philadelphians in 1990—in England and Wales.

Smaller Cities

A voyager into the past would search in vain for the sprawling urban complexes which have dominated the continent since the Industrial Revolution transformed it some two hundred years ago. In 1500 the three largest cities in Europe were Paris, Naples, and Venice, with about 150,000 each. The only other communities with more than 100,000 inhabitants were situated by the sea, rivers, or trading centers: Seville, Genoa, and Milan, each of them about the size of Reno, Nevada; Eugene, Oregon; or Beaumont, Texas. Even among the celebrated *Reichsstädte* of the empire, only Cologne housed over 40,000 people. Other cities were about the same: Pisa had 40,000 citizens; Montpellier, the largest municipality in southern France, 40,000; Florence 70,000; Barcelona 50,000; Valencia 30,000; Augsburg 20,000; Nuremberg 15,000; Antwerp and Brussels 20,000. London was by far England's largest town, with 50,000 Londoners; only 10,000 Englishmen lived in Bristol, the second-largest.

Twentieth-century urban areas are approached by superhighways, with skylines looming in the background. Municipalities were far humbler then. Emerging from the forest and following a dirt path, a stranger would confront the grim walls and turrets of a town's defenses. Visible beyond them would be the gabled roofs of the well-to-do, the huge square tower of the donjon, the spires of parish churches, and, dwarfing them all, the soaring mass of the local cathedral.

If the bishop's seat was the spiritual heart of the community, the donjon, overshadowing the public square, was its secular nucleus. On its roofs, twenty-four hours a day, stood watchmen ready to strike the alarm bells at the first sign of attack or fire. Below them lay the council chamber, where el-

The Italian Image of Civility

Though there is much about everyday life in the Renaissance that is appalling from a modern perspective, the period marked the emergence of new ideals of behavior and comportment. As scholar J.H. Plumb observes, the Italian writer Castiglione inspired a more sophisticated and cultivated model of aristocratic manners, a model that influenced Europe throughout the Renaissance.

Castiglione depicted [the princes of Italy] as they desired themselves to be, just as Titian painted them as they wished to look—distinguished, set apart by their *virtù* and destiny from other men, yet full of ease, grace, nobility, and charm. The image created by Castiglione and his imitators, for his book enjoyed a vast success, increased the civility of Italians, made their courts a byword for sophisticated living. The cleanliness of their homes, the decorum at their tables, the beauty of their clothes and furnishings, the elegance of their manners, became models for the rude provincial gentry of the northern countries. Indeed for many generations Italy became an obsession for the less sophisticated nations of Europe, for it provided Europe not only with images of men, but also with a mirage of aristocratic and courtly life. Of course between image and reality there was frequently enough of a chasm. Most men could not live like Castiglione. Crude manners, vulgar habits, coarse pleasures, the instinctive life of which Aretino sang, lurked even in the Courtier. The importance of Castiglione lies in the fact that men thought they *ought* to be like his Courtier, and valued men who seemed to achieve it.

J.H. Plumb, *The Italian Renaissance*, 1965, p. 124.

ders gathered to confer and vote; beneath that, the city archives; and, in the cellar, the dungeon and the living quarters of the hangman, who was kept far busier than any executioner today. Sixteenth-century men did not believe that criminal characters could be reformed or corrected, and so there were no reformatories or correctional institutions. Indeed, prisons as we know them did not exist. Maiming and the lash were common punishments; for convicted felons the rope was commoner still.

The donjon was the last line of defense, but it was the wall, the first line of defense, which determined the propinquity inside it. The smaller its circumference, the safer (and cheaper) the wall was. Therefore the land within was invaluable, and not an inch of it could be wasted. The twisting streets were as narrow as the breadth of a man's shoulders, and pedestrians bore bruises from collisions with one another. There was no paving; shops opened directly on the streets, which were filthy; excrement, urine, and offal were simply flung out windows.

And it was easy to get lost. Sunlight rarely reached ground level, because the second story of each building always jutted out over the first, the third over the second, and the fourth and fifth stories over those lower. At the top, at a height approaching that of the great wall, burghers could actually shake hands with neighbors across the way. Rain rarely fell on pedestrians, for which they were grateful, and little air or light, for which they weren't. At night the town was scary. Watchmen patrolled it—once clocks arrived, they would call, "One o'clock and all's well!"—and heavy chains were stretched across street entrances to foil the flight of thieves. Nevertheless rogues lurked in dark comers.

Changing Trade Practices

One neighborhood of winding little alleys offered signs, for those who could read them, that the feudal past was receding. Here were found the butcher's lane, the papermaker's street, tanners' row, cobblers' shops, saddlemakers, and even a small bookshop. Their significance lay in their commerce. Europe had developed a new class: the merchants. The hubs of medieval business had been Venice, Naples, and Milan—among only a handful of cities with over 100,000 inhabitants. Then the Medicis of Florence had entered banking. Finally, Germany's century-old Hanseatic League stirred itself and, overtaking the others, for a time dominated trade.

The Hansa, a league of some seventy medieval towns centering around Bremen, Hamburg, and Lübeck, was originally formed in the thirteenth century to combat piracy and overcome foreign trade restrictions. It reached its apogee when a new generation of rich traders and bankers came to power. Foremost among them was the Fugger family. Having started as peasant weavers in Augsburg, not a Hanseatic town, the Fuggers expanded into the mining of silver, copper, and mercury. As moneylenders, they became immensely wealthy, controlling Spanish customs and extending their power throughout Spain's overseas empire. Their influence stretched from Rome to Budapest, from Lisbon to Danzig, from Moscow to Chile. In their banking role, they loaned millions of ducats to kings, cardinals, and the Holy Roman emperor, financing wars, propping up popes, and underwriting new adventures—putting up the money, for example, that King Carlos of Spain gave Magellan in commissioning his voyage around the world. In the early sixteenth century the family patriarch was Jakob Fugger II, who first emerged as a powerful figure in 1505, when he secretly bought the crown jewels of Charles the Bold, duke of Burgundy. Jakob first became a count in Kirchberg and Weisserhorn; then, in 1514 the emperor Maximilian I—*der gross Max*—acknowledged the Fuggers' role as his chief financial supporter for thirty years by making him a hereditary knight of the Holy Roman Empire. In 1516, by negotiating complex loans, Jakob made Henry VIII of England a Fugger ally. It was a tribute to the family's influence, and to the growth of trade everywhere, that a year later the Church's Fifth Lateran Council lifted its age-old prohibition of usury.

Each European town of any size had its miniature Fugger, a merchant whose home in the marketplace typically rose five stories and was built with beams filled in with stucco, mortar, and laths. Storerooms were piled high with expen-

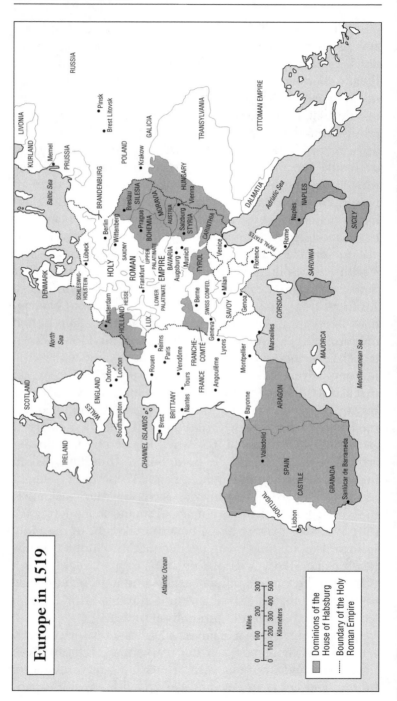

Europe in 1519

Dominions of the
House of Habsburg

Boundary of the Holy
Roman Empire

sive Oriental rugs and containers of powdered spices; clerks at high desks pored over accounts; the owner and his wife, though of peasant birth, wore gold lace and even ignored laws forbidding anyone not nobly born to wear furs. In the manner of a grand seigneur the merchant would chat with patrician customers as though he were their equal. Impoverished knights, resenting this, ambushed merchants in the forest and cut off their right hands. It was a cruel and futile gesture; commerce had arrived to stay, and the knights were just leaving. Besides, the adversaries were mismatched. The true rivals of the mercantile class were the clerics. Subtly but inexorably the bourgeois would replace the clergy in the continental power structure.

Rural Life

The town, however, was not typical of Europe. In the early 1500s one could hike through the woods for days without encountering a settlement of any size. Between 80 and 90 percent of the population (the peasantry; serfdom had been abolished everywhere except in remote pockets of Germany) lived in villages of fewer than a hundred people, fifteen or twenty miles apart, surrounded by endless woodlands. They slept in their small, cramped hamlets, which afforded little privacy, but they worked—entire families, including expectant mothers and toddlers—in the fields and pastures between their huts and the great forest. It was brutish toil, but absolutely necessary to keep the wolf from the door. Wheat had to be beaten out by flails, and not everyone owned a plowshare. Those who didn't borrowed or rented when possible; when it was impossible, they broke the earth awkwardly with mattocks.

Knights, of course, experienced none of this. In their castles—or, now that the cannon had rendered castle defenses obsolete, their new manor houses—they played backgammon, chess, or checkers (which was called *cronometrista* in Italy, *dames* in France, and draughts in England). Hunting, hawking, and falconry were their outdoor passions. A visitor from the twentieth century would find their homes uncomfortable: damp, cold, and reeking from primitive sanitation, for plumbing was unknown. But in other ways they were attractive and spacious. Ceilings were timbered, floors tiled (carpets were just beginning to come into fashion); tapestries covered walls, windows were glass. The great central hall of the crumbling castles had been replaced by a vestibule at the entrance, which led to a living room dominated by its massive hearth, and, beyond that, a "drawto chamber," or "(with)drawing room" for private talks and a "parler" for general conversations and meals.

Gluttony wallowed in its nauseous excesses at tables spread in the halls of the mighty. The everyday dinner of a man of rank ran from fifteen to twenty dishes; England's earl of Warwick, who fed as many as five hundred guests at a sitting, used six oxen a day at the evening meal. The oxen were not as succulent as they sound; by tradition, the meat was kept salted in vats against the possibility of a siege, and boiled in a great copper vat. Even so, enormous quantities of it were ingested and digested. On special occasions a whole stag might be roasted in the great fireplace, crisped and larded, then cut up in quarters, doused in a steaming pepper sauce, and served on outsized plates.

Unsanitary, Close Quarters

The hearth excepted, the home of a prosperous peasant lacked these amenities. Lying at the end of a narrow, muddy lane, his rambling edifice of thatch, wattles, mud, and dirty brown wood was almost obscured by a towering dung heap in what, without it, would have been the front yard. The building was large, for it was more than a dwelling. Beneath its sagging roof were a pigpen, a henhouse, cattle sheds, corncribs, straw and hay, and, last and least, the family's apartment, actually a single room whose walls and timbers were coated with soot. According to Erasmus, who examined such huts, "almost all the floors are of clay and rushes from the marshes, so carelessly renewed that the foundation sometimes remains for twenty years, harboring, there below, spittle and vomit and wine of dogs and men, beer . . . remnants of fishes, and other filth unnameable. Hence, with the change of weather, a vapor exhales which in my judgment is far from wholesome."

The centerpiece of the room was a gigantic bedstead, piled

high with straw pallets, all seething with vermin. Everyone slept there, regardless of age or gender—grandparents, parents, children, grandchildren, and hens and pigs—and if a couple chose to enjoy intimacy, the others were aware of every movement. In summer they could even watch. If a stranger was staying the night, hospitality required that he be invited to make "one more" on the familial mattress. This was true even if the head of the household was away, on, say, a pilgrimage. If this led to goings-on, and the husband resumed to discover his wife with child, her readiest reply was that during the night, while she was sleeping, she had been penetrated by an incubus. Theologians had confirmed that such monsters existed and that it was their demonic mission to impregnate lonely women lost in slumber. (Priests offered the same explanation for boys' wet dreams.) Even if the infant bore a striking similarity to someone other than the head of the household, and tongues wagged as a result, direct accusations were rare. Cuckolds were figures of fun; a man was reluctant to identify himself as one. Of course, when unmarried girls found themselves with child and told the same tale, they met with more skepticism.

If this familial situation seems primitive, it should be borne in mind that these were *prosperous* peasants. Not all their neighbors were so lucky. Some lived in tiny cabins of crossed laths stuffed with grass or straw, inadequately shielded from rain, snow, and wind. They lacked even a chimney; smoke from the cabin's fire left through a small hole in the thatched roof—where, unsurprisingly, fires frequently broke out. These homes were without glass windows or shutters; in a storm, or in frigid weather, openings in the walls could only be stuffed with straw, rags—whatever was handy. Such families envied those enjoying greater comfort, and most of all they coveted their beds. They themselves slept on thin straw pallets covered by ragged blankets. Some were without blankets. Some didn't even have pallets.

Food and Famine

Typically, three years of harvests could be expected for one year of famine. The years of hunger were terrible. The peasants might be forced to sell all they owned, including their pitifully inadequate clothing, and be reduced to nudity in all seasons. In the hardest times they devoured bark, roots, grass; even white clay. Cannibalism was not unknown. Strangers and travelers were waylaid and killed to be eaten, and there are tales of gallows being torn down—as many as twenty bodies would hang from a single scaffold—by men frantic to eat the warm flesh raw.

However, in the good years, when they ate, they *ate*. To avoid dining in the dark, there were only two meals a day— "dinner" at 10 A.M. and "supper" at 5 P.M.—but bountiful harvests meant tables which groaned. Although meat was rare on the Continent, there were often huge pork sausages, and always enormous rolls of black bread (white bread was the prerogative of the patriciate) and endless courses of soup: cabbage, watercress, and cheese soups; "dried peas and bacon water," "poor man's soup" from odds and ends, and during Lent, of course, fish soup. Every meal was washed down by flagons of wine in Italy and France, and, in Germany or England, ale or beer. "Small beer" was the traditional drink, though since the crusaders' return from the East many preferred "spiced beer," seasoned with cinnamon, resin, gentian, and juniper. Under Henry VII and Henry VIII the per capita allowance was a gallon of beer a day— even for nuns and eight-year-old children. Sir John Fortescue observed that the English "drink no water, unless at certain times upon religious score, or by way of doing penance."

Life Expectancy and Clothing

This must have led to an exceptional degree of intoxication, for people then were small. The average man stood a few inches over five feet and weighed about 135 pounds. His wife was shorter and lighter. Anyone standing several inches over six feet was considered a giant and inspired legends— Jack the Giant Killer, for example, and Jack and the Beanstalk. Folklore was rich in such violent tales, for death was their constant companion. Life expectancy was brief; half the people in Europe died, usually from disease, before reaching their thirtieth birthday. It was still true, as Richard

Rolle had written earlier, that "few men now reach the age of forty, and fewer still the age of fifty." If a man passed that milestone, his chances of reaching his late forties or his early fifties were good, though he looked much older; at forty-five his hair was as white, back as bent, and face as knurled as an octogenarian's today. The same was true of his wife—"Old Gretel," a woman in her thirties might be called. In longevity she was less fortunate than her husband. The toll at childbirth was appalling. A young girl's life expectancy was twenty-four. On her wedding day, traditionally, her mother gave her a piece of fine cloth which could be made into a frock. Six or seven years later it would become her shroud.

Clothing served as a kind of uniform, designating status. Some raiment was stigmatic. Lepers were required to wear gray coats and red hats, the skirts of prostitutes had to be scarlet, public penitents wore white robes, released heretics carried crosses sewn on both sides of their chests—you were expected to pray as you passed them—and the breast of every Jew, as stipulated by law, bore a huge yellow circle. The rest of society belonged to one of the three great classes: the nobility, the clergy, and the commons. Establishing one's social identity was important. Each man knew his place, believed it had been foreordained in heaven, and was aware that what he wore must reflect it.

The Darker Side of Renaissance Society

Philip Lee Ralph

Renaissance scholar Philip Lee Ralph analyzes in this essay the curious paradox that the dominant mood of the early Renaissance was very optimistic, even though social and political conditions were dismal and tumultuous. While the mood of the later Renaissance became more disillusioned due to political power struggles and widespread violence, these later years also saw some of the greatest artistic and literary accomplishments of the Renaissance.

The mood of the early Renaissance—illogical as it may seem—was predominantly optimistic. The Black Death, one of the most devastating calamities in the whole of Western history, failed to dispel the mood or to destroy initiative. Boccaccio's *Decameron* tales, which celebrated the delights of human wit and appetite, were composed while Florence was suffering an epidemic of the plague. The most notable progress toward a democratic state in Florence was accomplished by the generation following the Black Death; at the end of the century Florence emerged as champion of free republics against the tyrants of Milan, and her citizens, though still few in numbers, engaged in an ambitious program of territorial expansion. Italian publicists of the fourteenth and early fifteenth centuries expressed confidence rather than defeatism. The humanist chancellors Salutati and Bruni proudly cited Florence's wealth, her "flourishing" population, and the magnitude of her affairs—at a time when, judging from statistical records, population had dropped by at least one-third and the output of woolen cloth by two-thirds since their early fourteenth-century peak, and when the number of banks and the volume of their business were diminishing. The current of optimism was especially strong in Florence between about 1380 and 1420, reflecting both an economic upturn in the second decade of the fifteenth century and the satisfaction of the closely knit oligarchy that had gained control of the government of the republic. This favored and highly prosperous group could afford to be optimistic and could afford to express its gratitude by patronizing "civic humanism" and engaging in "an activism perhaps unparalleled in the annals of a city-state bourgeoisie since the halcyon days of the Roman Republic." The optimistic outlook of Florentines was matched by inhabitants of other Italian centers. Contemporary chroniclers boasted of the size, wealth, and grandeur of their cities with such fervor that even modern historians, until recently, were inclined to accept their inflated testimonials. . . .

The mood of optimism did not persist indefinitely. The High Renaissance of the late fifteenth and early sixteenth centuries, while producing the ripest works of genius, was colored by shades of doubt, resignation, and disillusionment, partly attributable to dwindling economic prospects and the collapse of political hopes. But if time had run out for the Italian cities, it was because they had not made the wisest use of the time allotted them. The distortions and injustices within their own societies—far more than the eclipse of the Levant trade or the vicissitudes of banking and industrial establishments—may be blamed for a deepening despondency and the slackening of civic and cultural vigor.

Society in Turmoil

The process of social change that characterized the later Middle Ages became so pronounced during the Renaissance that it makes the medieval order appear stable by comparison. The dissolution of old bonds of allegiance led to conflict, confusion, and uncertainty as to the location and extent of authority. The notorious violence of the age has given it a certain lurid fascination. Some shocked observers have interpreted the violence as a sign of moral degeneracy, but it is better understood as a symptom of stress and strain within the social fabric. The changes taking place held the possibility of a freer and more productive society, with a wider range of opportunities, though their more immediate effect was to disrupt traditional restraints and to leave the weak at the mercy of the strong.

Whatever uncertainties attended the upper reaches of society, there is no doubt as to the abject state of the people at the bottom. Increasing social mobility did not bring equality or an improvement in living standards for the majority. Serfdom was disappearing in the more progressive agrarian regions, such as England, France, and the Netherlands, largely because it had ceased to be profitable, but the lowest class of rural labor—unorganized, undefended before the law—sank to the condition of a commodity. In the industrially advanced sections of Europe, merchant entrepreneurs who handled the exporting and importing of valuable wares forced local craft guilds into a subsidiary role or displaced them altogether. Surviving guilds tended to become closed corporations of masters. Journeymen were kept perpetually as wage earners. Even more unfortunate were the unskilled workers outside the guild system or absorbed into newly developing industries which had no guild tradition. Although not yet equipped with factories and heavy machinery, the fifteenth and sixteenth centuries evidenced somber aspects of modern industrial society, including strikes, blacklisting, and exploitation of the labor of women and children.

The numerous towns of northern Italy in the thirteenth and fourteenth centuries successfully extended their rule over adjacent country districts, forced the rural inhabitants to pay heavy taxes while denying them the privilege of communal citizenship, and, in spite of their essentially mercantile character, assumed the position of a feudal lord in relation to the body of country folk who supplied them with food, timber, and other raw materials. Although serfdom was a negligible factor in northern Italy, the institution of slavery revived when the Black Death of the mid-fourteenth century created a labor shortage. Florence, Genoa, Venice, and Siena imported slaves from Near Eastern markets, employing them chiefly as domestic servants.

Excess and Violence

A scramble for wealth, power, and personal distinction generated emotional excess that readily found an outlet in violence. In the hands of talented desperadoes murder became a fine art, practiced with ingenuity and a variety of methods. The lurid tales of the Borgia family, though largely fabricated, could gain currency because they did not greatly exceed authenticated instances of mayhem and treachery. Benvenuto Cellini's Autobiography casually relates his success in dispatching his personal enemies and quotes a pope as excusing him on the ground that "men like Benvenuto, unique in their profession, stand above the law." Although Cellini was an exceptional case and prone to exaggeration, the age showed a remarkable tolerance for outrageous acts that were performed with skill or daring or that contributed to some supposedly laudable end: successful assassins were frequently converted into heroes. "Blessed be the Lord, blessed be the Duke, blessed be this murder"—expressed the popular approval when one rapacious cardinal and papal administrator was dispatched. The sordid accounts of Renaissance feuds suggest that no respect for sex, age, or sacred place could deter infuriated antagonists. The Pazzi conspiracy of 1478 against the Medici brothers called for the murder to be committed in the cathedral during high mass when the victims would be least prepared to resist. In the Romagna twenty people were butchered during one Sunday mass and their slayers absolved, for a consideration, by Pope Alexander VI.

While the most hideous crimes often went unpunished—or were privately avenged at compound interest—the judicial machinery of governments meted out senseless and cruel penalties for minor offences, especially when committed by the poor. The criminal codes of all the civilized states of Europe were barbarous, and remained so until affected by the humanitarian reform movements of the late eighteenth and nineteenth centuries. Counterfeiting, cattle-stealing, jailbreaking, and pocket-picking were only a few of a long list of capital offences. A condemned criminal might be hanged if he was fortunate; he might also be burned at the stake or boiled to death. Beating, branding, and mutilation were lesser forms of punishment, and torture was regularly employed to extract confessions. With the state, the law, and the judges setting such an example, it is no wonder that human sensibilities became blunted.

Armed Strife

If there had been no other disasters during the fifteenth and sixteenth centuries, the interminable conflicts raging up and down the continent of Europe were almost sufficient in themselves to prevent the growth of a healthy society. Armed strife has been a feature of practically every epoch of civilization, and the wars of the Renaissance era are not the most important in military history. But while the destructive capacity of Renaissance armies seems infinitesimal by today's standards, it was far greater than could be inflicted by a press of armored knights. Artillery was coming into use, and infantry—cheaper and more expendable than mounted warriors—had begun to play a major role in combat.

The real victims of the wars of the despots were not soldiers or the governments that hired them but civilian populations. Armies customarily lived off the land, robbing, pillaging, laying waste the fields, and raping and murdering the inhabitants. Troops that adhered to a disciplined restraint were a rare exception. It was cheaper for their employer to let them plunder than to pay wages, and *condottieri* found it necessary to offer the incentive of loot to hold the allegiance of their fighting men. Fortified towns might be starved into surrender by a long siege and then delivered to the lust and avarice of the captors. The famous sack of Rome in 1527 stands out as one of the most horrifying incidents of the wars of this epoch. The invading imperial forces, before which Pope Clement VII took refuge in the Castle of Sant' Angelo, included Spaniards and German Lutherans—all of them near the point of mutiny over arrears in pay. The sack, one of the most thorough on record, lasted a month. For days and nights the screams of victims—men, women, and children—rent the air; palaces were gutted, churches, hospitals, and tombs pillaged and smashed; corpses were left to rot in the streets. Almost half of the city's population is believed to have perished during this bestial visitation. The sack of Rome and its accompanying orgy of blood attracted wide attention because of the fame of the Eternal City, but the atrocities were only an extreme example of the common incidents of contemporary warfare.

The Art of War

The mores of the period looked upon war as a normal and necessary human activity. Baldassare Castiglione's idealistic treatise, *The Book of the Courtier*, starts with the assumption that "the principal and true profession of the courtier must be that of arms," and "the more our courtier excels in this art, the more he will merit praise." One of the speakers in the *Courtier*, who criticizes contemporary rulers for neglecting the tasks of peace, stipulates:

> princes ought not to make their people warlike out of a desire to dominate, but in order to defend themselves and their people . . . or in order to drive out tyrants and govern well those people who are badly treated; or in order to subject those who by nature deserve to become slaves, with the aim of giving them good government, ease, repose, and peace.

The escape clauses seem sufficient to cover every alleged *casus belli*, ancient or modern.

Influential writers supported the high priority given to military pursuits as a function of the body politic. Machiavelli taught that the prince's first duty was to master the art of war and to wage it successfully. Religious leaders, including the Protestant Reformers, regarded armed conflict as inevitable if not desirable. To the Reformers the scourge of war could be an instrument of divine judgment; and they taught that subjects must submit to the violence of their rulers, whether directed against themselves or against the people of a neighboring state. Erasmus stood almost alone among intellectual leaders in advocating pacifism. Not surprisingly, those who profited directly from the bloody business showed little interest in halting it. A group of *condottieri*, fearing that Peace might raise her timid head in Italy, exclaimed, "Where shall we go then? We shall have to return to the hoe. Peace is death to us. War is our life."

The Status of Women

If man's position was imperiled by the roughness of the times, woman's remained far worse. The alleged emancipation of women during the Renaissance is a myth. Among all classes of society, women were typically regarded as sex objects, of possible commercial value. Legislation relating to female workers was designed to make them available on the labor market rather than to protect them from exploitation. The degradation of women is evidenced by the large number of professional prostitutes (some seven thousand in Rome and upwards of eleven thousand in Venice during the High Renaissance). Both social convention and the law upheld a double standard of sexual morality. Adultery was an acceptable pastime for a husband; a wife's unfaithfulness could be—although rarely was—punished by death. Marriage among members of the middle and upper classes retained the character of a property transaction arranged by parents of the two parties with the girl's dowry serving as inducement to an advantageous contract. The prospective bride might be betrothed at the age of three and married before she entered her teens. Supposedly, women of the aristocracy, reared in luxury and often well educated, enjoyed a greater degree of independence. If marriageable, however, they served as pawns in the game of alliance-building that became an obsession with both large and petty principalities. Many an attractive and high-spirited young woman, sacrificed on the altar of political expediency, was sent off as consort to a total stranger in an uncongenial environment. Surprisingly, some of these bartered brides developed a genuine love for their husbands, overlooked their infidelities, and assisted in the governance of the state or enhanced its luster by holding court for artists and writers.

Amid the pressures and intrigues of a power-oriented society, only a rare woman could carve out a career and win recognition in her own right. To succeed in the arena of politics she had to be of uncommonly tough fiber, able to play a man's game while employing her feminine wiles to take advantage of the weaknesses of the opposite sex. Such a woman was Caterina Sforza, niece of Duke Lodovico of Milan and mother—by her second husband, Giovanni de' Medici—of the heroic captain Giovanni "of the Black Band." Inured to violence (her first husband and two of her lovers were murdered), she repaid her injuries in like coin and with interest, while also giving free rein to her prodigious sensuality. Determined to maintain her rule over two petty states in the Romagna, she pitted herself against Cesare Borgia and paid a high price for her audacity. When she became his prisoner, Cesare took his revenge on Caterina's handsome body and then incarcerated her in a Roman dungeon.

The brutal aspects of Renaissance life are not proof of wholesale corruption or decadence. An age that displayed such exuberance and left such enduring works cannot fairly be called decadent. The seamy incidents, however, do reflect serious flaws in society and institutions.

Witchcraft in Renaissance Europe

Merry E. Wiesner

The phenomenon of witchcraft persecution emerged in Europe in a climate of intellectual suspicion of women in general, according to Merry Wiesner, professor of history at the University of Wisconsin–Milwaukee. Women were considered weak and given to carnal lust, and such stereotypes facilitated accusations of experimenting with black magic. Wiesner also examines the Protestant Reformation and the ongoing social and economic upheaval of the period as factors contributing to the dramatic rise in witchcraft persecutions.

As for the first question, why a greater number of witches is found in the fragile feminine sex than among men . . . the first reason is, that they are more credulous, and since the chief aim of the devil is to corrupt faith, therefore he rather attacks them . . . the second reason is, that women are naturally more impressionable, and . . . the third reason is that they have slippery tongues, and are unable to conceal from their fellow-women those things which by evil arts they know. . . . But the natural reason is that she is more carnal than a man, as is clear from her many carnal abominations. And it should be noted that there was a defect in the formation of the first woman, since she was formed from a bent rib, that is, a rib of the breast, which is bent as it were in a contrary direction to a man. And since through this defect she is an imperfect animal, she always deceives. . . . And this is indicated by the etymology of the world; for Femina comes from Fe and Minus, since she is ever weaker to hold and preserve the faith. . . . To conclude. All witchcraft comes from carnal lust, which is in women insatiable.

> *Malleus maleficarum*, translated and quoted in
> Alan C. Kors and Edward Peters (eds.), *Witchcraft*
> *in Europe 1100–1700: A Documentary History*.

It is commonly the nature of women to be timid and to be afraid of everything. That is why they busy themselves so much about witchcraft and superstitions and run hither and thither, uttering a magic formula here and a magic formula there.

> Sermon by Martin Luther on I Peter, translated and
> quoted in Sigrid Brauner, *The Politics of Gender in Early*
> *Modern Europe*, Sixteenth Century Essays and Studies, 12.

And then the Devil said, "Thee art a poor overworked body. Will thee be my servant and I will give thee abundance and thee shall never want."

> Confession of Bessie Wilson, quoted in Christina
> Larner, *Enemies of God: The Witch Hunt in Scotland*.

These three statements, the first by two Dominican monks in the most influential witch-hunters' manual of the early modern period, the second by Martin Luther in a sermon on Christian marriage, and the third by a Scottish woman during her interrogation for witchcraft, represent widely varying assessments of the reasons why women were so much more likely to be accused and found guilty of witchcraft during the early modern period. Though they disagree, the three things they point to—sex, fear, and poverty—can in many ways be seen as the three most important reasons why the vast majority of those questioned, tried, and executed for witchcraft after 1500 were women.

Anthropologists and historians have demonstrated that nearly all pre-modern societies believe in witchcraft and make some attempts to control witches. It was only in early modern Europe and the English colony in Massachusetts, however, that these beliefs led to large-scale hunts and mass executions. Because so many records have been lost or destroyed, it is difficult to make an estimate for all of Europe, but most scholars agree that during the sixteenth and seventeenth centuries somewhere between 100,000 and 200,000 people were officially tried and between 50,000 and 100,000 executed. Given the much smaller size of the European population in comparison with today, these are enormous numbers.

Explanations for the Witch Hunts

This dramatic upsurge in witch trials, often labelled the "Great Witch Hunt" or the "Witch Craze," has been the subject of a huge number of studies during the last twenty-five years, and a variety of explanations have been suggested. Some scholars have chosen to emphasize intellectual factors. During the late Middle Ages, Christian philosophers and theologians developed a new idea about the most important characteristics of a witch. Until that period, in Europe, as in most cultures throughout the world, a witch was a person who used magical forces to do evil deeds (*maleficia*). One was a witch, therefore, because of what one *did*, causing injuries or harm to animals and people. This notion of witchcraft continued in Europe, but to it was added a demonological component. Educated Christian thinkers began to view the essence of witchcraft as making a pact with the Devil, a pact which required the witch to do the Devil's bidding. Witches were no longer simply people who used magical power to get what they wanted, but people used by the Devil to do what he wanted. (The Devil is always described and portrayed visually as male). Witchcraft was thus not a question of what one *did*, but of what one *was*, and proving that a witch had committed *maleficia* was no longer necessary for conviction. Gradually this demonological or Satanic idea of witchcraft was fleshed out, and witches were thought to engage in wild sexual orgies with the Devil, fly through the night to meetings called sabbats which parodied the mass, and steal communion wafers and unbaptized babies to use in their rituals. Some demonological theorists also claimed that witches were organized in an international conspiracy to overthrow Christianity, with a hierarchy modelled on the hierarchy of angels and archangels constructed by Christian philosophers to give order to God's assistants. Witchcraft was thus spiritualized, and witches became the ultimate heretics, enemies of God.

This demonology was created by Catholic thinkers during the fifteenth century, and is brought together in the *Malleus maleficarum (The Hammer of Witches)*, quoted above, written by two German Dominican inquisitors, Heinrich Krämer and Jacob Sprenger, and published in 1486. This book was not simply a description of witchcraft, however, but a guide for witch-hunters, advising them how to recognize and question witches. It was especially popular in northern Europe, and the questions which it taught judges and lawyers to ask of witches were asked over a large area; the fact that they often elicited the same or similar answers fuelled the idea that witchcraft was an international conspiracy. Though witch trials died down somewhat during the first decades after the Protestant Reformation when Protestants and Catholics were busy fighting each other, they picked up again more strongly than ever about 1560. Protestants rejected many Catholic teachings, but not demonology, and the *Malleus* was just as popular in Protestant areas as in Catholic ones. Protestants may have felt even more at the mercy of witches than Catholics, for they rejected rituals such as exorcism which Catholics believed could counter the power of a witch. The Reformation may have contributed to the spread of demonological ideas among wider groups of the population, for both Catholics and Protestants increased their religious instruction to lay people during the sixteenth century. As part of their program of deepening popular religious understanding and piety, both Protestants and Catholics attempted to suppress what the elites viewed as superstition, folk belief, and more open expressions of sexuality; some historians, most notably Robert Muchembled, view the campaign against witches as part of a larger struggle by elite groups to suppress popular culture, to force rural residents to acculturate themselves to middle-class urban values. The fact that women were the preservers and transmitters of popular culture, teaching their children magical sayings and rhymes along with the more identifiably Christian ones, made them particularly suspect.

The Reformation also plays a role in political explanations of the upsurge in witch trials. Christina Larner has effectively argued that with the Reformation Christianity became a political ideology, and rulers felt compelled to prove their piety and the depth of their religious commitment to their subjects and other rulers. They could do this by fighting religious wars or by cracking down on heretics and witches within their own borders. Because most of the people actually accused or tried were old, poor women, political authorities felt compelled to stress the idea of an international conspiracy of witches so as not to look foolish and to justify the time, money, and energy spent on hunting witches. Witchcraft was used as a symbol of total evil, total hostility to the community, the state, the church, and God. Only when authorities came to be more concerned with purely secular aims such as nationalism, the defense of property, or the creation of empires did trials for witchcraft cease.

Legal changes were also instrumental in causing, or at least allowing for, massive witch trials. One of these was a change from an accusatorial legal procedure to an inquisitorial procedure. In the former, a suspect knew her accusers and the charges they had brought, and an accuser could in turn be liable for trial if the charges were not proven; in the latter, legal authorities themselves brought the case. This change made people much more willing to accuse others, for they never had to take personal responsibility for the accusation or face the accused's relatives. Inquisitorial procedure involved intense questioning of the suspect, often with torture, and the areas in Europe which did not make this change saw very few trials and almost no mass panics. Inquisitorial procedure came into Europe as part of the adoption of Roman law, which also (at least in theory) required the confession of a suspect before she or he could be executed. This had been designed as a way to keep innocent people from death, but in practice in some parts of Europe led to the adoption of ever more gruesome means of inquisitorial torture; torture was also used to get the names of additional suspects, as most lawyers trained in Roman law firmly believed that no witch could act alone. Another legal change was the transfer of witchcraft trials from ecclesiastical to secular courts. Though the courts of the Spanish and Roman Inquisitions have a reputation for secrecy and torture, in actual practice they were much more lenient than secular courts or other types of ecclesiastical courts; judges of the Inquisition were more likely to send a woman accused of witchcraft home again with a warning and a religious penance.

Many historians see social and economic changes as also instrumental in the rise of witch trials. Europe entered a period of dramatic inflation during the sixteenth century and continued to be subject to periodic famines resulting from bad harvests; increases in witch accusations generally took place during periods of dearth or destruction caused by religious wars. This was also a time when people were moving around more than they had in the previous centuries, when war, the commercialization of agriculture, enclosure, and the lure of new jobs in the cities meant that villages were being uprooted and the number of vagrants and transients increased. These changes led to a sense of unsettledness and uncertainty in values, with people unwilling or unable to assist their neighbors, yet still feeling they should. The initial accusation in many witch trials often came from people who refused to help a fellow villager, and then blamed later misfortune on her anger or revenge; Hugh Trevor-Roper has suggested that in such a scenario, witchcraft accusations were used as a way of assuaging guilt over uncharitable conduct. This explanation can help us to understand the first accusation in a trial, but not the mass trials which might involve scores or hundreds of people.

Demographic changes may have also played a part. During the sixteenth century, the age at first marriage appears to have risen, and the number of people who never married at all increased. The reasons for these changes are not entirely clear, but this meant that there was a larger number of women unattached to a man, and therefore more suspect in the eyes of their neighbors. Female life expectancy may also have risen during the sixteenth century, either in absolute terms or at least in comparison with male life expectancy during this period when many men lost their lives in religious wars.

Social and intellectual factors have both been part of recent feminist analyses of the witch hunts. In perhaps the most radical of these, Mary Daly asserts that the women accused of witchcraft not only were perceived as a challenge to dominant ideas of women's subordinate place, but actively opposed male supremacy. She views the witch hunts as attempts by male authorities to suppress independent women, especially those who had spiritual knowledge or were healers. Barbara Ehrenreich and Deirdre English have also focussed on female healers, arguing that the witch hunts were primarily driven by male doctors trying to take over control of medicine from female healers; they point to a statement in the *Malleus maleficarum* in which midwives were specifically accused of having a special propensity for witchcraft. This emphasis on female healers and midwives has been challenged by other historians using actual trial records, for midwives were not accused more often than other women. Marianne Hester has stressed that this does not negate the value of radical feminist analysis, but argues that the emphasis should be placed on male sexual violence and the maintenance of male power through the eroticization of male-female relations rather than on the more narrow issue of male control of medicine. In her study of the New England witchcraft persecutions, Carol Karlsen also discusses the role of male-female power relations, not only sexual and ideological, but also economic; she finds that many of the women accused of witchcraft were widows or unmarried women who were a potential challenge to male economic control as they had inherited property or might do so, and that older women received harsher sentences than younger.

Medical issues have also been part of another area of investigation related to the witchcraze. Witches were often accused of mixing magic potions and creams, leading some scholars to explore the role that hallucinogenic drugs such as ergot and belladonna may have played, particularly in inducing feelings of flying. Such hallucinogens could have been taken inadvertently by eating bread or porridge made from spoiled grain. A problem with this is that witches were rarely accused of eating their concoctions or rubbing them on their bodies, but of spreading them on brooms or pitchforks, which they then rode to a sabbat. If delusions of flying came from eating spoiled grain, why was not the whole population of an area equally affected?

No one factor alone can explain the witch hunts, but taken together, intellectual, religious, political, legal, social, and economic factors all created a framework which proved deadly to thousands of European women. In the rest of this chapter, I would like to consider why the vast majority of European witches were women; to do this we must first examine how the stereotype of witch-as-woman developed, and then explore actual witch trials to develop a more refined view as to what types of women were actually accused and convicted.

The idea that women were more likely to engage in witchcraft had a number of roots in European culture. Women were widely recognized as having less physical, economic, or political power than men, so that they were more likely to need magical assistance to gain what they wanted. Whereas a man could fight or take someone to court, a woman could only scold, curse, or cast spells. Thus in popular notions of witchcraft, women's physical and legal weakness was a contributing factor, with unmarried women and widows recognized as even more vulnerable because they did not have a husband to protect them. Because women often married at a younger age than men and female life expectancy may have been increasing, women frequently spent periods of their life as widows. If they remarried, it was often to a widower with children, so that they became step-mothers; resentments about preferential treatment were very common in families with step-siblings, and the evil stepmother became a stock figure in folk tales. If a woman's second husband died, she might have to spend her last years in the house of a step-son or step-daughter, who resented her demands but was bound by a legal contract to provide for her; old age became a standard feature of the popular stereotype of the witch.

Women also had close connections with many areas of life

in which magic or malevolence might seem the only explanation for events—they watched over animals which could die mysteriously, prepared food which could become spoiled inexplicably, nursed the ill of all ages who could die without warning, and cared for children who were even more subject to disease and death than adults in this era of poor hygiene and unknown and uncontrollable childhood diseases. Some women consciously cultivated popular notions of their connection with the supernatural, performing rituals of love magic with herbs, wax figures, or written names designed to win a lover or hold a spouse. Though learned notions of witchcraft as demonology made some inroads into popular culture, the person most often initially accused of witchcraft in any village was an older woman who had a reputation as a healer, a scold, or a worker of both good and bad magic.

We might assume that women would do everything they could to avoid such a reputation, but in actuality the stereotype could protect a woman for many years. Neighbors would be less likely to refuse assistance, and the wood, grain, or milk which she needed to survive would be given to her or paid as fees for her magical services such as finding lost objects, attracting desirable suitors, or harming enemies. This can help to explain the number of women who appear to have confessed to being witches without the application or even threat of torture; after decades of providing magical services, they were as convinced as their neighbors of their own powers. Though we regard witchcraft as something which has no objective reality, early modern women and men were often absolutely convinced they had suffered or caused grievous harm through witchcraft.

This popular stereotype of the witch existed long before the upsurge in witch trials, and would continue in Europe centuries after the last witch was officially executed; in some more isolated parts of Europe people still mix magical love potions and accuse their neighbors of casting the evil eye. The early modern large-scale witch hunts resulted much more from learned and official ideas of witchcraft than from popular ones, and in the learned mind witches were even more likely to be women than they were in popular culture.

Chapter 3

Renaissance Discoveries and Transformations

Turning|Points

IN WORLD HISTORY

The European Conquest of the Americas

Norman Davies

Historian Norman Davies, a professor emeritus at the University of London, argues that the traditional view that the Americas were "discovered" should be replaced by the more realistic view that the Americas were brutally "conquered." Davies picks up the story of European conquest with the explorations and depredations of the Spanish. He describes the "vast exchange" of goods and people between Europe and the New World as a bargain that worked decidedly to the advantage of the Europeans, resulting in the suffering, exploitation, and death of countless Native Americans.

Europe overseas is not a subject that starts with Columbus or the Caribbean. One experiment, in the crusader kingdoms of the Holy Land, was already ancient history. Another, in the Canaries, had been in progress for seventy years. But once contact had been made with distant islands, Europeans sailed overseas in ever-increasing numbers. They sailed for reasons of trade, of loot, of conquest, and increasingly of religion. For many, it provided the first meeting with people of different races. To validate their claim over the inhabitants of the conquered lands, the Spanish monarchs had first to establish that non-Europeans were human. According to the Requirement of 1512, which the conquistadors were ordered to read out to all native peoples: 'The Lord Our God, Living and Eternal, created Heaven and Earth, and one man and woman, of whom you and I, and all the men of the world, were and are descendants . . .' To confirm the point,

Pope Paul III decreed in 1537 that 'all Indians are truly men, not only capable of understanding the Catholic faith, but . . . exceedingly desirous to receive it'.

The Great Explorers

The earlier voyages of exploration were continued and extended. The existence of a vast fourth continent in the West was gradually established by trial and error, some time in the twenty years after Columbus's first return to Palos. Responsibility for the achievement was hotly disputed. Columbus himself made three more voyages without ever knowing where he had really been. Another Genoese, Giovanni Caboto (John Cabot, 1450–98), sailed from Bristol aboard the *Matthew* in May 1497 under licence from Henry VII; he landed on Cape Breton Island, which he took to be part of China. The Florentine Amerigo Vespucci (1451–1512), once the Medicis' agent in Seville, made three or four transatlantic voyages between 1497 and 1504. He then obtained the post of *piloto mayor* or 'Chief Pilot' of Spain. It was this fact which determined, rightly or wrongly, that the fourth continent should be named after him. In 1513 a stowaway, Vasco Núñez de Balboa (d. 1519), walked across the isthmus of Panama and sighted the Pacific. In 1519–22 a Spanish expedition led by the Portuguese captain Ferdinand Magellan (*c.*1480–1521) circumnavigated the world. It proved beyond doubt that the earth was round, that the Pacific and Atlantic were separate oceans, and that the Americas lay between them.

The presence of a fifth continent in the antipodes was not suspected for another century. In 1605 a Spanish ship out of Peru and a Dutch ship out of Java both sailed to the Gulf of Carpentaria. The main outlines of the great *Zuidland* or 'Southland' (Australia and New Zealand) were charted by the Dutch navigator Abel Tasman (1603–59) in 1642–3.

The Portuguese were quickest to exploit the commercial opportunities of the new lands. They claimed Brazil in 1500, Mauritius in 1505, Sumatra in 1509, Malacca and the 'Spice Islands' (Indonesia) in 1511. To protect their trade, they established a chain of fortified stations stretching from Goa in

India to Macao in China. The Spaniards, in contrast, did not hesitate to apply their military might. Lured by the dream of El Dorado the *conquistadores*, who had so recently subdued Iberia, now turned their energies to the conquest of America. They settled Cuba in 1511 and used it as a base for further campaigns. In 1519–20 Hernando Cortez (1485–1547) seized the Aztec empire in Mexico in a sea of blood. In the 1520s and 1530s permanent settlements were established in Costa Rica, Honduras, Guatemala, and New Granada (Colombia and Venezuela). From 1532 Francisco Pizarro (*c.*1476–1541) seized the empire of the Incas in Peru.

Colonization and Sea Trade

European colonization in North America began in 1536 with the founding of Montreal in Canada by the Breton sailor Jacques Cartier (1491–1557) and in 1565 of St. Augustine in Florida by Pedro Menéndez. Menéndez had just destroyed a nearby Huguenot settlement (in the future South Carolina), where he hanged America's first religious exiles 'as Lutherans'. Three years later the Huguenots' compatriot, Dominique de Gourgues, arrived on the same spot and hanged the Spanish garrison 'as robbers and murderers'. Western civilization was on the move.

The Dutch and the English were relative latecomers to colonization, but in the late sixteenth century they both began to reap its benefits. Having founded Batavia in Java in 1597, the Dutch set out to wrest the East Indies from the Portuguese. The English colony of Virginia, discovered in 1598, received its first successful settlement at Jamestown in 1607. The *Mayflower*, carrying 120 puritan 'Pilgrim Fathers' and their families, landed in their Plymouth Colony on 11 (21) December 1620. The Massachusetts Bay Colony followed ten years later. Although religious refugees from England, they did not prove tolerant. The colony of Rhode Island (1636) was founded by dissenters expelled from Massachusetts. By that time the existence of a worldwide network of European colonies, and their seaborne lines of communication, was an established fact.

The international sea trade multiplied by leaps and

bounds. To the west, the transatlantic route was long dominated by Spain. By 1600, 200 ships a year entered Seville from the New World. In the peak decade of 1591–1600, 19 million grams of gold and nearly 3 billion grams of silver came with them. The southerly route via the Cape of Good Hope was worked first by the Portuguese and then by the Dutch, who also provided the main commercial link between the North Sea and the Mediterranean. To the east, the Dutch also pioneered a huge trade in Baltic grain. The growing demand for food in West European cities was met by the growing capacity of the Polish producers to supply. This Baltic grain trade reached its peak in 1618, when 118,000 *lasts* or 'boatloads' left Danzig for Amsterdam. The English trade in cloth to the Low Countries had reached record levels somewhat earlier, in 1550. English adventurers launched a Muscovy Company (1565), a Levant Company (1581), and the East India Company (1600).

The nexus of all these activities was located in the Low Countries. Antwerp, which was the main entrepôt of both the Spanish and the English trade, reigned supreme until the crash of 1557–60; thereafter the focus moved to Amsterdam. The year 1602, which saw the foundation both of the Dutch East India Company and of the world's first stock exchange in Amsterdam, can be taken to mark a new era in commercial history.

As overseas trade expanded, Europe received a wide range of new staple foods, as well as exotic 'colonial' products including pepper, coffee, cocoa, sugar, and tobacco. Europe's diet, cuisine, and palate were never the same again. The haricot bean, which was first recorded in France in 1542, the tomato, which spread far and wide via Italy in the same period, and the capsicum pepper, which was grown throughout the Balkans, were all American in origin.

A Vast Exchange

Europe's intercourse with America, heretofore a largely hermetic ecological zone, led to a vast Exchange of people, diseases, plants, and animals. This 'Columbian Exchange' worked decidedly in Europe's favour. European colonists braved hardship and deprivation, and in some places faced hostile 'Indians'. But their losses were minuscule compared to the genocidal casualties which they and their firearms inflicted. They brought some benefits, but with them depopulation and despoliation on a grand scale. Europe received syphilis; but its ravages were not to be compared to the pandemics of smallpox, pleurisy, and typhus which literally decimated the native Americans. The Europeans re-introduced horses; in return they received two foods of capital importance, potatoes and maize, as well as the turkey, the most substantial and nutritious of domestic poultry. Potatoes were adopted in Ireland at an early date, and moved steadily across northern Europe, becoming the staple of Germany, Poland, and Russia. Maize, which was variously known as 'American corn' and 'American fallow', enriched exhausted soil and greatly facilitated both crop rotation and livestock farming. It was well established in the Po valley in the sixteenth century. It was inhibited from crossing the Alps until climatic conditions improved some hundred years later, but its long-term impact was enormous. There is good reason to count American additions to the food supply as one of the major factors underlying the dramatic growth of Europe's population at the end of the early modern period.

Descriptions of the arrival of Europeans in America have recently undergone fundamental revision. They have been 'decolumbianized'. What was once 'the discovery' is now called an 'encounter' or a 'meeting of cultures'. It would be better to be honest and call it a conquest. Columbus, too, has been downgraded. The primacy of his voyages has been handed to Vikings or Irishmen, or even to a Welshman in a coracle. His landing on San Salvador (Watling Island) has been relocated to Samana Cay in the Bahamas. The 'peerless navigator' is now said to have been a ruthless and rapacious 'colonialist pirate', alternatively a quixotic Jew sailing in search of the lost tribes of Israel. He is even said to have heard about the other continent from American women already in Europe. The sources for Columbus's activities are meagre, the myths abundant. The real discoverers of America are those who went in the steps of the *conquistadores*, often friars like Bernardino de Sahagún, 'the world's first anthropologist', and who tried to understand what was happening.

Intercourse with America had a profound impact on European culture. A gulf began to open between those countries which had ready access to the New World and those which did not. [As modern French scholar Jacques Attali maintains:] 'Philosophy is born of the merchant. Science is born of commerce. Henceforth, Europe is almost cut into two. The West is preoccupied with the sea. The East is preoccupied with itself.'

Renaissance Neoplatonism

Charles G. Nauert Jr.

The reputation of the Greek philosopher Plato increased dramatically during the Renaissance, while the status of the Greek philosopher Aristotle declined somewhat. This was due in large measure to the efforts of the Italian humanists, especially Marsilio Ficino, who translated Plato for a much larger audience. Ficino was also responsible for the revival of an intellectual movement called Neoplatonism, which emphasized a mystical kind of spirituality and glorified human creativity and freedom of choice. This philosophy spread throughout Europe during the Renaissance, influencing such diverse figures as Michelangelo and Shakespeare.

The influence of Plato and his Neoplatonic interpreters had already strongly affected Christian thought in the Middle Ages, but then it was indirect, coming from the writings of authors such as Cicero, St. Augustine, Dionysius the Areopagite, and other Church Fathers, and from medieval Arab philosophers such as Avicenna. Only one work of Plato himself, the *Timaeus*, was widely available in Latin during the Middle Ages.

Yet Plato's ancient reputation as a philosophical rival to his pupil Aristotle was well known. When humanists such as Petrarch began attacking scholastic Aristotelianism, they often cited Plato as a countervailing authority, though they knew virtually no details of his thought. The successful introduction of Greek studies into Italy by Chrysoloras at the end of the fourteenth century changed matters somewhat, for several of his pupils produced translations of a number of Platonic dialogues. . . .

Many Florentine intellectuals were attracted by [Greek scholar Georgios] Pletho's claim that fundamentally all the rival Greek philosophical systems agreed with one another and that a thorough knowledge of Plato could lead to philosophical concord and a religious unity which they, unlike Pletho, conceived in broadly Christian terms. Marsilio Ficino (1433–99) later claimed that Cosimo de'Medici dreamed of creating a new Platonic Academy in Florence and so selected young Ficino and supported his preparation to become the restorer of Platonic philosophy. In reality, Ficino seems to have begun his philosophical studies independently as part of his preparation to become a physician, receiving a traditional scholastic education and failing (to his later regret) to develop the elegant Latin style typical of the humanists.

Translations of Plato

The main cause of Ficino's turning from the scholastic Aristotle to study of Plato was his distress over the tendency of Aristotelian philosophy to deny the immortality of the human soul. While a student of philosophy, he experienced a personal religious crisis which he ultimately resolved through his conviction that Plato's philosophy had been given by divine providence to prepare the pagan world for conversion to Christianity. By about 1460 he drew a clear distinction between the philosophy he wanted to pursue, which dealt with the spiritual health of the soul and was based on Plato, and the secular Aristotelian philosophy of the universities. In 1462, Cosimo gave him a country house at Careggi near Florence; and from about that period, Ficino began giving lectures to an informal group (never a school in the formal sense) which became known as the Platonic Academy. Cosimo also urged him to translate the works attributed to Hermes Trismegistus, which were believed to represent a distillation of the wisdom of ancient Egypt. In 1463, Ficino presented Cosimo with a Latin translation of the most important of these vaguely Platonic tracts, the *Pimander*. Before Cosimo's death in 1464, Ficino had given him several other translations of works by ancient Platonists, including ten dialogues of Plato. Indeed, though Ficino was not yet an ordained priest, he reports that he ministered words of consolation from the Platonic writings to the dying patriarch of the Medici clan. Ficino continued his lectures and his work of translation, producing a Latin text of all thirty-six of Plato's known dialogues. The first edition was printed in 1484. For the first time, the full text of all surviving Platonic dialogues was available for readers of Latin. It was a superb translation, far superior to earlier versions of individual dialogues; and it remained the standard text for students of Plato until the nineteenth century. In subsequent years, he produced influential Latin translations of major pagan Neoplatonists such as Plotinus and of the Christian Platonist Dionysius the Areopagite.

Ficino was a professional philosopher, not a humanist, even though he did not teach in a conventional academic setting and had the social elite of Florence rather than undergradu-

Beauty as an Attribute of the Soul

Renaissance Neoplatonism influenced a wide range of thinkers and artists in many countries, from Castiglione and Michelangelo in Italy, to Copernicus, More, and Shakespeare in Northern Europe. The Neoplatonic emphasis on beauty, for example, is linked inextricably with the artistic fascination with the nude human body in the Renaissance. Some modern scholars have even argued that Neoplatonism is the most significant intellectual influence on the work of Michelangelo.

Renaissance artists, absorbed in the study of man, were attracted to Neoplatonic philosophy because it seemed to offer a means of interpreting the natural world, including human passions, in terms of man's highest potentialities. It enabled them to treat of love and beauty—and to embellish these perennial themes of art—while at the same time appealing to the intellectual and moral faculties; and by drawing upon the rich storehouse of pagan mythology they could invest subtle metaphysical concepts with a warm and radiant symbolism.

Straightforward as it appears to be, the art of the High Renaissance can be apprehended only superficially unless the deep

ates for his audience. His own philosophical works, such as the *Platonic Theology* and *On the Christian Religion*, applied Plato to uphold Christian doctrines such as personal immortality. His translations, treatises, and commentaries on Plato gave him a great reputation, first in Florence and eventually throughout all of Europe. His concept of Platonic love (purely spiritual, free from bodily and material desires) became a major influence on the poetry of all European literatures.

The Influence of Ficino

But the mere excellence of Ficino's philosophical translations is not an adequate explanation of his great impact on Florentine culture. Why did his works, why did Plato himself, rapidly become a major force in Florentine intellectual life? Plato, of course, is one of the world's greatest philosophers. But some recent studies have shown that the cultural shift in

influence of Neoplatonism is taken into account. The abundance of nudes, for example, reflects—along with an undeniable fascination with the human body—the boldly expressed conviction that reality is independent of external trappings, that truth is unadorned. Erotic themes, while utilizing the traditional figures of mythology, were made to symbolize the Neoplatonic conception of love as a divine force leading its object upward from the earthly plane. . . .

The discerning critic Erwin Panofsky goes so far as to assert that only Michelangelo among his contemporaries adopted Neoplatonism "in its entirety," not merely as a philosophical system but as "a metaphysical justification of his own self." According to Neoplatonic doctrine, physical beauty is evanescent, a mere image or echo; true beauty is an attribute of the soul, a spiritual state which the soul remembers from a precorporeal existence. On the mortal plane the soul is a prisoner of the body, and the soul's struggle to attain beauty and freedom is an agonizing process. No other artist pursued this paradox so relentlessly as Michelangelo.

Philip Lee Ralph, *The Renaissance in Perspective*, 1973, pp. 169–174 passim.

mid-century Florence was not just a movement toward Plato. It was also a movement by a large segment of the cultural elite away from rhetorical culture and the ideal of ethical commitment to the active life of family, business, and politics and toward a consciously chosen philosophical culture that devalued these things. The generation of Alberti, Palmieri, and Manetti were still disciples of Bruni and glorified the active life of the lay citizen. Hence most of that generation avoided philosophy because they thought that, except for ethics, it was useless for the life of laymen. This 'civic humanism' no longer had much attraction for the young intellectuals who came of age after mid-century. Ficino's lectures eventually became the focal point of the new outlook. . . .

What Ficino offered his hearers was a sort of elegant, gnostic, perfectly spiritualized brand of Christianity that appealed to their own sense of being superior to ordinary people. He conceived himself as a physician of troubled and delicate souls, guiding them (and himself) toward a contemplative equilibrium which would free them from the depressing distractions of the everyday world and lead them toward the eternal happiness that could be found only through the intellectual vision of God. There can be no doubt that he thought of his philosophy as thoroughly—indeed, especially—Christian. For him, Jesus Christ was the perfect fulfilment of all the spiritual aspirations of humanity, the goal only partially glimpsed by pagan sages like Plato. He was particularly hostile to the prevailing Aristotelian philosophy (the only system taught in the universities) because its rationalism tended to undermine faith, especially faith in immortality. His preference for Plato was based on the Platonic depreciation of the material world and the exaltation of the spiritual and eternal. He found the same advantages in the works of Hermes Trismegistus, the Jewish Cabalists, and pseudo-Dionysius. Being quite without any sensitivity to the issues raised by humanistic textual critics like Valla, he firmly believed that these other texts (all of which were products of late Antiquity) were preclassical and went back (except for Dionysius) to the very beginnings of human civilization, in fact to a sort of preliminary revelation by God to ancient sages.

The Magical Renaissance

One aspect of his Platonic philosophy was his interest in magic, which was historically linked to some of the post-Platonic texts he translated, such as Hermes. While he had some interest in the kind of magic that could perform material works, he was mainly interested in spiritual magic, in which he combined asceticism, meditation, music, and astrological influences to strengthen his soul and thus to gain power over material objects, other persons, and especially himself. His spiritual magic was intended to relieve and control the spirit of melancholy which supposedly afflicted scholars like himself. Thus for Ficino the magical aspect of Platonism constituted a sort of do-it-yourself psychotherapy which gave calm and power to the soul.

The foundation of Ficino's philosophy and of his magic was a hierarchical view of the universe which was based ultimately on Plato's famous doctrine of ideas but derived more directly from Alexandrian Neoplatonists like Plotinus. In this hierarchy, the highest rank was held by the uncreated and purely spiritual being, God; and all other beings were ranged in order, from the more spiritual down to the more material. The position of any particular being (animate or inanimate) in this great interconnected chain is the determinant of its true value in the total picture of reality. The various parts of the universal hierarchy are intimately and mysteriously interrelated, and the whole of being is likened to a great musical instrument on which parts tuned to the same pitch vibrate sympathetically in harmony with one another. This theory provided a supposedly rational foundation for occult pseudo-sciences such as astrology, in which the higher rank of celestial beings causes them to influence corresponding beings at lower levels.

A rational being who understands the celestial correspondences and other mysterious relations between things can use that understanding to affect and control one thing by the power of another thing which stands above it in the hierarchy. This is the theoretical foundation of magic, which in late Antiquity was closely linked with vaguely Platonic notions (in the Hermetic books, for instance). The person who understands and uses these occult connections between things is the *magus*, or magician. Since the Neoplatonic world is permeated by spiritual force, the *magus* may be able to produce works not only by using the interrelationships between material things (natural magic) but also by summoning spiritual beings, demons. This practice is potentially dangerous, since some of the spirits or demons are good, while others are servants of Satan and evil. No one denied that attempts to conjure with the power of evil demons was a sin; but even efforts to employ good spirits were risky, for evil spirits might disguise themselves as good in order to lure souls into bondage. Ficino himself actively practiced natural magic and even (good) demonic magic, though he was very cautious in expressing his beliefs, because he believed that the immense power of demonic magic would be turned to evil uses if the knowledge on which it was based fell into the hands of evil men, or into the hands of the rabble, who would easily be misled into idolatry—that is, devil-worship. Magical knowledge and practice must be confined to a small inner circle of educated, select, and pure spirits like Ficino and his intimate friends.

Glorification of Human Nature

As this discussion shows, Ficino attributed great cosmic significance and supernatural power to human nature. In the great hierarchy of being, humanity occupied a crucial middle position, the sole point of contact between the spiritual world and the material world. Human beings, having both body and soul, had power in both realms; and humankind, as the point of connection that guaranteed the unity of creation, was especially dear to God. The *magus* has access to that power because he has prepared himself spiritually and has acquired the necessary knowledge (of astrological signs, for example) to command the powers of all created beings to do his will. This power, Ficino taught, also inheres (though not in so sublime a way) in the artist, who has a vision of God, even a kind of spiritual madness (*furor*) which inspires him to create. Each person faces the moral choice between cultivating the material and bodily side of human nature, and so falling away from God, and cultivating the spiritual side, and so becoming united with God.

Ficino's glorification of human nature repeated a theme expressed earlier in the century by humanists like Bruni, Alberti, Palmieri, and Manetti. But his glorification of man differed in that he presented it within the metaphysical framework of the Platonic hierarchy. The earlier humanistic descriptions of human nature avoided speculative philosophy and described human greatness in terms of moral excellence, solidarity with society, political commitment, and daily family and business relations—in terms of the active life. Ficino's glorification of human nature, on the other hand, defined human glory in contemplative terms and repudiated the values of everyday life. Inevitably, such a system could appeal only to a small elite of persons who had the leisure to become enlightened and closely linked to God. Ficino had little to offer to the politically disfranchised or even to solid middle-class Florentines whose economic and social condition precluded intensive study and directed their efforts to the worldly realms of family and business. His spiritual universe was elegant and aloof, and he felt remote disdain for the more traditional and plebeian spirituality promoted by the popular sermons of the friars. . . .

Pico and the Dignity of Man

Aside from Ficino himself, the most distinguished philosophical figure in the group was the young prince Giovanni Pico della Mirandola (1463–94), though his philosophical background was independent of Ficino, based on study of scholasticism at the University at Padua and at Paris. As early as 1485, he engaged in a published debate with the prominent Venetian humanist Ermolao Barbaro, defending the superiority of philosophy to the central humanistic subject, rhetoric, which he belittled as mere play on words. Pico shared Ficino's belief in a continuous tradition of ancient spiritual wisdom which ran through the works of all the ancient sages, such as Hermes, the Cabalists, Zoroaster, and Orpheus, as well as Plato and the later Platonists. Indeed, he adopted a philosophical and religious universalism even more expansive than that of Ficino, for he thought that all religious traditions contained some truth (though not in equal degree) and that it would be possible by studying the writings of the wise men of all nations to distil from their works a common set of true doctrines on which concord of all philosophies and all religions could be built. Pico studied Hebrew as well as Greek and Latin and was especially hopeful of proving that Jewish religion, if properly understood from the books of the Cabalists (Jewish mystics believed to be ancient but really medieval in date), would fully agree with Christianity. He sought to investigate the beliefs of all known religions, seeking the basis for universal peace and harmony. He assumed that Platonic philosophy was the key to discovering the underlying points of agreement and resolving all conflicts, and that the ultimate beliefs would be identical with a purified Christianity. Yet without intending to do so, both he and Ficino relativized all religions and jeopardized Christianity's claim to a unique status among the world's religions and to a monopoly of truth. When in 1486 he offered to sustain in public debate a list of 900 propositions, many of them derived from the Cabala and the Hermetic books, he was charged at Rome with heresy and found it expedient to retire to France for a time.

Pico's most famous work is the little treatise now known as the *Oration on the Dignity of Man*, published in 1496. As the modern title suggests, it does deal in part with the theme of human dignity, and both because of its inherent attractiveness and because of its brevity, it is commonly studied not only as the quintessential statement of Renaissance views on the nature of man but also as a work that expresses *the* humanistic philosophy of human nature. Neither of these judgments is sound. As for humanism, any reader of Machiavelli (to offer just one example) should be aware that Pico's poetic and glowing praise of human nature is not typical of all humanists. And while many humanists did write in praise of human nature, the union of that theme with an otherworldly metaphysic sets the works of Pico and Ficino quite apart from works on human dignity by humanists like Bruni, Alberti, Palmieri, and Manetti.

Freedom of Choice

Pico adopts many of Ficino's opinions. Yet there is one significant difference, rooted in Pico's Aristotelian background. In Aristotelian philosophy, the nature of any object determines what it is and hence imposes strict limits. For example, because a newborn puppy is by nature a dog, it can never become anything but a dog. From this perspective, Ficino's decision to place humanity at one specific point in the hierarchical order of creation seemed deterministic. Man may hold an especially honourable place as the one creature that consists of both soul and body. But by being the middle link in the chain of being, man is bound and limited. His potential is determined by his nature. Pico did not accept this view. He offers a striking alternative. Presenting a hypothetical narrative of creation, he declares that first God created the natures of all things, spiritual and material, to form a complete and perfect universe. Only then did God create man. But since the hierarchy of creation was already complete and all possible natures had been given out, he gave man no fixed place in the hierarchy and no nature at all. Instead of a nature, man—and only man, not even the angels—received freedom, the freedom to choose his own place in the hierarchy and to choose for himself any created nature. The man who makes the right choice will cultivate the spiritual part of his being and become spiritual. Of course the man who makes an unwise choice, who follows his baser instincts, will become like a beast. The true 'nature' of man is to have no nature that rigidly determines what he becomes. By his own free choice, man creates himself. Eugenio Garin has described this position well: every other created being is a *quid*, a something; man alone among all creatures is a *quis*, a someone, a person; and this is a condition he shares only with God himself. Thus he is truly made in the image of God, in a way that no other creature can be. This is an optimistic view indeed, so optimistic that one may wonder whether Pico really meant it to apply to man after the fall of Adam. But his own treatise imposes no limitation to prelapsarian times. It is important to recall, however, that this view of human nature is Pico's special blend of Neoplatonic and

Aristotelian philosophy and may not be equated with 'humanism'. It must be regarded as the opinion of only this one philosopher. His view of human nature seems to leave no need at all for the action of divine grace, no need for a crucified and resurrected Saviour: it seems totally Pelagian.

The cultural interests of the humanists, and still more, those of the Platonic Academy of Florence, may seem very esoteric to modern readers. Yet the elegant Florentine aristocrats who heard Ficino's lectures and the gatherings of chancery secretaries who read classical literature and perused humanistic commentaries and treatises were trend-setters, precisely because they were an elite group and hence caught the attention of all aspirants to elite status. The eagerness of the urban ruling class in most of Italy's small towns to provide humanistic Latin schools for their sons demonstrates that both humanism proper and the Platonist philosophy that was loosely associated with it penetrated the upper and middle classes of Italian cities very thoroughly. This new culture, expressed in both humanism and Neoplatonism, engaged a surprisingly broad audience.

Art of the High Renaissance: Leonardo, Michelangelo, Raphael

De Lamar Jensen

The fruitful decades from 1500 to 1520 in Italy are called the High Renaissance period, and these years saw the greatest artistic achievements of the Italian Renaissance in the works of Leonardo, Michelangelo, and Raphael. De Lamar Jensen, professor of history at Brigham Young University, assesses in this essay the self-confidence, drive, and spirit of creativity shared by these three versatile artists, and he analyzes the philosophy of art underlying the work of each artist.

The High Renaissance (especially the years between 1500 and 1520) was the culmination and fulfillment of the aspirations and techniques of the earlier Renaissance artists. The problems of perspective, light and shade, foreshortening, space composition, painting in oil, texture, and movement had all been variously solved. Artists could now apply the techniques they had learned to creating masterpieces of harmony and strength to glorify their great age. As the painters' techniques were perfected, they concentrated more on using this medium for powerful portrayals of man's personal accomplishments and also his partnership with God. In architecture, sculpture, painting, and music, as well as in the lofty Latin epics and vernacular histories, this was a period of reconciliation and culmination. Projects of artists and patrons were on a grand and heroic scale—building the richest homes in Rome, the finest palaces in Italy, and the largest churches in the world. The affinity felt with the ancients also made this par excellence, the age of classicism. Now, as masters of their media, Renaissance artists and builders could create the kind of art they deeply felt, the kind of art the ancient Greeks and Romans had conceived. Nature was no longer something merely to be copied—it was to be transcended.

The High Renaissance coincides also with the decline, and in some cases the collapse, of political democracy in Italy and with the growing power and importance of the aristocracy. Art of this period was the art of the great princes, popes, and potentates, reflecting their thoughts and aspirations. In almost any sector one chooses to look—religious, economic, political, intellectual, or artistic, in deeds of virtue, heroism, or villainy—one will find proof that the High Renaissance was an age of giants. Whatever the enterprise, it was neither too vast nor too difficult for a Leonardo da Vinci, Ariosto, Machiavelli, Julius II, Christopher Columbus, Amerigo Vespucci, Cortés, Charles V, Martin Luther, Francis I, Thomas More, Erasmus, Rabelais, Henry VIII, or Michelangelo. Whereas Florence had been the focus of Quattrocento culture, now Rome became the center to which the greatest artists converged and out of which the finest art emerged. But Rome was not the only center of artistic production; Milan too had its moments of glory and disgrace in the High Renaissance, as did Florence and especially Venice. This was also the age when Renaissance art ceased being primarily an Italian phenomenon and spread rapidly to other parts of Europe in the wake of the French invasions.

In the arts we have been describing, three figures tower above all the rest in the High Renaissance: Leonardo, Michelangelo, and Raphael. Each was unique in personality, style, and significance; yet all three shared the spirit of creative genius and left masterpieces conceived in heroic proportions.

Leonardo da Vinci

Of the three artists, Leonardo da Vinci (1452–1519) was born the earliest. Chronologically, he belongs with Botticelli and Ghirlandaio and the artists of the late Quattrocento, and his almost complete rejection of Roman models is unlike the flowering classicism of the early sixteenth century. But his powerful, protean mind and versatile style place him on the frontier of his age. His grandiose projects mark him as a man of the High Renaissance. He was born at Anchiano, near the village of Vinci just west of Florence, of a lawyer father and peasant mother, but was Florentine by training. Leonardo received his early apprenticeship under Verrocchio, who soon recognized his pupil's precocity and provided him with opportunities to work on some of the most important contracts. His *Baptism of Christ* and *Annunciation* are now legendary. In 1481 Leonardo was commissioned to paint an *Adoration of the Kings* for a monastery outside Florence. This unfinished work (and most of Leonardo's works are unfinished) is one of the finest examples of his mastery of composition and movement, and the figures that are completed reveal his unrivaled facility for interpretive facial expression. Two years later, he was in Milan where he painted the controversial *Virgin of the Rocks*. During the last years of the century, Leonardo worked in the monastery of Santa Maria della Grazie, in Milan, on his most famous masterpiece, the *Last Supper*. Here is a supreme example of artistic composition, rhythmically arranging the apostles in groups of three contrasting types, balancing each other as they harmonize the whole in the person of Christ at the moment of emotional drama evoked by the Lord's pronouncement that one of his apostles would betray him.

With the fall of Milan to the French in 1499, Leonardo left the Sforza employ and returned to Florence where he remained for the next six years, creating, in addition to the *Mona Lisa*, a charming *Madonna and Child with Saint Anne*, numerous preliminary studies for great paintings that were never finished, and a mammoth fresco of the *Battle of Anghiari* for a wall of the Great Hall of the Palazzo Vecchio in Florence, which he was employed by the *Signoria* to paint in competition with his archrival Michelangelo. He also served as military engineer to Cesare Borgia during that tyrant's campaign through the Romagna. He then returned to Milan, this time in the employ of Milan's new ruler, the king of France. For four years (1513–17), he resided in Rome under the patronage of Giulio de' Medici before accepting Francis I's offer to come to France, where he joined other Italian artists invited by the king to carry Renaissance ideas and art to that country. He was given a home and shop in Amboise near the court, where he died two years later at the age of sixty-seven.

A Restless Brilliance

From whatever position he is viewed, Leonardo was a remarkable and unusual man, gifted beyond most of his contemporaries in the intellectual and technical skills of his profession. But he was not satisfied with being only an artist, although he considered painting the highest of all callings. His restless mind and thirst for knowledge would not allow him repose as he vacillated between painting, engineering, designing, writing, sketching, building, dissecting, and contemplating. During much of his wandering, he kept notebooks in which he jotted down thoughts and impressions on innumerable subjects and sketched hundreds of objects and figures from life. Some of these were used in his paintings, most of them were not, but they reveal the turmoils and trials of his life, as well as the brilliance of his insights and his ability to describe them in pictures.

His philosophy of art is important for understanding his own mind and for appreciating his painting and other art of the Renaissance. Like Alberti, Leonardo believed painting was a science because it is based on mathematical perspective and on the study of nature. No other artist of the Renaissance made such close and detailed observations of nature, including anatomy, as did Leonardo. Surface appearance was not sufficient. He had to know the inner construction and functions of all parts and organs before he felt he could adequately paint the human body in lifelike actions and moods. For this reason, he performed many dissections of animal and human bodies and in so doing added much to his knowledge of human anatomy. But Leonardo believed the artist's role was different from that of other scientists, for in the end it resulted in a creative work of art. Thus the painter is both scientist and creator. In his *Treatise on Painting*, Leonardo argued that painting is superior to science, because it transcends it, being both contemplative and operative. He also maintained that painting is a higher art than sculpture, architecture, and music, and is equal, if not superior, to philosophy and poetry (considered since ancient times the greatest of the liberal arts).

Leonardo's artistic genius is best shown in his complete mastery of the art of composition and in his ability to penetrate beyond the outward appearance of things and reveal their inner reality. His portraits breathe character as well as personality; even his landscapes possess a quality of "lifeness" through the delicate and misty gradations of light, known as *sfumato*, that are the hallmarks of Leonardo's paintings.

Michelangelo

Like the versatile Leonardo, Michelangelo Buonarroti (1475–1564) was also a universal man. He was a painter of unequaled power and feeling, an imaginative architect, an engineer, a poet of depth and sensitivity, a knowledgeable authority on anatomy, and the greatest sculptor of all time. Yet in a sense, he was a simpler person than Leonardo, motivated and unified by a single driving passion to create. Whereas Leonardo found it difficult, usually impossible, to carry a project through to completion, Michelangelo was so compulsively impelled to finish a sculpture once begun that he frequently worked day and night without food or sleep until it was completed. Leonardo was fragmented by his conflicting interests and talents, and by his restless, inquisitive mind, which drank in knowledge as fast as he could find it. Michelangelo was integrated by his powerful urge to produce, to create, in whatever medium available or with whatever technique required. His capacity for work was almost inhuman, yet he drove himself even further because of the unquenchable fire that burned within him. He was full of majestic and noble art that had to be released. The very walls and stones contained magnificent forms and ideas that had to be liberated. It was his life's work to free them.

Michelangelo's ideal of beauty was related to nature; yet true beauty, spiritual beauty in the Platonic sense, transcended nature. It was the divine reflection of God in the material sphere. He disclosed this conception of beauty in his poems as well as in his art:

> He who made the whole made every part;
> Then from the whole chose what was most beautiful,
> To reveal on earth, as He has done here and now
> His own sublime perfections.

The spark of this Divine beauty is revealed to people both physically, as we see, hear, and absorb the visible and audible world about us, and spiritually as we receive an inner image of ideal beauty from the interaction of mind and soul. In other words, true beauty is communicated from God to people, and from one person to another, not just by the senses or even by a rational faculty of "beauty-truth," as Alberti maintained, but by a combination of sensory, rational, and spiritual manifestations:

> The beauty you behold indeed emanates from her [the
>   visual image]
> But it grows greater as it flows
> Through mortal eyes to its nobler abode—the soul.
> Here it becomes divine, pure, perfect
> To match the soul's immortality.
> It is this beauty, not the other,
> Which ever outruns your vision.

Born in Florence, Michelangelo was the son of a petty shopkeeper and merchant (a descendant of a minor noble family) who would have liked nothing better than to have his son carry on the Buonarroti family business and eventually acquire land and nobility. It was with deep disappointment, therefore, that he finally consented to apprentice young Michelangelo, who was interested in nothing but art, to the painter Ghirlandaio. The arrangement was only a compromise, however, for the boy's real passion was sculpture. As an infant, he had been sent to a stonecutter's wife to nurse. Vasari proudly quotes Michelangelo as saying to him, "Giorgio, if I am good for anything, it is because I was born in the good mountain air of your Arezzo and suckled among the chisels and hammers of the stonecutters." Michelangelo was a bright student and learned much about the technique of fresco painting in the Ghirlandaio workshop. Soon, however, he was taken into Lorenzo de' Medici's circle of artist friends and trainees, where he became acquainted with many important people, with the intellectual impact of Plato, and with the prominent sculptors of Florence.

With the fall of the Medici in 1494, Michelangelo went to Bologna and from there to Rome in 1496. Here he began the most productive period in his long career. His first significant sculpture was the famous and long-loved *Pietà*, remarkable for its combination of naturalistic beauty and deep religious feeling. It stands in the Capella della Pietà in Saint Peter's Basilica. Michelangelo's fame was well established when he returned to Florence at the age of twenty-six to begin work on several commissions from the Florentine *Signoria*. One of these was the giant white marble statue of *David*, poised in classical masculine beauty and power anticipating the encounter with Goliath. This masterpiece of grandeur and dignity, which stands proudly under the cupola of the Academia in Florence, has probably been copied and reproduced more than any other statue. It has become a symbol of Michelangelo and of Renaissance art. While in Florence, he also completed other sculptures, including the life-size Bruges *Madonna and Child* and a tempera painting of the Holy Family, and competed with Leonardo da Vinci's battle scene on the wall of the council chamber with a cartoon for his own *Battle of Cascina*.

Employee of the Popes

Michelangelo was recalled to Rome in 1505 by the 62-year-old Pope Julius II who, like the artist himself, was a restless and impatient doer. Julius not only set himself the task of expelling the French from Italy and establishing a politically powerful Papal State but also began the creation of a new and more beautiful Rome, complete with grandiose plans for statues and paintings equal to the heroic history of the city, and a mammoth new cathedral that would be the wonder of Christendom. He did not live to see his vast ambitions fulfilled, but he did bring the greatest artists and builders to

Rome and inaugurated a brief age of Roman splendor. Michelangelo's first commission from Julius was for a huge tomb requiring no fewer than forty greater-than-life-size statues and innumerable smaller figures and designs. As it turned out, this work became the continuing burden of Michelangelo's life. No sooner had he begun work on the immense project than Julius's money ran out, and Michelangelo was forced to divert his energies to other work, including a bronze statue of Julius in Bologna and the fresco painting of the Sistine Chapel ceiling. After Julius's death, the contract was renegotiated with his heirs for a new tomb, this one considerably smaller and less expensive. But the fortunes of Italian politics were such that few long-range projects could be carried to conclusion. Eventually, five separate contracts were signed, each contradicting the former and causing endless litigation and recriminations over a period of forty years, before the remnant of Julius's original idea was completed. In its greatly diminished form, the tomb now stands in the small church of San Pietro in Vincoli (Saint Peter in Chains), crowned with the majestic marble statue of *Moses.*

The Sistine ceiling is a saga of its own, an unbelievable undertaking of fortitude, inspiration, and grandeur. The ceiling, covering some 6,300 square feet and containing, when finished, over 300 figures and all that goes with them, was completed by Michelangelo in the amazingly short time of four years. He was offered assistants but refused them (except for two men who mixed pigments and helped transfer Michelangelo's cartoons to the wet plaster), insisting on designing and executing the entire work himself, most of it while straining on his back or crouching over scaffolding in a feverish act of creation. Despite discomfort, fatigue, pain, and sickness (and violent disagreements with Pope Julius), Michelangelo not only completed the massive work but produced a masterpiece of such power and impact as to constitute the supreme Renaissance harmonization of the mortal and divine. In eight huge center panels, the completed vault depicts the story of Genesis from the Creation to Noah, surrounded on the sides of the vaulting by other scenes from the Bible, colossal figures of prophets and sibyls, and in the remaining arches and lunettes, the ancestors of the Virgin, suggesting the expectation and preparation for Christ's coming. Not only is the total rendition monumental, but each individual figure is a masterpiece of composition, movement, and deep meaning surpassing anything that had been painted before. Raphael, who was at the same time painting the Stanza della Segnatura only a few corridors away, pronounced them divine.

The Sistine ceiling notwithstanding, Michelangelo considered himself a sculptor, not a painter, and with hammer and chisel in hand he returned to the pope's tomb. During the next four years, he completed the *Moses* and two *Captives* for the tomb, and a life-size *Christ Risen* for another Roman patron. In the meantime, Julius II was succeeded by Leo X, Lorenzo de' Medici's second son. Leo ordered the abandonment of Julius's tomb and sent Michelangelo to Florence to design and build a new façade for the church of San Lorenzo, the Medici family church. After two years of designing, quarrying, and cutting Carrara marble, and fighting with his patrons, the project was abandoned because of excessive expenditures on Saint Peter's and other lavish papal projects. In 1520 Michelangelo was put to work on a tomb for the Medici family, to be located in the New Sacristy of San Lorenzo, which, after many interruptions (once to rebuild the fortification of Florence against the assault of an imperial army), he completed in 1534, under the aegis of another Medici pope, Clement VII.

The last thirty years of Michelangelo's life were spent in Rome in the successive employ of four more popes, while shunning the invitations of such princes as Charles V, Suleiman the Magnificent, Francis I, and the *doge* of Venice. At the age of sixty, Michelangelo began work on his *Last Judgment*, a mammoth fresco commissioned by Pope Paul III, covering the entire west wall of the Sistine Chapel. More than any of his other works, the *Last Judgment* shows the effects on Michelangelo of the great religious upheaval that was then tearing Europe apart. Here again he displayed a grandiose conception of his subject, but much of the grace and beauty of his earlier works was missing, not because his hand was failing but because he was no longer so interested in physical beauty for its own sake. Now, more than ever before, he employed art for conveying an idea, or more precisely, for revealing a spiritual condition. Deep religious feeling pervades most of Michelangelo's later works and reveals the impact of the Reformation and Counter-Reformation on Renaissance art, transforming it into what art critics now call manneristic—tense, disturbed, exaggerated, distorted, and above all, symbolic and allegorical. Michelangelo's long, productive life (he died in his ninetieth year, still working on the cupola of Saint Peter's Basilica) extended far into the period of Mannerism, and provided a sturdy bridge from the High Renaissance.

Raphael

The youngest of the artistic trio to make the High Renaissance a period of fulfillment and synthesis, as well as the culmination of classicism, was Raffaello Sanzio (1483–1520). Son of a court painter and poet in Urbino, Raphael grew up in the same courtly atmosphere that Castiglione found so attractive under Urbino's cultured duke, Guidobaldo da Montefeltro. After the early death of his parents, Raphael learned painting from a minor local artist before moving to Perugia in 1500 to study under the renowned Pietro Perugino. Perugino taught him much about space composition and form, but young Raphael was soon ready to move on to other ideas and styles. At the age of twenty-one, he settled in Florence in order to learn from the celebrated Leonardo da Vinci. With his unique ability to learn and absorb from many sources and styles and to synthesize and utilize without imitating any of them, Raphael was able to assimilate the best of Umbrian, Perugian, and Florentine art without sacrificing his own originality and style. When he moved to Rome in 1508, he was only twenty-five but already one of the finest painters of Italy.

Julius II invited Raphael to Rome to redecorate some of the rooms in the Vatican Palace at the same time Michelangelo was brought there to paint the Sistine ceiling. Here, in the Stanza della Segnatura, Raphael completed some of his greatest compositions, including the *School of Athens*, which depicts, in almost flawless harmony of composition and arrangement, the Greek philosophers Plato and Aristotle surrounded by numerous other scientists and thinkers of Europe and Asia; the *Dispute of the Sacrament (La Disputà)*, which brings together many heavenly figures, representing saints and prophets surrounding the Savior, the Virgin Mary, and John the Baptist, overlooking an assembly of church dignitaries on earth taking part in the controversy over the Eucharist; and *Parnassus* (sometimes called *Apollo and the Muses)*, another group fresco, which glorifies poetical life and cultural refinement. Many other noteworthy frescoes, depicting the cardinal virtues, civil and canon law, poetry, astronomy, justice, theology, and several scenes from the Bible and from history, adorn the walls and ceilings of the Raphael rooms. All of these Stanze paintings, from the *Jurisprudence* (personifying fortitude, prudence, and temperance), the *Mass of Bolsena*, and *The Expulsion of Heliodorus from the Temple*, to *The Liberation of Saint Peter, Fire in the Borgo*, and *The Meeting of Pope Leo I and Attila the Hun*, achieve near perfection in the techniques of figure painting and at the same time unrivaled skill in composition and visual imagery. The grandeur and scope of these Vatican paintings reflect the High-Renaissance style at its best.

Unlike Leonardo, Raphael was a prolific painter. Working quickly and almost effortlessly, he completed literally hundreds of frescoes, portraits, and oils. He was also a versatile artist, adapting his style to the requirements of the subject or patron. Undoubtedly, Raphael is most famous for his portraits and for his soft and modeled Madonnas. While in the employ of Popes Julius II and Leo X, Raphael made several portraits of these pontiffs and of the cardinals. The best known are portraits of Julius II, Leo X with Cardinals Ludovico de' Rossi and Giulio de' Medici, and Baldassare Castiglione. Raphael's most renowned Madonnas are the *Sistine Madonna* (Dresden), *Madonna di Foligno* (Vatican), the *Ansidei Madonna* (London), *Madonna del Gran' Duca* (Florence), and *Madonna in the Meadow* (Vienna). In all of these, and in the 114 other identified Raphael paintings (plus some sixty done by students from his sketches and under his supervision), we see the variety and scope of an artist who assimilated his surroundings assiduously and transformed his experiences into graceful and imaginative compositions that will always delight the lover of beauty. In 1520 Raphael succumbed to pneumonia and died, at the age of thirty-seven. . . .

The Artist in Renaissance Society

The social position of Renaissance artists has been alluded to but not yet examined or explained. Unlike the fifteenth-century humanists, who were predominantly wealthy and influential, the artists of the Renaissance were in most cases from the lower classes, men of modest means whose social and economic fate depended entirely on their patrons. Quattrocento artists were almost all attached to the workshops of master craftsmen who kept, taught, and worked their apprentices in much the same way as other medieval and Renaissance guildsmen did theirs. . . .

But by the early sixteenth century, artists with genuine talent were able not only to acquire wealth but also to occupy a position of respect and admiration in society. No one provides a better example of this triumphal rise than the artists we have just discussed, especially Michelangelo, Raphael, and Titian. Here were men no longer looked upon as laborers or craftsmen; they were at least "gentlemen" and at best—in the case of Michelangelo—"divine." Indeed, it is more than a coincidence that the art of the High Renaissance was stately, majestic, sublime, and pretentious; this is what the artist had become.

Northern Renaissance Art: Dürer and Brueghel

Bruce Cole and Adelheid Gealt

The significant artistic achievements of the Italians did not go unnoticed by the rest of Europe. One artist who took inspiration from Italian artists was the German painter and engraver, Albrecht Dürer. As art historians Bruce Cole and Adelheid Gealt observe, Dürer's fascination with measurement and proportion and his range of subject matter and media make him easily the most versatile and innovative of all Northern artists. Less influenced by Italian art was Pieter Brueghel of the Netherlands, who took as his subject matter the relation of man to nature, and who painted many scenes of everyday humanity at work and play.

In a culture where tradition was powerful and the future was regarded with trepidation, the art of the North remained codified and ritualized; at the end of the [fifteenth] century it looked to the past for protection and guidance, rather than to the future.

Nonetheless, humanism also flourished in the North, and was especially channeled into religious reforms. Erasmus of Rotterdam, Thomas More of England, and Martin Luther of Germany were the leaders of a movement based on humanistic training and a close reading of biblical texts to challenge the authority of the corrupt and secular papacy in Rome. In 1517, Martin Luther had nailed his ninety-five theses to the door of Wittenberg Cathedral, crystalizing the Reformation movement and setting the Reformers on a path that would ultimately rend the fabric of the unified church.

Reprinted with the permission of Simon & Schuster, Inc., from *Art of the Western World*, by Bruce Cole and Adelheid Gealt. Copyright ©1989 by Bruce Cole and Adelheid Gealt.

The Genius of Dürer

Germany was home at that time not only to the founder of the Lutheran faith but to a number of important artists, including the greatest engraver, draftsman, and painter of the late fifteenth and early sixteenth century, Albrecht Dürer. Born in Nuremberg in 1471, where he died in 1528, Dürer closed one era and opened another. He was deeply pious and remained a lifelong Catholic, yet he admired both Erasmus and Luther, the founders of the Reformation. The themes of Dürer's early work reflect the lingering mentality of the waning Middle Ages, but his later work is an enlightened and original discourse on the Italian Renaissance. Dürer's meticulous craftsmanship and his obsession with detail place him squarely in the tradition of Jan van Eyck and his followers; but in his search for ideals of proportion, and for mathematical systems by which to structure his vision, and in his insatiable visual appetite, Dürer became the German counterpart to Leonardo da Vinci.

Like Leonardo, Dürer drew incessantly. His drawings, watercolors, and diary entries trace his many journeys to observe and record. Dürer's watercolor studies of clumps of grass, animals, and landscapes are precociously scientific in their objective transcription and range of subjects, though latently medieval in their unquestioning acceptance of surface reality without any systematic attempt to penetrate to underlying principles.

The landscapes Dürer produced on his numerous travels are among the earliest independent treatments of the theme and anticipate the interest landscape would generate among Northern artists of the seventeenth century. His *Willow Mills on the Pegnitz* may have been painted some time after he returned from his first trip to Venice, about 1496. For Dürer, the river that flowed on the outskirts of Nuremberg became the subject of a watercolor simply because he saw it as he walked about his city. Atmospheric effects, the local flora, including the wispy river willows, and the high-peaked houses, are masterfully described but also interpreted. Dürer's watercolor has transcended mere topographic description and has made nature into art.

Dürer's first great success as a printmaker was connected with Europe's obsession with the century's end: people were gripped by the fear that the year 1500 would bring the end of the world. Dürer responded to the moment by producing, in 1498, an illustrated *Apocalypse*, showing what the revelations of Saint John had to say about an anticipated end. The result was fourteen full-page woodcuts that translate Saint John's written descriptions into compelling images.

The most famous of Dürer's *Apocalypse* scenes is the *Four Horsemen of the Apocalypse* who bring with them war, famine, death, and hell. Using the linear visual language that was his heritage, Dürer powerfully described the scene in vivid detail. The entire image explodes with movement as horses trample people underfoot. Anxiety emanates from every line and form. A bishop falls into a monster's open jaws, while God's destructive forces reclaim the earth and cleanse it of its evil, as the horsemen move forward, sparing no one. Intended for the general public, Dürer's *Apocalypse* was an immediate success, bringing him fame in Germany, Italy, and throughout Europe.

Dürer not only mastered the woodcut, he became an unparalleled engraver. His ability to make the copper plate yield diverse effects of line, light, shade, and texture is the union of infinite patience and brilliant technique. One of his most celebrated engravings is *Adam and Eve*, done in 1504, the year that Michelangelo completed his famous *David*. Here Dürer joined the quest for the ideal beauty and proportions of the human figure that had inspired Italian masters of the time to look at surviving works of antiquity. Dürer's *Adam and Eve* reflects the antique *Apollo Belvedere* found in 1489–1490 and an antique Venus of the type exemplified by the *Medici Venus* in Florence. He placed these gods in the gloomy precincts of a dark German forest, surrounded by local as well as exotic fauna.

Disobedience and Melancholy

For Dürer, Adam and Eve provided the opportunity to describe the most perfect of God's creations, who, through their disobedience to Him, doomed their descendants to physical as well as spiritual imperfection. Thus these medieval symbols of human corruption stand before the viewer as embodiments of Renaissance ideals of flawless beauty and grace. Dürer's methodical burin has transcribed every wave of Eve's luxuriant tresses, and every hair of the cat's thick coat. Symbolically, the cat and all the other forest creatures explain the nature and consequences of the Fall: as the cat traps the mouse, Eve caught Adam, and their sin of disobedience brought into being the four temperaments, or humors—the phlegmatic, choleric, sanguine, and melancholic personalities.

Subject to fits of melancholy himself, Dürer endured its torments and regarded melancholy as the natural temperament of the artist. In this respect Dürer shared with his contemporaries in Italy a new understanding of the artist, as someone apart from and above the rest of society because of his creative spirit. One of Dürer's greatest engravings is a cautionary discourse on the nature of melancholy.

Produced in 1514, Dürer's *Melancholia I* anticipates the doubts and frustrations about the creative quest that later found expression in Italy. Slumped into tormented passivity, Melancholia stares into space. Implements of thought, measurement, and creation lie about, discarded and useless in the pursuit of artistic perfection. Obsessed with thought, Melancholia embodies its futility. Utilizing his unlimited technical abilities, Dürer, in his *Melancholia*, set about describing the nature of his own artistic limitations. To Dürer, technical mastery was achievable, but artistic endeavors often led the artist to the unknown and the unreachable. What the human mind pursues is ultimately elusive and mysterious; Dürer's portrayal of Melancholia was one of the earliest expressions of artistic frustration. His message was destined to be echoed by many other voices over the centuries, by artists liberated from their role as pure craftsmen and confounded by their freedom.

Dürer stands alone in Northern art for the range of his subject matter, which includes not only traditional themes but, as in his *Melancholia*, new concepts. . . .

Shortly after Dürer . . . had died, a painter was born who

was destined to establish the theme of man and nature as one of Northern Europe's most important subjects. Pieter Brueghel the Elder was born c. 1525 in the Netherlands, around Brueghel or Breda. He, like Dürer and other Northern artists, made his way to Italy, where the trip through the mountains, forests, and valleys of Europe may have inspired his enthusiasm for nature. In contrast to the prevailing fashion of his day, Brueghel did not emulate Italian art but retained his own, indigenous approach. He was an insightful student of human nature and a lover of the natural environment.

Images of Folly and Dignity

Working in the aftermath of the Reformation, in a period that witnessed peasant revolts, wars of religion, persecutions, class struggle, and economic upheavals, Brueghel embedded in his images an understanding of human folly as well as an appreciation of human dignity and endurance. Brueghel's portrayals of the months of the year, produced about 1565, show both the scope of his vision and his sensitivity to nature. *Hunters in the Snow* belongs to this series. Depicting Winter, it is singular in its concentration on human efforts within a broad natural setting. Filled with anecdotal details that balance the panoramic sweep of the scene, the work shows humanity as part of nature. Seasons, weather, the contour of the landscape and the vegetation that grows upon it, all affect the lives of the people who live and work in, and reap the bounty of, the natural world.

An astute observer of humanity, Brueghel understood life in its broadest sense. His *Magpie on the Gallows* is a haunting evocation of human suffering, mortality, and cruelty, set within the grander scheme of social order, human folly, and endurance. Peasants dance, sing, laugh, and carouse in the shadow of gallows that have temporarily become the roost for a harmless magpie. Like the bird, the peasants are greedy for life, and hardy and industrious even in the face of death. The gallows, an instrument of death made by humans for use against others of their kind, are a stark reminder of the violence of the age, while the dancing people are symbolic of human indifference as well as human survival.

Unlike his Italian counterparts, who made the human figure their subject and its perfection their challenge, Brueghel took as his subject the reality of human existence. Quotidian in its approach, anecdotal in its treatment, and epic in its sweep, Brueghel's art made both humanity as it really was and nature as it actually looked the central subjects for artists of the next century. The great landscape painters of Holland and Flanders, such as Ruisdael, Cuyp, and Koninck, all studied Brueghel, while such great students of human nature and peasant life as Brouwer, van Ostade, Hals, and Steen also have roots in his work. Through Brueghel's efforts, satire, humor, pathos, and the vast parade of peasant and village life had joined the mainstream of artistic expression.

Brueghel's forthright and honest portrayal of life was worlds away from the art of the Italian Renaissance. When Brueghel died in 1569, Titian was still active and Tintoretto had another quarter of a century of work ahead of him. While Brueghel knew, absorbed, and transformed Italian sources, the Italians ignored his contributions. The human figure of nearly mythic proportions was and remained for them the supreme subject. In Italy during the sixteenth century, the unvarnished reality that Brueghel championed was ignored in favor of a heroic interpretation of the human form. Whereas Brueghel examined humanity for all its internal and external flaws, the Italian masters of the sixteenth century stripped them away, and celebrated the human form as a paradigm of perfection and beauty such as would never be created again.

The Reformation and Counter-Reformation

J.M. Roberts

The Protestant Reformation arrived just as the Renaissance in Italy reached its peak and before the Renaissance in Northern Europe had fully taken hold. The rejection of the Catholic Church by large numbers of Europeans threw the countries north of Italy into decades of religious turmoil and political conflict. In the following essay, British historian J.M. Roberts assesses the problems in the Catholic Church and social conditions that led to the Reformation, and he explicates the fundamental premises of the new Protestant religion as promoted by the passionate Protestant leader Martin Luther.

In 1500, one Church united Europe—and almost defined it. Within fifty years, this was no longer so and that might be taken as the end of the Middle Ages. This was the result of a great upheaval, later called the Protestant Reformation. It marked a new era of European civilization and was to be of outstanding importance in world history. Yet, like so many great changes, few could have foreseen the Reformation and those who launched it would have been horrified had they been able to glimpse the final outcome of what they were doing. They were men with what we should now think of as medieval minds, but they broke a tradition of respect for religious authority going back a thousand years. They ended the unity of Christendom which they deeply believed in. They created new political conflicts though they often thought they were concerned only with unworldly matters. Looking back, we can see too that they were taking the first

Excerpted from *A Concise History of the World*, by J.M. Roberts. Copyright ©1993 by J.M. Roberts. Reprinted by permission of Sterling Lord Literistic, Inc.

and most important steps towards greater individual freedom of conduct, more tolerance of different opinions and much more separation between the secular and religious sides of life. All these things would have appalled them. In short, they launched much of modern history.

In theory, Europe had been wholly Christian since the Dark Age conversions of the barbarians. Only in Spain did Christian kings in 1500 rule any large number of non-Christian subjects; in other countries a few Jews lived apart from Christians, segregated in their ghettos, taxed and not usually enjoying the same legal protection as Christians. Apart from these special cases, all Europeans were Christians: the words almost mean the same thing in the Middle Ages. Religion was the one Europe-wide tie and Christendom was an undivided whole, held together by a common faith and the work of the Church, Europe's only continent-wide legal institution. Church law operated in every land through courts alongside and separate from the lay system. All universities were governed and directed by churchmen. Finally, in every country the same sacraments were administered and imposed the same pattern on the great events of people's lives—birth, marriage and death.

Early Reformers

In spite of its unrivalled position, there had always been plenty of criticism of the Church. There was nothing new about it. Evils which were still worrying critics when the sixteenth century began had been much denounced in the Middle Ages—the ignorance of clergymen, for example, or their misuse of power for personal gain, or their worldly lives. Many such ills—and others—had long been attacked, often by clergymen themselves, and writers had long poked plenty of fun at priests who liked drinking and chasing girls more than attending to their spiritual duties, and had contrasted poor priests devoted to their flocks with their rich, self-indulgent superiors. Yet anti-clericalism—that is, attacking the clergy—did not mean that people wished to forsake the Church itself or doubted the truth of Christianity.

There had long been efforts made by the clergy to put

their house in order. As the fifteenth century went on, some critics—many priests among them—began to suggest that it might be necessary to turn back to the Bible for guidance about the way to live a Christian life, since so many of the clergy were obviously not making a very good job of it. They were often labelled heretics and the Church had powerful arms to deal with them. Some of these men, the Oxford scholar Wyclif or the Czech John Hus (who was burnt), for example, had strong popular support, and appealed to the patriotic feelings of fellow-countrymen who felt that the papacy was a foreign and unfriendly institution. Some heretics could draw also on social unrest; no Christian could easily forget what the Bible had to say about the injustices of life.

The followers of Wyclif and Hus, 'Lollards' and 'Hussites' as they were called, were harried and chased by the authorities. It was not they who were to pull down the Church they often criticized. It was still very strong in 1500 and by no means in much worse shape then than at earlier times, even if we seem suddenly to hear more about what is going wrong. Its influence was still taken for granted at every level of society, controlling, moulding, setting in familiar grooves and patterns the accidents of each individual's life, watching over him or her from the cradle to the grave. Religion was so tangled with everyday life that their separation was almost unthinkable. In most villages and little towns, for instance, there was no other public building than the church; it is not surprising that people met in it for community business, and for amusement, at 'church-ales' and on feast days (when even dances were held in it).

Problems in the Church

Being mixed up in the everyday world was not always good for the Church. Bishops who played a prominent part in the affairs of their rulers had always been in danger of being too busy to be good shepherds of their flocks. The great Cardinal Wolsey, archbishop of York and favourite of the English Henry VIII, never visited his see until sent there in disgrace after falling from favour and power. At the very centre of the Church, the popes themselves often seemed to worry too much about their position as temporal princes. Because the papal throne and the papal bureaucracy had both fallen more or less entirely into Italian hands, foreigners especially felt this. Pluralism—holding many offices and neglecting their duties while drawing the pay for them—was another problem the Church had long faced and did not seem to be able to put right. One reason was that for all the grandeur of the way many bishops and abbots lived, for all the extravagance of the papal court at Rome ('Since God has given us the papacy', one pope is supposed to have said, 'let us enjoy it'), there never seemed to be enough money to go round and, as a result, jobs had to be dished out to reward services. Poverty created other difficulties too. It was unusual for a pope to have to go so far as Sixtus IV, who was finally reduced to

Calvin Compared with Luther

After breaking from the Catholic Church, the Protestant movement fragmented into several large contingents. The two largest were led by the most influential Protestant leaders, Martin Luther and John Calvin. Scholar Karl Dannenfeldt here examines the prominent similarities and differences between these figures. In spite of much agreement, they differed notably in their conception of God and in Calvin's emphasis on predestination.

Calvin was deeply influenced by Luther, and there were many similarities between the Wittenberg reformer's fully developed theology and that of Calvin. Both were much indebted to St. Augustine in their assertions that man is morally helpless and entirely dependent on God's grace for salvation. Both accepted Scripture as the sole source of Christian doctrine, and both discarded as unscriptural purgatory, the papacy, Mariolatry, the cult of the saints and of relics, the Mass as a sacrifice, monasticism, the celibacy of clergy, and many other medieval developments. Both stressed that any useful secular work is a "calling" from God. Both accepted as true sacraments only those sacred actions that had an explicit "promise of Christ" attached to them: Baptism and the Lord's Supper. Man was saved only by God's grace pawning the papal tiara, but using juridical and spiritual power to increase papal revenues was an old complaint, and it had its roots in the need to find revenue.

Money was short in the parishes, too. Priests became more rigorous about collecting tithes—the portion of the parishioners' produce (usually a tenth or twelfth) to which they were entitled. This led to resentment and resistance which then tempted churchmen into trying to secure their rights by threatening to refuse people the sacraments—to excommunicate them—if they did not pay up. This was a serious business when men believed they might burn in hell for ever as a result. Finally, poverty was also a cause of clerical ignorance (though not the only one). The standard of education among the clergy had improved since the twelfth

---

through faith; good works were ineffective for salvation.

Despite these similarities, there were also fundamental differences in the theology and practice of the two reformers. Calvin's theology was much more legalistic than Luther's. The latter stressed the God of love as portrayed in the New Testament, a God who so loved the world that He sent His only-begotten Son to redeem mankind. Calvin was more influenced by the Old Testament in his vision of God as the Lawgiver who demanded obedience to His divine precepts. . . .

Much more than Luther, Calvin placed special importance on the traditionally orthodox belief in predestination. Calvin went beyond the view of St. Augustine in asserting a double predestination in which God had not only selected some for eternal life but had also damned all the rest to everlasting damnation. God had from all eternity *willed* the salvation of some and the damnation of others irrespective of merit. . . . Many readers of Calvin's works were repelled by this concept of predestination, for it seemed to make God the author of sin, but to Calvin this example of God's judgments and undeserved mercy was an appalling mystery beyond man's limited understanding.

Karl H. Dannenfeldt, *The Church of the Renaissance and Reformation*, 1970, pp. 73–76 passim.

century (this owed much to the universities) but many parish priests in 1500 were hardly less ignorant or superstitious than their parishioners.

Against this background, when the papacy began to build a great new cathedral in Rome—the St Peter's which still stands there—it had to find new ways to raise money. One of these ways was licensing more salesmen of 'indulgences'. These were preachers who, in return for a contribution to the funds needed for St Peter's, gave the pope's assurance that subscribers would be let off a certain amount of time in Purgatory, that part of the after-world in which the soul was believed to be purged and cleansed of its worldly wickedness before passing to heaven.

Luther and the Protestant Revolt

It was the unexpected spark for a religious revolution. In 1517 a German monk, Martin Luther, decided to protest against indulgences as well as several other papal practices. Like the old-fashioned scholar he was, he followed tradition by posting his arguments in a set of ninety-five 'theses' for debate on the door of the castle church in Wittenberg, where he was a professor at the university. Here began the Protestant Reformation. Soon his arguments were translated from their original Latin into German. They ran through Germany like wildfire—printing gave them a wider audience than that for earlier criticisms of the papacy. Unknowingly, Luther was becoming a maker of world history, but he had the temperament for the task. He was a Saxon, the son of peasants, impulsive and passionate, who at the age of twenty-one had become a monk after an emotional upheaval set off by a thunderstorm which broke on him as he was trudging along the highway. Overcome by terror and a feeling of his own sinfulness which made him sure he was fit only to go to hell if he was struck by lightning and killed, Luther suddenly felt the conviction that God cared for him and would save him. It was rather like St. Paul's conversion on the road to Damascus in its suddenness and violence. Luther's first celebration of Mass was another overwhelming experience, so convinced was he of his personal unworthiness to be a priest. Later he was to believe Satan appeared to him—and he even threw his ink-pot at him. Luther's nature was such that, when convinced he was right, he was immovable and this explains his impact. Germany may have been ripe for Luther, but the Reformation would not have been what it was without him.

An enormous dislike of the Italian papacy waited to be tapped in Germany. Luther turned to writing and preaching with a will when the primate of Germany, the archbishop of Mainz, tried to silence him. His fellow-monks abandoned him, but his university stood by him and so did the ruler of Saxony, the state he lived in. Eventually his writings divided Germans into those who came to be called 'Lutherans' (though he was first called a 'Hussite') and those who stood by the pope and the emperor. Support came to him not only from clergy who disapproved of the teaching and practice of the Roman clergy, but from humble folk with grievances against tithe-gatherers and church courts, from greedy princes who coveted the wealth of the Church, and from others who simply took his side because their traditional or habitual rivals came out against him.

Luther in the end set out his views in the form of new theological doctrines—that is to say, statements about the beliefs a Christian ought to hold in order to be sure that he really was a Christian and that he would be saved from Hell after death. He said that the Church itself and even attendance at the sacraments was not absolutely necessary to salvation, but that men might be saved if they had faith in Jesus Christ. This was very important. He was teaching that in the last resort it was possible to hope to be saved even without the Church, by simply relying on your own private relationship with God. It has been said that he dethroned the pope and enthroned the Bible, God's Word, which every believer could consult without the Church coming between him and it. A view putting such stress on the individual conscience was revolutionary. Not surprisingly, Luther was excommunicated, but he went on preaching and won wider and wider support.

The political quarrels Luther's teaching aroused between Germany's rulers broke out in wars and revolts. After a long period of turmoil, a general settlement had to be made. By the peace of Augsburg of 1555 (nine years after Luther's death) it was agreed that Germany should be divided between Catholic and Protestant (the word had come into use after the signing of a 'Protestation' against the papacy in 1529). Which religion prevailed in each state was to be decided by its ruler. Thus yet another set of divisions was introduced into that divided land. The emperor Charles V had to accept this; it was the only way of getting peace in Germany, though he had struggled against the Reformers. For the first time Christian princes and churchmen acknowledged that there might be more than one source of religious authority and more than one recognized Church inside western Christendom.

Something else, of which Luther himself disapproved, had already begun to happen by then. Protestantism tended to fragment, as more and more people began to make up their own minds about religious questions. Other Protestants had soon appeared who did not share his views. The most important were to be found in Switzerland, where a Frenchman, John Calvin, who had broken with Catholicism, began to preach in the 1530s. He had great success at Geneva, and set up there a 'theocratic' state—that is, one governed by the godly where it had been born. The result in any case, was further division—there were now three Europes, two Protestant and one Catholic, as well as several minor Protestant sects.

One country where Protestantism was to be particularly important for the future was England. In that country many of the forces operating elsewhere in favour of throwing off allegiance to the papacy were at work, and so was a very personal one, the wish of Henry VIII to get rid of his queen who was not able to give him a son and heir. Yet Henry was a loyal son of the Church; he had actually written a book against Luther which earned him papal approbation as 'Defender of the Faith', a title still borne by his descendant today. It is very likely that he would have been able to get his marriage to his queen 'annulled'—that is, deemed not to have been a valid marriage—by the pope, had she not been aunt to the emperor Charles V, whose support was needed by the Church against the German heretics. So, as the papacy would not help, Henry quarrelled with the pope, England broke away from allegiance to Rome, and the lands of the English monasteries were seized by the Crown. Some Englishmen also hoped to make the English Church Lutheran, but that did not happen.

Protestantism's successes forced change on Rome. Whatever hopes Roman Catholics might have of returning to the former state of affairs, they would have to live for the foreseeable future in a Europe where there were other claimants to the name of Christian. One effect was that Roman Catholicism became more rigid and intransigent—or, to put it in a different way, better disciplined and more orderly. This was the 'Counter-Reformation'. Several forces helped but the most important of them was a general Council of the Church which opened at Trent in north Italy in 1545 and sat, on and off, until 1563. It redefined much of the Church's doctrine, laid down new regulations for the training of priests and asserted papal authority. Putting its decisions into practice was made a little easier by the work of a remarkable Spaniard, Ignatius Loyola, who had founded a new order of clergy to serve the papacy, the Society of Jesus, or 'Jesuits'. Sanctioned in 1540 and bound by a special vow of obedience to the pope himself, the Jesuits were carefully trained as an elite corps of teachers and missionaries (Loyola was especially concerned to evangelize the newly discovered pagan lands). More than any other clergy they embodied the combative, unyielding spirit of the Counter-Reformation. This matched Loyola's heroic temper, for he had been a soldier and always seems to have seen his Society in very military terms; Jesuits were sometimes spoken of as the militia of the Church. Together with the Inquisition, a medieval institution for the pursuit of heresy which became the final court of appeal in heresy trials in 1542, and the 'Index' of prohibited books first issued in 1557, the Jesuits were part of a new armoury of weapons for the papacy.

Reformation and Counter-Reformation divided Europeans bitterly. The Orthodox world of the east was little affected, but everywhere in what had been Catholic Europe there were for more than a century religious struggles [and] political struggles envenomed by religion. Some countries successfully persecuted minorities out of existence: Spain and (in large measure) Italy thus remained strongholds of the Counter-Reformation. Rulers usually made up their minds for themselves and their subjects often fell in with their decisions. Foreigners occasionally tried to intervene; Protestant England had the Channel to protect her, and was in less danger than Germany or France. Yet religion was not the only explanation of the so-called 'religious wars' which devastated so much of Europe between 1550 and 1648. Sometimes, as in France, what was really going on was a struggle for dominance between great aristocratic families who identified themselves with different religious parties. . . .

Although even then many people still thought of religion as well-worth fighting over and certainly as something which justified murdering or torturing your errant neighbours, statesmen for the most part began to take more account of other matters in dealing with one another. The world became a tiny bit more civilized when they turned their attention back to arguments about trade and territory, and away from religion. Europe by then, in the second half of the seventeenth century, was divided into states, most of which did not officially tolerate more than one dominant religion, but in some of which—in particular, England and the United Provinces—a fair degree of tolerance was practised.

The Renaissance Influence on the Reformation

C. Black et al.

At first glance, the Renaissance and Reformation would appear to be vastly different historical phenomena, even though the Reformation occurred in the middle of the Renaissance era. In spite of their differences, there are important overlaps, as the following essay makes clear. Both movements involve a critique of the contemporary society and a thrust to return to the original texts and sources of the Western intellectual and spiritual heritage. Further, the textual and scholarly achievements of Renaissance humanism served to support the Protestant critique of the Catholic Church.

The Renaissance and the Reformation appear to have little in common. The Renaissance links the European experience to the classical past in one great continuum. The Reformation cuts across it as a unique divide. . . . The contrasts may be extended. The Renaissance of the 15th century was "secular"—or at least it acknowledged that the whole of human history could not be contained entirely within a Christian framework. The Reformation was first and foremost a religious phenomenon, expressing criticism of the Church and responding to ordinary believers' thirst for spiritual succor. The Renaissance was something to which all the regions of Europe could relate, albeit in different ways. To that extent the Renaissance tended to promote cultural unity. The Reformation demanded a stance for or against and so proved profoundly divisive, setting Protestant north against Catholic south.

Excerpted from *Atlas of the Renaissance*, by C. Black, M. Greengrass, D. Howarth, J. Lawrance, R. Mackenney, M. Rady, E. Welch. Copyright ©1993 by Andromeda Oxford Ltd. Reprinted by permission of Andromeda Oxford Ltd.

Nevertheless, on closer inspection there is evidence of an important legacy of the "secular" Renaissance to the "religious" Reformation. The intellectual thrust of humanism was toward a pure original text, a return to sources. Although this tendency is often related to classical texts, the religious implications were never far removed. In the first instance, there was the matter of Church history. The great scholar Lorenzo Valla (1407–57)—who enjoyed papal patronage—was able to demonstrate in 1440 that the Donation of Constantine was an 8th-century forgery. This grant by Emperor Constantine was alleged to have established the authority of the papacy over Italy and the western Church. Valla showed that words used in the text could not have been applied to or employed by the emperor or his agent. Valla also produced a set of notes on the New Testament, writings that were to exercise a profound influence on the thinking of Erasmus. It was entirely consistent with Valla's approach to apply the principles of humanist scholarship to the text of the Bible. In doing so he demonstrated that many of the most obvious manifestations of ecclesiastical power—particularly those associated with the papacy and with monasticism—had little if any foundation in Scripture. Set in the context of the revival of Platonic philosophy, which encouraged the individual to seek God without recourse to a priestly intermediary, the potential of Renaissance humanism became explosive. It offered not only a systematic critique of ecclesiastical institutions, but also alternative versions of the spiritual life. It did so by returning to sources.

Protestant Debt to Humanism

One of Luther's most durable and monumental achievements was the translation of the Bible into German so the ordinary man and woman could read the pure Word of God. The Protestant reformer John Calvin (1509–64) might seem a world away from the Italian Renaissance, yet his scholarship owed much to the techniques of the humanists. His earliest surviving work is a humanistic exercise, a commentary on Seneca's *On Clemency* (1532). Although Calvin was no slavish imitator of Italian learning, the monumental and systematic exposition of his *Institutes of Christian Religion* (1536) demonstrate his debt to the scholarly techniques of the humanists. What is so exciting about the text of his most famous work is the conviction that the Scriptures enable Christians to get as close as possible to the Word of God.

It is somewhat surprising, but nonetheless significant, to recognize the intensely secular dimension of the *Institutes*. For in them Calvin makes much of the history of the papacy. Calvin tended to write human history as a parallel to the Bible: the history of the papacy was seen as the Old Testament of fallen man, with the Reformed Church promising a New Testament of redemption. All the same, his argument draws strength from the use of historical examples to demonstrate the corruption of the papacy through its involvement in worldly affairs. So even Calvin made use of the secular branches of Renaissance learning. The ancient Greeks and Romans had constructed secular states without knowledge of Christianity. The papal fraud was the creation of a secular state under the flag of Christianity. In a profoundly important way, humanist historical studies, by examining a non-Christian past, had exposed the worldliness of the papacy.

The Authority of the Princes

It is curious to think of Calvin in the same intellectual context as Niccolò Machiavelli (1469–1527), until it is remembered that religious reform gave enormous impetus to the formation of sovereign secular states. When Machiavelli, in *The Prince* (c. 1513), asserted that he merely wrote of human affairs "as they really are", then it was perfectly logical to point to the worldly ambitions of the papacy. If the popes could use Christianity to reinforce their secular power, could not secular rulers do the same? This message was highly significant for Catholic and Protestant alike. The kings of France enjoyed rights of intervention in ecclesiastical appointments: this "Gallicanism" was reaffirmed in an agreement reached by Catholic monarch and Roman pope (the Concordat of Bologna, 1516). The Spanish Inquisition was responsible to the monarchs, not to Rome. Henry VIII became head of the Church of England—not as a Protestant, merely as a schismatic Catholic. When religious peace finally came to the states of Germany in 1555, its mainstay was the principle that the territorial ruler could determine whether his lands were to be Lutheran or Catholic, a principle later defined as *cuius regio, eius religio* ("to whom the kingdom, his the religion").

While princely authority was enhanced by claims to power in religious affairs, claims that owed a good deal to the ideas of the humanists, the stature of princes was enhanced by the use of Renaissance art. Princely magnificence found expression in pageants and ceremonies, and patronage at court. The French king Francis I appeared as a Gallic Hercules, Henry VIII of England as an imperial sovereign, Charles V of the German Empire as the supreme expression of knighthood.

The Reformation, then, derived something of its character from the secular and religious implications of humanism; the princes who gained power from the religious upheaval used the visual arts of the Renaissance to emphasize their secular authority. The religious potential of the visual arts, however, was also to serve the purposes of the Catholic revival, the Counter-Reformation. The Council of Trent met intermittently between 1545 and 1563 to reform abuses in the Catholic Church. Among many reaffirmations of traditional doctrine, it established that the targets of Protestant criticism—shrines, the cult of the Virgin and the saints, the sacramental role of the priesthood—should be extolled and exalted in the decoration of church interiors all over the world.

Chapter 4

Achievements and Developments of the Later Renaissance

Turning Points

IN WORLD HISTORY

The Printing Press and the Spread of Humanist Ideas

Peter Gay and R.K. Webb

The Renaissance in Northern Europe came at the heels of the greatest accomplishments of the later Italian Renaissance, and it was fueled by the increasing power of the printing press, and shaped by the religious tone of Northern humanism. Historians Peter Gay and R.K. Webb contend that while the Northern Renaissance was hugely influenced by Italian culture, it nevertheless reflected, in its earlier stages, the scholarship, religious piety, and satiric temper of the leading Northern humanists, Erasmus and Sir Thomas More.

The Northern Renaissance flourished later than the Renaissance in Italy. Its most celebrated Humanist, artist, and scientist—Erasmus, Dürer, and Copernicus—did their enduring work after 1500. This late date suggests that the Renaissance originated in Italy and expanded northward, to spawn a Renaissance there. The evidence in favor of this view is impressive. Leonardo da Vinci, who died in France, and lies buried at the French château of Amboise, did little in his last years in the service of Francis I, but the French king's eagerness to have this great Italian with him indicates how much prestige the Italian Renaissance had for its northern admirers. Albrecht Dürer was only one, and the greatest, among northern painters to enter the ambiance of Italian artists and theoreticians; when he said, in perfect candor, that the rebirth of the arts had begun in Italy, with Giotto, he was voicing an accepted opinion. English and French Humanists traveled to Italy, Italian Humanists traveled to

Excerpted from *Modern Europe*, by Peter Gay and R.K. Webb (New York: Harper & Row, 1973). Reprinted by permission of the authors. (Endnotes in the original have been omitted from this reprint.)

France and England, and in these exchanges it was understood that the Italians were the teachers, the northerners their disciples. . . .

The Impact of Moveable Type

When Johann Gensfleisch zum Gutenberg of Mainz perfected or invented printing by movable type in the 1440s—the precise sequence of events and influences remains, and must always remain, somewhat obscure—the idea of multiplying information mechanically was not new. But in the hands of Gutenberg and of the financiers and printers associated with him, the convenient new device spread rapidly. The Gutenberg Bible, set from 1452 on and published in 1456, remains the most precious relic of these heroic days. While the cultural effects were not immediate, the technical transformation was indeed nothing less than a revolution; this was not handwriting speeded up, it was a new mode of communication altogether: "A hard-working copyist," Elizabeth L. Eisenstein has said, "turned out two books in little less than a year. An average edition of an early printed book ranged from two hundred to one thousand copies. Chaucer's clerk longed for twenty books to fill his shelf; ten copyists had to be recruited to serve each such clerk down to the 1450s, whereas one printer was serving twenty before 1500."

The phenomenal growth of the printing industry reflects the widespread hunger for books. The spread of lay learning, at once cause and effect of the Renaissance mentality, called for reading material in ever larger quantities, and printers across Europe soon supplied it. Mainz, Gutenberg's home city, was the first center; before 1460, there were printers in Bamberg and Strasbourg; by the early 1470s, the major German and Italian cities all had printing presses, and by the early 1480s, so did Stockholm and Valencia, Budapest and Antwerp, Cracow and Paris. Printing was an industry calling for considerable capital; it was part not merely of the intellectual, but also of the commercial, revolution of the age.

For the Humanists who accepted printing—and gradually more and more of them did—it meant a wide public for their editions of classical authors and for their writings: Erasmus, who in his wandering life spent eight months in 1508 with the Venetian printer Aldus Manutius, was thoroughly modern in his quick recognition and shrewd exploitation of movable type. He wrote quite deliberately for the press, with gratifying results. His European reputation, already established, grew with the thirty-four editions of his *Adages* and the many thousands of copies that were sold all over Europe of his *Praise of Folly*. The ancients—both the pagan and the Christian classics—became available to a new reading public, and as scholars enjoyed the new audience printing gave them, this audience in turn provided a stimulus for further scholarly efforts.

But this was by no means all. As today so at its very beginning, printing mainly served a public that had no interest in scholarship. Printers turned out textbooks, books of devotion, collections of saints' lives, and political tracts in impressive quantities. "Printing," Luther said, "was God's highest act of grace," and this single observation, made about half a century after printing had been invented, illuminates its cultural possibilities. The printing press, after all, was a docile and neutral instrument. It could produce a learned edition of St. Jerome but also, and with far less trouble, an inflammatory broadside or a papal indulgence. Printing made information immeasurably easier to produce and disseminate; truths and lies traveled faster and further than ever before. In the long run, the invention radically altered the tone and even the content of political and social life, the mode and matter of education, the distribution of fashion, and man's very way of perceiving the world. The effects were incalculable and, in the early modern centuries, no one even tried to calculate them. All one could say was said by Bacon early in the 1600s: the three inventions that the ancients had not known and that had "changed the appearance and state of the whole world," he wrote, were gunpowder, the compass, and printing.

The Growth of Northern Humanism

If printing was a unique contribution of the North to the Renaissance, northern humanism, although not unique, was distinctive. Its single-minded campaign to purify religion has earned it an epithet of doubtful validity: "Christian humanism." It is doubtful because the Italian Humanists, for all their flirtations with esoteric doctrines, remained Christians too; it is doubtful also because the northern Humanists, for all their intentions, sometimes strayed perilously close to infidelity.

Moreover, it is plain that French, British, German, and Netherlands scholars acted under the impress of ideas and personalities native to the Mediterranean regions. By the 1480s, Paris was saturated with Italian and Greek Humanists teaching Greek and denigrating Scholastic philosophy. The two most influential figures in the French Renaissance, Guillaume Budé and Jacques Lefèvre d'Etaples, eagerly consumed these southern dispensations; Lefèvre in fact absorbed Italian teachings quite directly in Florence and Padua. The same is true of English Humanists: William Caxton, the most distinguished printer in the country—and in this movement, printers were not simply technicians or businessmen but influential molders of learned opinion as well—resorted to Italian scholars in England as editors and advisers; and the leading English Humanists—John Tiptoft, William Grocyn, Thomas Linacre, John Colet—all studied in Italy during the second half of the fifteenth century and bore the marks of Italian tastes and Italian scholarship. Sir Thomas More, the exemplar of English humanism—the English Erasmus—is only an apparent exception. He never set foot in Italy, but he acquired the methods and aims of the Mediterranean Renaissance through his circle of learned friends and through Italians resident in England.

The German Humanists, too, beginning early in the fifteenth century with the versatile theologian Nicolas of Cusa and ending a century later with the political knight Ulrich von Hutten, looked to the South for instruction and inspiration; they disseminated their new learning at courts and in universities, in literary societies and academies. The members of these societies encouraged the study of antiquity, the writing of Latin verse, the study of the German past—and one another. Perhaps the best known of these informal but influential groups centered around Mutianus Rufus at Erfurt, and Rufus was a disciple of the Florentine Neoplatonists.

Yet all across northern Europe the Humanists applied what they had acquired on their memorable journeys—the doctrines of Neoplatonism, the restored works of Aristotle, respect for precise scholarship, and Greek—in their own way and for their own purposes. The German movement nourished, and was nourished by, a series of new Humanist universities—between 1450 and 1510 there were eight new foundations, including Wittenberg in 1502—and fed the stream of religious discontent that was to become the German Reformation. Elsewhere, too, northern Humanists wrote treatises and founded institutions in the service of a purified Christian faith. Their very ideal of learned piety— *docta pietas*—had first been proclaimed by the Italian Petrarch, but in the North it acquired special force. The northern Humanists were certain that the shortest and perhaps the only path to true religion was through scholarship. Accurate learning alone could clear away the trivia, the superstitions, and the worldliness that had accumulated around Christianity and that were threatening to choke it. The truth would make men pious, and the truth lay in the sacred texts themselves; in the Scriptures carefully read, devoutly interpreted, and accurately translated; and in the writings of the church fathers, printed and edited with religious care. Secular learning—the study of languages, the law, and the natural sciences—were forms of, and often preparations for, authentic piety. The northern Humanists did not denigrate religious feeling and did not doubt miracles; they were not unbelievers in clerics' disguise. But they saw danger in the general sway of ignorance, and a place for the exercise of the intellect—was not reason itself, honestly and humbly used, a divine gift? . . .

Humanism in England

In England, Humanist learning penetrated the court and the church. It even touched the universities: this was a time of college foundations, mainly at Cambridge, devoted to the study of the ancient languages, including Hebrew. The Humanist message was carried to wide reaches of society by an impressive collection of scholars, nearly all of them in holy orders. The career of John Colet is representative. Born in London around 1467 of a substantial family, he became a priest, but while his eyes were on higher things, he did not neglect the blessings of reason. With inherited money he opened St. Paul's School in 1512, dedicated to the realization of *docta pietas*. Even more significant, perhaps, for the cause of Christian learning were his public lectures on the Epistles of St. Paul, which he delivered to large and distinguished audiences at Oxford in 1496. One modern student has not hesitated to call these lectures on 1 Corinthians and Romans, "a milestone in the history of Christian scholarship." Medieval exegetes, delighting in number mysticism, allegorical readings, and obscure depths beyond obscure depths, had treated sacred texts as material for elegant or esoteric dialectical games. Colet broke with all this, and the effect was electrifying. He was not a modern rationalist or a radical philologist; compared with other Humanists of his time he was not even much of a classicist. But his devotion, which has something mystical about it, was directed at the plain sense of the texts; he cut through logic-chopping and the manufacture of allegories to the meaning of St. Paul's message, its historical context, and the moral lesson it held for the time of Colet and his hearers. And this reform of method led to a demand, by Colet and his friends and disciples, for larger reform—in church and state alike. More than in the Mediterranean world, Humanism in the North was thoroughly political.

The Career of Erasmus

John Colet made memorable contributions to Christian scholarship, but his greatest achievement was doubtless Desiderius Erasmus. He found Erasmus a brilliant classicist without inner direction; he left him launched on a career of scholarly productivity and humane propaganda unequaled in his time.

Erasmus was born at Rotterdam, probably in 1466, an illegitimate child. Educated by an influential lay fraternity, the Brethren of the Common Life, he early made a misstep that took many years to rectify: around 1488 he took monastic vows. Until he met Colet he was not certain of his vocation, but he was certain that he had no vocation for the clerical life. He secured permission to study at the University of Paris, and with his first long stay there, beginning in 1495, he moved from one center of scholarship to another. Erasmus' peripatetic career testifies to the cosmopolitan quality of the Renaissance style; where there was a Humanist, Erasmus was at home. He visited England three times, he stayed at Louvain and Venice, and he ended his years at Basel, where he died in 1536, one of the most famous men in Europe, a private citizen of doubtful ancestry who had made his fame with his pen alone.

When Erasmus met Colet and other English Humanists on his first English visit in 1499, his erudition was already impressive. What Colet did for him was to channel his talents, to prove to him that learning and piety, even wit and piety, were by no means incompatible. Every reader of Erasmus has been impressed by his cool temper, that almost ostentatious moderation which he erected practically into a philosophy. If there were deep crises in his emotional and spiritual life, Erasmus knew how to keep them private. In his adolescence, he had been passionately attached to a friend and been rebuffed; from then on his letters contain no more intimate revelations. He was fastidious beyond the normal, but if his passion for cleanliness is indeed a neurotic symptom, he turned his neurosis to good purpose. He spent his life seeking to cleanse thinking, to purify texts, to bring the fresh air of decency and good sense into the affairs of the world.

Erasmus was both a scholar and a popularizer, and sometimes both at once. His first major work, the *Adages*, published in 1500 and often reprinted and greatly enlarged, consisted of a vast collection of sayings from the classical writers supplied with full annotations—all, of course, in Latin. The work made Erasmus famous and humanism popular. "Until this time the humanists had, to some extent, monopolized the treasures of classic culture," Johan Huizinga has written, "in order to parade their knowledge of which the multitude remained destitute, and so to become strange prodigies of learning and elegance. With his irresistible need of teaching and his sincere love for humanity and its general culture, Erasmus introduced the classic spirit, in so far as it could be reflected in the soul of a sixteenth-century Christian, among the people." The phrase "the people" should be taken in a restricted sense; the many were still illiterate, and to many who could barely read, Latin was still an alien tongue. Still, Erasmus pioneered in making classical education general by taking the classics out of the realm of mystery open to a few initiates alone. The vast success of his book was a tribute at once to the powers of the printing press and to his lively Latin style. Erasmus' great edition of St. Jerome and his corrected edition of the Greek New Testament, both published in 1516, reached a smaller public, but they were daring appeals to the text in defiance of tradition, all the more so as Erasmus joined to his Greek text of the Scriptures a Latin translation that varied considerably from the accepted Vulgate version.

Scholar and Satirist

Erasmus sought to disseminate his religious and social ideas in a wide variety of ways: his vast correspondence with publishers, cardinals, kings, and Humanists and his didactic treatises, like the *Manual for a Christian Knight* of 1503 and the *Education of a Christian Prince* of 1515. The most celebrated of these writings, the one book by Erasmus that is still widely read, is *The Praise of Folly* (1509), a lighthearted satire that says humorously what his other writings say, though with wit, gravely. Its original title, *Moriae encomium*, with its punning reference to Thomas More, reveals its origin: Erasmus conceived the book on his way to More's house, and wrote it there. Cast, like Valla's critique of the Donation of Constantine, in the form of a declamation, *The Praise of Folly* once again displays the hold of classical rhetoric on the Humanists. Cheerfully speaking in its own behalf, Folly declares itself necessary to human happiness, indeed human existence, and in the course of its demonstration surveys the contemporary world with a keen eye for its failings. All professions are legitimate targets for Erasmus' gentle yet biting scorn, but most of all the clergy, with their worldliness, their ignorance, their elevation of ritual over faith.

In *The Praise of Folly*, we penetrate to the core of Erasmus' thought. As the aim of scholarship must be to free texts from corrupt readings and ignorant misinterpretations, so in life the aim is to find the essence of things by discarding its trappings. This is what Erasmus meant by what he called "the philosophy of Christ"; his religious thought is a distillation of Christian morality at its purest. This set him apart from mystics or from unquestioning followers of Rome—some thought, in fact, from religion altogether. It is undeniable that the perfect marriage of antiquity and Christianity, consummated in Erasmus' mind, made him a stranger to religious fervor. Eventually, his way of thinking set him apart from the Reformers as well. He prized Christian unity too highly to participate in its destruction, cultivation and moderation too highly to enjoy the coarse fanaticism of Luther and his followers. While at first he welcomed Luther as a surgeon called by God to cure the corruptions of the Renaissance papacy, he later polemicized against him. It was this moderation that led Erasmus even to ridicule fellow Humanists for demonstrating the "purity" of their Humanism by slavishly imitating Cicero.

Strong spirits have always found Erasmus too mild for their tastes, but there is something vastly appealing about this self-made scholar and moralist, inveighing against corruption, superficiality, fanaticism, stupidity, and the love of war, and championing tolerance, reasonableness, accuracy, generosity of mind, and decency. Yet in the world of the Reformation, Erasmus was in the end a misfit, distrusted by Catholics for the tepidness of his support and detested by Protestants (whose cause he had done so much to advance with his criticisms and his scholarship) for his refusal to join them. In immoderate times, moderate men are sadly out of place.

The Career of Thomas More

Just as sadly, in an unprincipled world a man of principle is out of place. This is the lesson that forces itself on the student of Sir Thomas More. In the extravagant portrait Erasmus drew of him in a letter to Hutten, he appears a man "born for friendship," simple in his tastes, a charming and witty host, a generous husband and father, "the common advocate of all those in need," an excellent speaker, a consummate classicist versed in Greek, Latin, pagan and Christian writers alike, a splendid stylist, a good man even at court— "and then there are those who think that Christians are to be found only in monasteries!" Born in 1478, More came under the beneficent influence of Colet; the passionate humanitarianism of his *Utopia* owes much to Colet's articulate practical charity. Unlike most of the other English Humanists, More was not a cleric but a lawyer; yet his piety was as fervent and his scholarship as accurate as that of any priest. And he wrote, both English and Latin, better than anyone else in his day. His rise was rapid and his career, first as a lawyer and then as a statesman, was distinguished; Henry VIII employed him on diplomatic missions and in 1529 appointed him to his highest post, lord chancellor. But in the midst of his legal and public activities More never forgot his humanism; at Oxford, his university, he defended the teaching of Greek against detractors who feared that such Humanist interests would lead to impiety.

More's greatest work, a fine late flower of Renaissance humanism, is *Utopia*, published in 1516, a satire and program that has given its name and form to a large genre of writings for four and a half centuries. Erasmus, who had reason to know its author's intentions, said that it "was published with the aim of showing the causes of the bad condition of states; but was chiefly a portrait of the British State, which he has thoroughly studied and explored." The first book, written last, is a vehement indictment of war, the idle rich, an unjust social system that first turns men into thieves and then cruelly punishes them, and the enclosure movement which has led the mild sheep of England to grow voracious and wild, so that (in More's savage simile) they eat men, and "devour whole fields, houses, and cities." The second book, written first, portrays a perfect commonwealth, rationally divided into regions and cities, reasonably and justly governed, tolerant of religious dissent, and above all, free from the curse of private property. Some critics have dismissed these utopian proposals as a Humanist's intellectual pastime or as the longing of a reactionary for the medieval communal ideal that was being destroyed by nascent capitalism. On the other side, Socialists have hailed them as an early version of their own designs. While there is some point to the Socialist view of More, both parties are wrong: More was neither a belated Scholastic nor a premature Marxist, but a keenly observant student of his own time and a radical reformer. And his satire was not a game; it was serious—satires usually are.

As soon as he accepted employment under Henry VIII in 1518, More was compelled to recognize that he could not act in government and realize the principles he had so seriously advocated; neither toleration nor communism seemed a possibility in the world of sixteenth-century England. Then came Henry VIII's divorce and his break with Rome, both incompatible with More's legal and religious principles. He retired from office, refused to take the required oath of supremacy, and paid for his principles with his life. In 1535 he went to his execution, his wit unimpaired to the end. Speaking from the scaffold, he told the throng that he "died the King's good servant but God's first." They were brave and potent words, but they could not hide the reality that had brought him to his fall. Politics was made by ideas, but in the clash of the two, politics must win.

The Literary Renaissance in Northern Europe

Lewis W. Spitz

The Renaissance in Northern Europe peaked in the latter half of the sixteenth century, and its cultural achievements are primarily literary rather than artistic. As Stanford historian Lewis W. Spitz notes, the Italian models continued to be very influential in both France and England throughout the century. Such innovative writers as the Frenchman Montaigne and the Englishmen Sidney, Spenser, Marlowe, and Shakespeare, however, took their influences from the plethora of cultural choices available to them: Italian writers, classical writers, and the history and culture of their own countries.

The imitation of classical models and the influence of Italian Renaissance thought continued to be very much in evidence in French literature. A group of writers known as the Pleiades cultivated the French language, but at the same time believed that literary perfection was to be achieved by a close study and imitation of classic authors such as Cicero and Virgil. Joachim du Bellay's *Defense and Illustration of the French Language* (1549) developed these theories of the Pleiades. Du Bellay (1522–1560), inspired by both Plato and Christ, adhered to theories of tender and delicate love. Pontus de Tyard, an exquisite poet, was a student of Marsilio Ficino's writings and reflected his Neoplatonic theories of love. Pierre de Ronsard (1524–1585), the best known of the group, met du Bellay in a hostel in Touraine and became his fast friend. Ronsard was voluptuous, sensual, even lewd, not at all in the spirit of Ficino, but his theories of poetic mad-

Excerpted from *The Renaissance and Reformation Movements*, by Lewis W. Spitz (St. Louis: Concordia, 1987). Copyright ©1987, Concordia Publishing House. Used with permission of the publisher.

ness were derived from Plato. He spoke of France as the "mother of the arts.". . .

The Achievement of Montaigne

The greatest man of French letters in that era, some would say in all times, was that urbane, exquisite intellectual Michel de Montaigne (1533–1592). Montaigne was the scion of a wealthy Bordeaux family and grew up with all the advantages of skilled tutors and schooling. He studied at the College of Guyenne for seven years, then spent two years in logic and dialectics at Bordeaux and studied law before entering public life as a counselor and member of the parliament. At the age of thirty-eight he retired to the Château de Montaigne, where from 1571 to 1580 he wrote his *Essays*. He spent a year and a half traveling through Alsace, Switzerland, Bavaria, Venice, and Rome, recording his experiences in his *Journal*. His life in his rural retreat was reminiscent of the *vita solitaria*, the contemplative life away from the marketplace cultivated by Petrarch, Sadoleto, and other humanists. Embellished by a library of classics and the company of intellectual friends, his urbane style of life anticipated the eighteenth-century salon. Through the wit and charm of his writing shines the evanescent quality that Matthew Arnold must have had in mind when he spoke of a "sad lucidity of soul."

The *Essays* are a long, polished relation of Montaigne's reflections and recollections, his experiences garnered in life and gained vicariously by reading. Although he himself is the subject of the book, it reflects the foibles and strengths of all humanity. Highly rational, Montaigne had a strong sense of the limitations of reason when confronted by the big questions of life. When he considered the variety of customs and ethical and aesthetic standards revealed in the cultures of Asia, Africa, and the New World, he concluded that such matters are relative to the cultural experience of the people concerned. His skepticism has brought down upon him charges of Pyrrhonism. "I generally observe," he commented wryly, "that when a matter is set before them, men are more ready to waste their time in seeking the reason of it than in seeking the truth of it . . . so much uncertainty is there in all things." An unbending elitist as a young man, he learned that the unlettered peasant and fisherman may possess a practical wisdom not to be found in books. Montaigne's humane, witty, pithy, and often wise observations on the human condition place him in the best humanist tradition. Many of his theories on education were very influential in later years. But his acute sense of the limitations of human reason and the frailty of mankind set him apart from the ebullience and naïveté of some Renaissance men. In that sense his work marks the end of an era.

The Spanish Golden Age

During the reign of Philip II Spain experienced its golden age of culture. Thomist theology revived and an Erasmian tradition persisted in letters. Lope de Vega and Pedro Calderón de la Barca flourished. But above all the incomparable Miguel de Cervantes (1547–1616), author of the classic *Don Quixote*, raised Spanish literature to new triumphs. In painting, the names of Velázquez and El Greco became immortal.

The Spanish cultural efflorescence is an intriguing phenomenon, coming as it did in a period of absolutistic tendencies and inquisitorial repression. Perhaps the imperial glory proved inspiring, so that for the first time in their history Spaniards felt themselves culturally superior to other Europeans. In art and literature Spain developed strong traditions of its own and Spanish intellectuals exuded a new confidence, revealing a predilection for ethical, legal, and religious problems rather than for science and philosophy. The decline from greatness was gradual but seemingly inevitable in the century that followed.

The English Renaissance

It can be argued with some plausibility that the real English Renaissance began during the age of Elizabeth. The earlier efflorescence of culture during the reigns of Henry VII and Henry VIII, the days of Latimer, Grocyn, Linacre, Colet, More, and Erasmus, were pale compared with the flowering of native genius during Elizabeth's reign. The first phase was indispensable to the second and the Italian influence was of critical importance to both. Essential carriers were the English who went to Italy, such as the earl of Surrey and Sir Thomas Wyatt. "They," wrote the Elizabethan poet and critic Richard Puttenham, "having traveled into Italy, and there tasted the sweet and stately measures of the Italian poesie, greatly polished our rude and homely manner." Italians who came to England, such as Polydore Vergil, brought with them the finest literary products of the Renaissance, and courtly manners in addition.

The new and improved schools spread learning among increased numbers of Englishmen. In 1531 Sir Thomas Elyot, in *The Boke Named the Gouvenour*, fused the literary aims of Vives and Erasmus with the idea of the "gentleman" promoted by Castiglione. He urged a Renaissance approach to education, Latin as a living language, tutors for the children of "governors" or public servants, and the teaching of music, art, and physical education. The aim of education was

The Last Great Renaissance Poet

Though John Milton wrote his greatest works after the Renaissance in England had largely run its course, the achievement of his poetry places him squarely in the Renaissance epic tradition. His passion for ancient Greek and Roman authors, along with his deep involvement in the religious and political controversies of his day, make Milton an example of the well-rounded "Renaissance man." According to Robert E. Lerner, in Paradise Lost *Milton achieves an unsurpassed fusion of classical poetic form and Christian content.*

Though less versatile than Shakespeare, not far behind him in eloquent grandeur stands the Puritan poet John Milton (1608–1674). The leading publicist of Oliver Cromwell's regime, Milton wrote the official defense of the beheading of Charles I as well as a number of treatises justifying Puritan positions in contemporary affairs. But he was also a man full of contradictions who loved the Greek and Latin classics at least as much as the Bible. Hence he could write a perfect pastorial to be the cultivation of wisdom learned from the ancients and applied for the good of society. In this humane tradition the greatest English educator of all, Roger Ascham (1515–1568), wrote *The Schoolmaster*, published two years after his death. It was the best treatise in English on classical education, and stressed the need for gentleness in teaching the very young and for cultivating "hard wits" rather than "quick wits." Ascham argued that by education a man learns vicariously and safely in one year what would take twenty to learn by experience. The educational theories and curricula recommended by such distinguished Renaissance humanists as Juan Luis Vives were put into practice in schools even in remote northern provinces. As humanist learning spread out from court circles to a larger segment of the population, the way was prepared for the secular cultural rejuvenation in the age of Elizabeth. There is a unity in the cultural developments that came to a climax in the triumphs at the end of the century and ripened to maturity in the decades after Elizabeth's death. . . .

elegy, *Lycidas*, mourning the loss of a dear friend in purely classical terms. Later, when forced into retirement by the accession of Charles II, Milton, though now blind, embarked on writing a classical epic, *Paradise Lost*, out of material found in Genesis concerning the creation of the world and the fall of man. This magnificent poem, which links the classical tradition to Christianity more successfully than any literary work written before or since, is surely one of the greatest epics of all time. Setting out to "justify the ways of God to man," Milton in *Paradise Lost* first plays "devil's advocate" by creating the compelling character of Satan, who defies God with boldness and subtlety. But Satan is more than counterbalanced in the end by the real "epic hero" of *Paradise Lost*, Adam, who learns to accept the human lot of moral responsibility and suffering, and is last seen leaving Paradise with Eve, the world "all before them."

Robert E. Lerner, *Western Civilizations: Their History and Their Culture*, 1993, p. 516.

History attracted some of the strongest minds of the age. Francis Bacon's *History of Henry VII* had real literary quality and gained considerable renown. But perhaps the most remarkable achievement was Sir Walter Raleigh's outstanding *History of the World*, written to keep his mind occupied during his long years of imprisonment. His preface reveals some of the presuppositions of the age about history. Hearing boys outside his prison window arguing over things that had happened only a short time before, he reflected upon how much more difficult it is to be certain about events of ages gone by. The general notions of a cyclical pattern in history, the pragmatic use of history as philosophy, the assumption that the lessons of history can be applied to daily life and present times—these were typical Renaissance conceptions and were derived immediately from classical theories of history. The fact that Shakespeare's historical plays (*King John, Richard II, Richard III, Henry IV, Henry V*) belong to the years between 1592 and 1600 may suggest that the historical subject matter is related not only to Shakespeare's personal development, but also to the exuberant patriotism and interest in England's national dynastic history in that period.

Classical and Italian models were important to the development of *belles lettres*. Translations became increasingly numerous and some gained lasting fame, such as Chapman's version of Homer's *Iliad*, Harrington's translation of Ariosto's *Orlando furioso*, and Fairfax's rendition of Tasso's *Jerusalem Delivered*. But the classical forms were now filled by native genius. Secular literature came to replace religious poetry as sonnets, lyrics, odes, and popular ballads and madrigals rose to prominence. In a beautiful treatise *In Defence of Poesie* Sir Philip Sidney vindicated the power of the poetic imagination against the dull and prosaic limitations that mere nature imposes upon man. Nature, he wrote, "never set forth the earth in so rich tapestry as divers poets have done, neither with so pleasant rivers, fruitful trees, sweet-smelling flowers, nor whatsoever else may make the too much loved earth more lovely. Her world is brazen; the poets only deliver a golden." Sidney offered a noble argument for the glories of Elizabethan letters. His own masterpiece was his *Arcadia*, which in a somewhat confused mixture of medieval and classical surroundings offered a pastoral story of love and chivalry, setting a high standard for the age. His sonnets reflected his own love experiences and helped to popularize that relatively easy Italianate poetic form. Sidney was important in his own times as the exemplar of the new ideal of Protestant knighthood. In later centuries Raleigh and Essex came to represent the epitome of Elizabethan courtier culture, but their Protestant gentlemen contemporaries saw Sidney as the cultural hero of the age.

Elizabethan men of letters, like the men of affairs, were concerned for the most part with the real world about them. There is very little romantic longing for an imagined golden age of the past. With some justification literary historians have traditionally dated the birth of Elizabethan letters from the *Shepheards Calendar* of 1579, a satire by Edmund Spenser. Spenser was educated at Cambridge, was patronized by the earl of Leicester, and in 1580 went to Ireland as secretary to the viceroy. He lived there, near Cork, for nearly two decades, until the Irish rebels under Tyrone burned his house and forced him to flee to England in 1598. He died in London a year later. A friend of Sir Walter Raleigh, active in Munster, Spenser was close to the Elizabethan scene in spite of his seclusion in Ireland. His *Faerie Queen* was the great epic of the age, revealing the influence of Tasso and Ariosto. Spenser imagined a day when chivalry was more than idle form, peopled his world with such knights and ladies as never were, and carried his readers with him on rhythmic waves of poetry to a land of aesthetic delight. And yet it would be a mistake to interpret his poetry as merely romantic in its use of old forms, for his legends and chivalric symbols carry the spirit of a new age in politics and religion. The *Faerie Queen* is quite simply a masterpiece, and in his devotion to the Protestant ethic as well as his literary concerns, Spenser was a spokesman for his age.

Few men of the time so incorporated in their own persons the Renaissance gentleman, the Elizabethan politician and man of affairs, the genial man of letters, and the serious philosopher as did Francis Bacon. This courtier was only forty-two when Elizabeth died. His career as rival of the formidable legist Sir Edward Coke, his disgrace, and his trial for bribery came during the reign of James I, but he was formed as an Elizabethan, published his famed *Essays* during her reign (1597), and was in many ways typical of the brash, aggressive, profane circle of Elizabethan statesmen. His thoughts on society and science have had enduring influence. His moral essays reflect practical political wisdom derived from an unsentimental observation of Elizabethan politics. His thoughts were weighty but of a practical kind, expressed in short, pithy sayings easily transformed into clichés. Like Erasmus' *Adages*, Bacon's essays grew in number from ten in the first edition to fifty-eight in the edition of 1625. In later life he displayed his pride in the English past by writing a *History of Henry VII*, a lively narrative with a skillful characterization of the monarch.

The fame of Francis Bacon will always rest on his philosophical treatises, which contributed so much, though deviously, to the rise of the modern scientific method. While still a student at Cambridge he came to the conclusion that the methods employed in various sciences were erroneous and sterile. Although he retained a certain respect for Aristotle as a thinker, he reacted strongly against the prevailing Aristotelian philosophy. "The knowledge whereof the world is now possessed," he wrote, "especially that of nature, extendeth not to magnitude and certainty of works." All his life Bacon poured out a stream of treatises, some, such as *On the Advancement of Learning*, of enduring value. His major work on natural philosophy, *Novum organum* (1620), was written in Latin, the language of scholars. . . .

Elizabethan Drama

The true genius of that dramatic age was given its most perfect expression in Elizabethan drama. Christopher Marlowe began to write in the turbulent years just before the Armada. Marlowe lived a wild, dissolute life, and was stabbed to death in a tavern brawl in 1592, when he was only twenty-eight. His dramas, too, displayed the lack of restraint and the *terribilità* of the Italian Renaissance, giving vent to the most extravagant passions and fearful deeds. In his *Tamburlaine the Great*

(1586) he portrays the Tatar emperor caught up in *hybris*, false pride that tempts fate, as he rages against God and man. In *The Rich Jew of Malta* (1589) he has Machiavelli recite a prologue, mocking religion as "a childish toy" and holding that "there is no sin but ignorance." His most famous play was *Dr. Faustus* (1588), based on the medieval legend of the Rhenish doctor who sold his soul to the devil in exchange for knowledge and the power it gives. Marlowe's characters, like the Elizabethan adventurers, all seemed larger than life-size.

There were others in Marlowe's day much like him, though less skillful. Notable among them was Robert Greene (1560?–1592), a pamphleteer, novelist, and dramatist who managed to live a little longer than Marlowe but no less extravagantly. After leaving Cambridge he wandered through Italy and Spain, and was impressed by Italian literary models. A restless soul, he did as he pleased, abandoned his wife, and followed the precept that "what is profitable ceases to be bad." His own dramas were hurriedly written and did not approach the excellence of Marlowe's. Yet he ventured to call young William Shakespeare an "upstart crow beautified with our feathers," a mere actor who dared to invade the profession of the playwright.

Shakespeare came to London when Marlowe's earliest play was first appearing. The son of a Stratford tradesman down on his luck, Shakespeare was only nineteen when he married Anne Hathaway, who was eight years older. Poverty and a charge of poaching on a noble's land led him to abandon Stratford to try his fortunes in London, where he became an actor at twenty-two. His invasion of the dramatists' guild was a most happy event. He began with comedies. His earliest play, *Love's Labor Lost*, was a spoof on pedantry and contrived style and verbiage. His *Comedy of Errors* was an adaptation of a Latin play, amusing but lacking in depth of ideas and characterization. In his *Midsummer Night's Dream* he conjured up a fairyland of elves and clumsy clowns. As his fame grew, Queen Elizabeth herself listened with delight, and it is said that he wrote *The Merry Wives of Windsor* to amuse the queen, who had expressed a wish to see Falstaff in love.

After the premature death of so many leading playwrights, Shakespeare virtually had the stage to himself from 1592 to the end of the century, years in which his historical plays responded to the patriotic fervor of the English. From 1601 to 1608 a pessimistic strain crept into his "gloomy comedies," such as *Measure for Measure* and *All's Well That Ends Well*, and into his tragedies, *Hamlet, Othello, King Lear, Macbeth*, and *Timon of Athens*. During the last eight years he softened some, toning down the harsh, tragic element and adding a note of tolerance and romance to leaven the disillusionment and futility in his last plays, as in *The Winter's Tale* and *The Tempest*.

Shakespeare was the universal genius, surpassing all others in depth of insight, in inventiveness, in power of characterization, in versatility and charm. He was a culmination and summation not only of the Elizabethan awakening, but of the entire Renaissance. The major themes of Renaissance humanism found unexcelled expression in the lines of Shakespeare. Consider, for example, how the whole Renaissance discussion of the dignity and misery of man is given its ultimate poetic expression in Hamlet's soliloquy (Act II, Scene 2):

> What a piece of work is a man! How noble in reason! how infinite in faculty! in form, in moving, how express and admirable! in action how like an angel! in apprehension how like a god! the beauty of the world! the paragon of animals! And, yet, to me, what is this quintessence of dust? man delights not me; no, nor woman neither, though, by your smiling, you seem to say so.

Shakespeare was a genius, but his genius was always controlled. He could drink with the cleverest wits of London at the Mermaid Tavern, but he bought land near Stratford and lived out his last years in ease and comfort. He died there in 1616 at the age of fifty-two. Not even Ben Jonson, whose plays *Volpone, or the Fool* (1605), *Epicene, or the Silent Woman* (1609), *The Alchemist* (1610), and *Bartholemew Fair* (1614) were of high order, equaled Shakespeare's sympathetic bond with all mankind.

The Scientific Revolution

Robert E. Lerner

Renaissance humanists were not generally proponents of science or radical new theories about the universe. Conversely, the leading scientists of the Renaissance found much to reject in the rudimentary scientific theories of ancient Rome and Greece. Still, as scholar Robert E. Lerner points out, certain intellectual trends of the Renaissance, especially the philosophy of Neoplatonism, did much to prepare the way for the great scientific advances of Copernicus, Galileo, and Kepler.

Some extraordinarily important accomplishments were made in the history of science during the sixteenth and early seventeenth centuries, but these were not preeminently the achievements of Renaissance humanism. The educational program of the humanists placed a low value on science because it seemed irrelevant to their aim of making people more eloquent and moral. Science for humanists like Petrarch, Leonardo Bruni, or Erasmus was part and parcel of the "vain speculation" of the Scholastics which they attacked and held up to ridicule. Accordingly, none of the great scientists of the Renaissance Age belonged to the humanist movement.

Renaissance Foundations of Modern Science

Nonetheless, at least two intellectual trends of the period did prepare the way for great new scientific advances. One was the currency of Neoplatonism. The importance of this philosophical system to science was that it proposed certain ideas, such as the central position of the sun and the supposed divinity of given geometrical shapes, that would help lead to crucial scientific breakthroughs. Although Neopla-

Excerpted from *Western Civilizations*, 12th ed., vol. 1, by Robert Lerner et al. Copyright ©1993, 1988, 1984, 1980, 1973, 1968, 1963, 1958, 1954, 1949, 1947, 1941 by W.W. Norton and Company, Inc. Reprinted by permission of W.W. Norton and Company, Inc.

tonism seems very "unscientific" from the modern perspective because it emphasizes mysticism and intuition instead of empiricism or strictly rational thought, it helped scientific thinkers to reconsider older notions that had impeded the progress of medieval science; in other words, it helped them to put on a new "thinking cap." Among the most important of the scientists who were influenced by Neoplatonism were Copernicus and Kepler.

A second trend that contributed to the advance of science was very different: the growth in popularity of a *mechanistic* interpretation of the universe. Renaissance mechanism owed its greatest impetus to the publication in 1543 of the works of the great Greek mathematician and physicist Archimedes. Not only were his concrete observations and discoveries among the most advanced and reliable in the entire body of Greek science, but Archimedes taught that the universe operates on the basis of mechanical forces, like a great machine. Because his view was diametrically opposed to the occult outlook of the Neoplatonists, who saw the world as inhabited by spirits and driven by supernatural forces, it took some time to gather strength. Nonetheless, mechanism did gain some very important late Renaissance adherents, foremost among whom was the Italian scientist Galileo. Ultimately mechanism played an enormous role in the development of modern science because it insisted upon finding observable and measurable causes and effects in the world of nature.

One other Renaissance development that contributed to the rise of modern science was the breakdown of the medieval separation between the realms of theory and practice. In the Middle Ages Scholastically trained clerics theorized about the natural world but never for a moment thought of tinkering with machines or dissecting corpses because this empirical approach to science lay outside the Scholastic framework. On the other hand, numerous technicians who had little formal education and knew little of abstract theories had much practical expertise in various aspects of mechanical engineering. Theory and practice began to come together in the fifteenth century. One reason for this was that the highly respected Renaissance artists bridged both areas of endeavor: not only were they marvelous craftsmen, but they advanced mathematics and science when they investigated the laws of perspective and optics, worked out geometric methods for supporting the weight of enormous architectural domes, and studied the dimensions and details of the human body. In general, they helped make science more empirical and practically oriented than it had been earlier. Other reasons for the integration were the decline in prestige of the overly theoretical universities and a growing interest in alchemy and astrology among the leisured classes. Thus although alchemy and astrology are today properly dismissed as unscientific superstitions, in the sixteenth and seventeenth centuries their vogue led some wealthy amateurs to start building laboratories and measuring the courses of the stars. Thereby scientific practice was rendered eminently respectable. When that happened modern science was on the way to some of its greatest triumphs.

The Copernican Revolution

The actual scientific accomplishments of the Renaissance period were international in scope. The achievement par excellence in astronomy—the formulation and proof of the heliocentric theory that the earth revolves around the sun— was primarily the work of the Pole Copernicus, the German Kepler, and the Italian Galileo. Until the sixteenth century the Ptolemaic theory that the earth stands still at the center of the universe went virtually unchallenged in Western Europe. Nicholas Copernicus (1473–1543), a Polish clergyman who had absorbed Neoplatonism while studying in Italy, was the first to posit an alternative system. Copernicus made few new observations, but he thoroughly reinterpreted the significance of the old astronomical evidence. Inspired by the Neoplatonic assumptions that the sphere is the most perfect shape, that motion is more nearly divine than rest, and that the sun sits "enthroned" in the midst of the universe, "ruling his children the planets which circle around him," Copernicus worked out a new heliocentric theory. Specifically, in his *On the Revolutions of the Heavenly Spheres*—which he completed around 1530 but did not publish until 1543—he argued that the earth and the planets move around the sun in concentric circles. Copernicus's system itself was still highly imperfect: by no means did it account without difficulties for all the known facts of planetary motion. Moreover, it asked people to reject their common-sense assumptions: that the sun moves since they observe it moving across the sky and that the earth stands still since no movement can be felt. More serious, Copernicus contradicted passages in the Bible, such as the one wherein Joshua commands the sun to stand still. As a result of such problems, believers in Copernicus's heliocentric theory remained distinctly in the minority until the early seventeenth century.

It was Kepler and Galileo who ensured the triumph of Copernicus's revolution in astronomy. Johann Kepler (1571–1630), a mystical thinker who was in many ways more like a magician than a modern scientist, studied astronomy in order to probe the hidden secrets of God. His basic conviction was that God had created the universe according to mathematical laws. Relying on the new and impressively accurate astronomical observations of the Dane Tycho Brahe (1546–1601), Kepler was able to recognize that two assumptions about planetary motion that Copernicus had taken for granted were simply not in accord with the observable facts. Specifically, Kepler replaced Copernicus's view that planetary orbits were circular with his "First Law" that the earth and the other planets travel in elliptical paths around the sun, and he replaced Copernicus's belief in uniform planetary velocity with his own "Second Law" that the speed of planets varies with their distance from the sun. He also argued that magnetic attractions between the sun and the planets keep the planets in orbital motion. That approach was rejected by most seventeenth-century mechanistic scientists as being far too magical, but in fact it paved the way for the law of universal gravitation formulated by Isaac Newton at the end of the seventeenth century.

Galileo's Confirmation of Copernicus

As Kepler perfected Copernicus's heliocentric system from the point of view of mathematical theory, so Galileo Galilei

(1564–1642) promoted acceptance for it by gathering further astronomical evidence. With a telescope that he manufactured himself and raised to a magnifying power of thirty times, he discovered the moons of Jupiter and spots on the sun. He was also able to determine that the Milky Way is a collection of celestial bodies independent of our solar system and to form some idea of the enormous distances of the fixed stars. Though many held out against them, Galileo's discoveries gradually convinced the majority of scientists that the main conclusion of Copernicus was true. The final triumph of this idea is commonly called the *Copernican Revolution.* Few more significant events have occurred in the intellectual history of the world, for it overturned the medieval worldview and paved the way for modern conceptions of mechanism, skepticism, and the infinity of time and space. Some thinkers believe that it contributed also to the degradation of man, since it swept man out of his majestic position at the center of the universe and reduced him to a mere particle of dust in an endless cosmic machine.

In the front rank among the physicists of the Renaissance were Leonardo da Vinci and Galileo. If Leonardo da Vinci had failed completely as a painter, his contributions to science would still entitle him to considerable fame. Not the least of these were his achievements in physics. Though he actually made few complete discoveries, his conclusion that "every weight tends to fall toward the center by the shortest way" contained the kernel of the law of gravity. In addition, he worked out the principles of an astonishing variety of inventions, including a diving board, a steam engine, an armored tank, and a helicopter. Galileo is especially noted as a physicist for his law of falling bodies. Skeptical of the traditional theory that bodies fall with a speed directly proportional to their weight, he taught that bodies dropped from various heights would fall at a rate of speed that increases with the square of the time involved. Rejecting the Scholastic notions of absolute gravity and absolute levity, he taught that these are purely relative terms, that all bodies have weight, even those which, like the air, are invisible, and that in a vacuum all objects would fall with equal velocity. Galileo seems to have had a broader conception of a universal force of gravitation than Leonardo da Vinci, for he perceived that the power that holds the moon in the vicinity of the earth and causes the satellites of Jupiter to circulate around that planet is essentially the same as the force that enables the earth to draw bodies to its surface. He never formulated this principle as a law, however, nor did he realize all of its implications, as did Newton some fifty years later.

Advances in Medicine

The record of Renaissance achievements in medicine and anatomy is also impressive. Attention must be called above all to the work of the German Theophrastus von Hohenheim, known as Paracelsus (1493–1541), the Spaniard Michael Servetus (1511–1553), and the Belgian Andreas Vesalius (1514–1564). The physician Paracelsus resembled Copernicus and Kepler in believing that spiritual rather than material forces governed the workings of the universe. Hence he was a firm believer in alchemy and astrology. Nevertheless, Paracelsus relied on observation for his knowledge of diseases and their cures. Instead of following the teachings of ancient authorities, he traveled widely, studying cases of illness in different environments and experimenting with many drugs. Above all, his insistence on the close relationship of chemistry and medicine foreshadowed and sometimes directly influenced important modern achievements in pharmacology and healing. Michael Servetus, whose major interest was theology but who practiced medicine for a living, discovered the pulmonary circulation of the blood, in an attempt to prove the veracity of the Virgin birth. He described how the blood leaves the right chambers of the heart, is carried to the lungs to be purified, then returns to the heart and is conveyed from that organ to all parts of the body. But Servetus had no idea that the blood returned to the heart through the veins, a discovery that was made by the Englishman William Harvey in the early seventeenth century.

Purely by coincidence the one sixteenth-century scientific treatise that came closest to rivaling in significance Copernicus's work in astronomy, Vesalius's *On the Structure of the*

Human Body, was published in 1543, the same year that saw the issuance of Copernicus's *Revolutions of the Heavenly Spheres.* Vesalius was born in Brussels and studied in Paris but later migrated to Italy where he taught anatomy and surgery at the University of Padua. He approached his research from the correct point of view that much of ancient anatomical doctrine was in error. For him the ancient anatomy of Galen (so to speak, the Ptolemy of medicine) could only be corrected on the basis of direct observation. Hence he applied himself to frequent dissections of human corpses to see how various parts of the body actually appear when the skin covering is stripped away. Not content with merely describing in words what he saw, Vesalius then collaborated with an artist—Jan van Calcar, a fellow Belgian who had come to Italy to study under the Renaissance master Titian—in portraying his observations in detailed engravings. Art historians are uncertain as to whether van Calcar was directly inspired in executing his illustrations for Vesalius by knowledge of earlier anatomical drawings of Leonardo da Vinci, but even if he was not, he certainly relied on a cumulative tradition of expert anatomical depiction bequeathed to him by Italian Renaissance art. Gathered in Vesalius's *Structure of the Human Body* of 1543, van Calcar's plates offered a new map of the human anatomy just when Copernicus was laying out a new map of the heavens. Since Vesalius in the same work offered basic explanations of how parts of the body move and interact, in addition to discussing and illustrating how they look, he is often counted as the father of modern physiology as well as the father of modern anatomy. With his landmark treatise we come to a fitting end to our survey of Renaissance accomplishments inasmuch as his *Structure of the Human Body* represented the fullest degree of fruitful international intellectual exchanges as well as the fullest merger of theory and practice, and art and science.

Chapter 5

The Significance of the Renaissance

Turning Points
IN WORLD HISTORY

A Revolution of Consciousness

Richard Tarnas

The Renaissance cannot be called a period of "all light and splendor," according to intellectual historian Richard Tarnas. Yet the fact remains that in a few short generations, Europe was turned upside down by exploration, by religious innovation, by new theories of the universe, and by powerful art the like of which had never been seen before. As Tarnas contends, the human potential unleashed by these radical innovations justifies calling the European Renaissance a revolution in human consciousness.

The phenomenon of the Renaissance lay as much in the sheer diversity of its expressions as in their unprecedented quality. Within the span of a single generation, Leonardo, Michelangelo, and Raphael produced their masterworks, Columbus discovered the New World, Luther rebelled against the Catholic Church and began the Reformation, and Copernicus hypothesized a heliocentric universe and commenced the Scientific Revolution. Compared with his medieval predecessors, Renaissance man appeared to have suddenly vaulted into virtually superhuman status. Man was now capable of penetrating and reflecting nature's secrets, in art as well as science, with unparalleled mathematical sophistication, empirical precision, and numinous aesthetic power. He had immensely expanded the known world, discovered new continents, and rounded the globe. He could defy traditional authorities and assert a truth based on his own judgment. He could appreciate the riches of classical culture and yet also feel himself breaking beyond the ancient boundaries to reveal entirely new realms. Polyphonic music, tragedy and comedy, poetry, painting, architecture, and

Excerpted from *The Passion of the Western Mind*, by Richard Tarnas. Copyright ©1991 by Richard Tarnas. Reprinted by permission of Frederick Hill Associates as agents for the author.

sculpture all achieved new levels of complexity and beauty. Individual genius and independence were widely in evidence. No domain of knowledge, creativity, or exploration seemed beyond man's reach.

With the Renaissance, human life in this world seemed to hold an immediate inherent value, an excitement and existential significance, that balanced or even displaced the medieval focus on an afterworldly spiritual destiny. Man no longer appeared so inconsequential relative to God, the Church, or nature. On many fronts, in diverse realms of human activity, Pico's proclamation of man's dignity seemed fulfilled. From its beginnings with Petrarch, Boccaccio, Bruni, and Alberti, through Erasmus, More, Machiavelli, and Montaigne, to its final expressions in Shakespeare, Cervantes, Bacon, and Galileo, the Renaissance did not cease producing new paragons of human achievement. Such a prodigious development of human consciousness and culture had not been seen since the ancient Greek miracle at the very birth of Western civilization. Western man was indeed reborn.

Yet it would be a deep misjudgment to perceive the emergence of the Renaissance as all light and splendor, for it arrived in the wake of a series of unmitigated disasters and thrived in the midst of continuous upheaval. Beginning in the mid–fourteenth century, the black plague swept through Europe and destroyed a third of the continent's population, fatally undermining the balance of economic and cultural elements that had sustained the high medieval civilization. Many believed that the wrath of God had come upon the world. The Hundred Years' War between England and France was an interminably ruinous conflict, while Italy was ravaged by repeated invasions and internecine struggles. Pirates, bandits, and mercenaries were ubiquitous. Religious strife grew to international proportions. Severe economic depression was nearly universal for decades. The universities were sclerotic. New diseases entered Europe through its ports and took their toll. Black magic and devil worship flourished, as did group flagellation, the dance of death in cemeteries, the black mass, the Inquisition, tortures and burnings at the stake. Ecclesiastical conspiracies were routine, and included such events as a papally backed assassination in front of the Florentine cathedral altar at High Mass on Easter Sunday. Murder, rape, and pillage were often daily realities, famine and pestilence annual perils. The Turkish hordes threatened to overwhelm Europe at any moment. Apocalyptic expectations abounded. And the Church itself, the West's fundamental cultural institution, seemed to many the very center of decadent corruption, its structure and purpose devoid of spiritual integrity. It was against this backdrop of massive cultural decay, violence, and death that the "rebirth" of the Renaissance took place.

Technological Advances

As with the medieval cultural revolution several centuries earlier, technical inventions played a pivotal role in the making of the new era. Four in particular (all with Oriental precursors) had been brought into widespread use in the West by this time, with immense cultural ramifications: the magnetic compass, which permitted the navigational feats that opened the globe to European exploration; gunpowder, which contributed to the demise of the old feudal order and the ascent of nationalism; the mechanical clock, which brought about a decisive change in the human relationship to time, nature, and work, separating and freeing the structure of human activities from the dominance of nature's rhythms; and the printing press, which produced a tremendous increase in learning, made available both ancient classics and modem works to an ever-broadening public, and eroded the monopoly on learning long held by the clergy.

All of these inventions were powerfully modernizing and ultimately secularizing in their effects. The artillery-supported rise of separate but internally cohesive nation-states signified not only the overthrow of the medieval feudal structures but also the empowerment of secular forces against the Catholic Church. With parallel effect in the realm of thought, the printing press allowed the rapid dissemination of new and often revolutionary ideas throughout Europe. Without it, the Reformation would have been limited to a relatively minor theological dispute in a remote German province, and the Scientific Revolution, with its dependence on international communication among many scientists, would have been altogether impossible. Moreover, the spread of the printed word and growing literacy contributed to a new cultural ethos marked by increasingly individual and private, noncommunal forms of communication and experience, thereby encouraging the growth of individualism. Silent reading and solitary reflection helped free the individual from traditional ways of thinking, and from collective control of thinking, with individual readers now having private access to a multiplicity of other perspectives and forms of experience. . . .

The Rise of Individualism

Concurrent with these advances was an important psychological development in which the European character, beginning in the peculiar political and cultural atmosphere of Renaissance Italy, underwent a unique and portentous transformation. The Italian city-states of the fourteenth and fifteenth centuries—Florence, Milan, Venice, Urbino, and others—were in many ways the most advanced urban centers in Europe. Energetic commercial enterprise, a prosperous Mediterranean trade, and continual contact with the older civilizations of the East presented them with an unusually concentrated inflow of economic and cultural wealth. In addition, the weakening of the Roman papacy in its struggles with the incohesive Holy Roman Empire and with the rising nation-states of the north had produced a political condition in Italy of marked fluidity. The Italian city-states' small size, their independence from externally sanctioned authority, and their commercial and cultural vitality all provided a political stage upon which a new spirit of bold, creative, and often ruthless individualism could flourish. Whereas in earlier times, the life of the state was defined by inherited structures of power and law imposed by tradition or higher authority, now individual ability and deliberate political action and thought carried the most weight. The state itself was seen as something to be comprehended and manipulated by human will and intelligence, a political understanding making the Italian city-states forerunners of the modern state.

This new value placed on individualism and personal genius reinforced a similar characteristic of the Italian Humanists, whose sense of personal worth also rested on individual capacity, and whose ideal was similarly that of the emancipated man of many-sided genius. The medieval Christian ideal in which personal identity was largely absorbed in the collective Christian body of souls faded in favor of the more pagan heroic mode—the individual man as adventurer, genius, and rebel. Realization of the protean self was best achieved not through saintly withdrawal from the world but through a life of strenuous action in the service of the city-state, in scholarly and artistic activity, in commercial enterprise and social intercourse. Old dichotomies were now comprehended in a larger unity: activity in the world as well as contemplation of eternal truths; devotion to state, family, and self as well as to God and Church; physical pleasure as well as spiritual happiness; prosperity as well as virtue. Forsaking the ideal of monastic poverty, Renaissance man embraced the enrichments of life afforded by personal wealth, and Humanist scholars and artists flourished in the new cultural climate subsidized by the Italian commercial and aristocratic elites.

The combined influences of political dynamism, economic wealth, broad scholarship, sensuous art, and a special intimacy with ancient and eastern Mediterranean cultures all encouraged a new and expansively secular spirit in the Italian ruling class, extending into the inner sanctum of the Vatican. In the eyes of the pious a certain paganism and amorality was becoming pervasive in Italian life. Such was visible not only in the calculated barbarities and intrigues of the political arena, but also in the unabashed worldliness of Renaissance man's interests in nature, knowledge, beauty, and luxury for their own sakes. It was thus from its origins in the dynamic culture of Renaissance Italy that there developed a distinctive new Western personality. Marked by individualism, secularity, strength of will, multiplicity of interest and impulse, creative innovation, and a willingness to defy traditional limitations on human activity, this spirit soon began to spread across Europe, providing the lineaments of the modern character.

The Integration of Contraries

Yet for all the secularism of the age, in a quite tangible sense the Roman Catholic Church itself attained a pinnacle of glory in the Renaissance. Saint Peter's Basilica, the Sistine Chapel, the Stanza della Segnatura in the Vatican all stand as astonishing monuments to the Church's final moments as undisputed sovereign of Western culture. Here the full grandeur of the Catholic Church's self-conception was articulated, encompassing Genesis and the biblical drama (the Sistine ceiling), classical Greek philosophy and science (the *School of Athens*), poetry and the creative arts (the *Parnassus*), all culminating in the theology and supreme pantheon of Roman Catholic Christianity (*La Disputa del Sacramento, The Triumph of the Church*). The procession of the centuries, the history of the Western soul, was here given immortal embodiment. Under the guidance of the inspired albeit thoroughly unpriestlike Pope Julius II, protean artists like Raphael, Bramante, and Michelangelo painted, sculpted, designed, and constructed works of art of unsurpassed beauty and power to celebrate the majestic Catholic vision. Thus the Mother Church, mediatrix between God and man, matrix of Western culture, now assembled and integrated all her diverse elements: Judaism and Hellenism, Scholasticism and Humanism, Platonism and Aristotelianism, pagan myth and biblical revelation. With Renaissance artistic imagery as its language, a new Pictorial Summa was written, integrating the dialectical components of Western culture in a transcendent synthesis. It was as if the Church, subconsciously aware of the wrenching fate about to befall it, called forth from itself its most exalted cultural self-understanding and found artists of seemingly divine stature to incarnate that image.

Yet this efflorescence of the Catholic Church in the midst of an era that was so decidedly embracing the secular and the present world was the kind of paradox that was altogether characteristic of the Renaissance. For the unique position in cultural history held by the Renaissance as a whole derives not least from its simultaneous balance and synthesis of many opposites: Christian and pagan, modern and classical, secular and sacred, art and science, science and religion, poetry and politics. The Renaissance was both an age to itself and a transition. At once medieval and modern, it was still highly religious (Ficino, Michelangelo, Erasmus, More, Savonarola, Luther, Loyola, Teresa of Avila, John of the Cross), yet undeniably worldly (Machiavelli, Cellini, Castiglione, Montaigne, Bacon, the Medici and Borgias, most of the Renaissance popes). At the same time that the scientific sensibility arose and flourished, religious passions surged as well, and often in inextricable combination.

The Renaissance integration of contraries had been foreshadowed in the Petrarchian ideal of *docta pietas*, and was now fulfilled in religious scholars like Erasmus and his friend Thomas More. With the Christian Humanists of the Renaissance, irony and restraint, worldly activity and classical erudition served the Christian cause in ways the medieval era had not witnessed. A literate and ecumenical evangelism here seemed to replace the dogmatic pieties of a more primitive age. A critical religious intellectuality sought to supersede naive religious superstition. The philosopher Plato and the apostle Paul were brought together and synthesized to produce a new *philosophia Christi*.

The Significance of Renaissance Art

But perhaps it was the art of the Renaissance that best expressed the era's contraries and unity. In the early Quattrocento, only one in twenty paintings could be found with a nonreligious subject. A century later, there were five times as many. Even inside the Vatican, paintings of nudes and pagan deities now faced those of the Madonna and Christ Child. The human body was celebrated in its beauty, formal harmony, and proportion, yet often in the service of religious subjects or as a revelation of God's creative wisdom. Renaissance art was devoted to the exact imitation of nature, and was technically capable of an unprecedented naturalistic realism, yet was also singularly effective in rendering a sublime numinosity, depicting spiritual and mythic beings and even contemporary human figures with a certain ineffable grace and formal perfection. Conversely, that capacity for rendering the numinous would have been impossible without the technical innovations—geometrical mathematization of space, linear perspective, aerial perspective, anatomical knowledge, *chiaroscuro*, *sfumato*—that developed from the striving for perceptual realism and empirical accuracy. In turn, these achievements in painting and drawing propelled later scientific advances in anatomy and medicine, and foreshadowed the Scientific Revolution's global mathematization of the physical world. It was not peripheral to the emergence of the modern outlook that Renaissance art depicted a world of rationally related solids in a unified space seen from a single objective viewpoint.

The Renaissance thrived on a determined "decompartmentalization," maintaining no strict divisions between different realms of human knowledge or experience. Leonardo was the prime exemplar—as committed to the search for knowledge as for beauty, artist of many mediums who was continuously and voraciously involved in scientific research of wide range. Leonardo's development and exploitation of the empirical eye for grasping the external world with fuller awareness and new precision were as much in the service of scientific insight as of artistic representation, with both goals jointly pursued in his "science of painting." His art revealed an uncanny spiritual expressiveness that accompanied, and was nurtured by, extreme technical accuracy of depiction. It was uniquely characteristic of the Renaissance that it produced the man who not only painted the *Last Supper* and *The Virgin of the Rocks*, but also articulated in his notebooks the three fundamental principles—empiricism, mathematics, and mechanics—that would dominate modern scientific thinking.

So too did Copernicus and Kepler, with Neoplatonic and Pythagorean motivations, seek solutions to problems in astronomy that would satisfy aesthetic imperatives, a strategy which led them to the heliocentric universe. No less significant was the strong religious motivation, usually combined with Platonic themes, impelling most of the major figures in the Scientific Revolution through Newton. For implicit in all these activities was the half-inarticulate notion of a distant mythical golden age when all things had been known—the Garden of Eden, ancient classical times, a past era of great sages. Mankind's fall from this primal state of enlightenment and grace had brought about a drastic loss of knowledge. Recovery of knowledge was therefore endowed with religious significance. And so once again, just as in classical Athens the religion, art, and myth of the ancient Greeks met and interacted with the new and equally Greek spirit of rationalism and science, this paradoxical conjunction and balance was attained in the Renaissance.

A Cultural Revolution

Although the Renaissance was in many senses a direct outgrowth of the rich and burgeoning culture of the high Middle Ages, by all accounts, between the mid-fifteenth and early seventeenth centuries, an unmistakable quantum leap was made in the cultural evolution of the West. The various contributing factors can be recognized in retrospect and listed—the rediscovery of antiquity, the commercial vitality, the city-state personality, the technical inventions, and so forth. But when all these "causes" of the Renaissance have been enumerated, one still senses that the essential thrust of the Renaissance was something larger than any of these factors, than all of them combined. Instead, the historical record suggests there was concurrently on many fronts an emphatic emergence of a new consciousness—expansive, rebellious, energetic and creative, individualistic, ambitious and often unscrupulous, curious, self-confident, committed to this life and this world, open-eyed and skeptical, inspired and inspirited—and that this emergence had its own raison d'être, was propelled by some greater and more subsuming force than any combination of political, social, technological, religious, philosophical, or artistic factors. It was not accidental to the character of the Renaissance (nor, perhaps, unrelated to its new sense of artistic perspective) that, while medieval scholars saw history divided into two periods, before and after Christ, with their own time only vaguely separated from the Roman era of Christ's birth, Renaissance historians achieved a decisively new perspective on the past: history was perceived and defined for the first time as a tripartite structure—ancient, medieval, modern—thus sharply differentiating the classical and medieval eras, with the Renaissance itself at the vanguard of the new age.

The events and figures converged on the Renaissance stage with amazing rapidity, even simultaneity. Columbus and Leonardo were both born in the same half decade (1450–55) that brought the development of the Gutenberg press, the fall of Constantinople with the resulting influx of Greek scholars to Italy, and the end of the Hundred Years' War through which France and England each forged its national consciousness. The same two decades (1468–88) that saw the Florentine Academy's Neoplatonic revival at its height during the reign of Lorenzo the Magnificent also saw the births of Copernicus, Luther, Castiglione, Raphael, Dürer, Michelangelo, Giorgione, Machiavelli, Cesare Borgia, Zwingli, Pizarro, Magellan, and More. In the same period, Aragon and Castille were joined by the marriage of Ferdinand and Isabella to form the nation of Spain, the Tudors succeeded to the throne in England, Leonardo began his artistic career with his painting of the angel in Verrocchio's *Baptism of Christ*, then his own *Adoration of the Magi*, Botticelli painted *Primavera* and *The Birth of Venus*, Ficino wrote the *Theologia Platonica* and published the first complete translation of Plato in the West, Erasmus received his early Humanist education in Holland, and Pico della Mirandola composed the manifesto of Renaissance Humanism, the *Oration on the Dignity of Man*. More than "causes" were operative here. A spontaneous and irreducible revolution of consciousness was taking place, affecting virtually every aspect of Western culture. Amidst high drama and painful convulsions, modern man was born in the Renaissance, "trailing clouds of glory."

Renaissance Society's Reverence of the Classical World

Bard Thompson

Though the validity of the premise has been long debated, Bard Thompson contends in the following essay that with the Renaissance came a new valuing of individual human beings and a "celebration of uniqueness and individual self-determination." Thompson, formerly professor emeritus of history at Drew University, retraces the steps by which the Renaissance embraced and interpreted classical values to apply to their own lives. The printing press, the voyages of discovery, and the scientific revolution all contributed to the re-evaluation of the individual's place in society.

Scholars since the eighteenth century have agreed that some sort of major change took place in western European civilization in the period from 1300 to 1600. However, the extent and nature of this change have been widely debated. Some have seen the period as one in which a radically new sense of the world and humanity emerged, whereas others have seen instead the gradual development of ideas that had long been current. Nevertheless, there are elements in Renaissance thought that recur frequently in comparison to earlier centuries.

In the Middle Ages, people typically yielded some of their identity to corporations—the church, the state, the feudal society, the guild, the university, and the monastic order. With the Renaissance came an increased sense of individuality and a celebration of uniqueness and individual self-determination. The literature of the period is filled with statements such as the following about the dignity, excellence, rationality, and power of individual human beings.

- Human beings are made "in the image of God," meaning that each one has the possibility of being a person of creativity and moral excellence.
- Human beings are free; we are not enslaved by sin or psychological obstructions; we are able to set our own course, determine our own destiny.
- Human beings are actors on the human scene; we are creators, second only to God; we are the God-appointed governors of the world.
- Human beings have immortal souls, which is God's way of verifying the preciousness of humankind.
- Human beings may achieve fame—the personal glory attained by an individual who thrusts himself or herself forward in some important, heroic, or prominent way.

Besides such statements in the literature, Renaissance art was equally powerful in expressing human individuality and dignity. The modern portrait, for example, came into existence during the age of the Renaissance precisely as a means of expressing the uniqueness, importance, and psychological complexity of a human being.

An Expansion of Horizons

For the fifteenth- and sixteenth-century European there occurred not only a new understanding of the individual, but also an expansion of human horizons—the exploration of the New World, for example, and the scientific conjectures of Copernicus (1473–1543). Such events shook people's confidence in medieval notions of the physical universe and finally began to undermine even the political philosophy and systems of divinity widely acknowledged in the Middle Ages. Older theories of church, state, and society were sacrosanct no longer. In *Utopia*, Thomas More questioned European civilization as he knew it, especially its political corruption, and presented an imaginary vision of a new society. In *The Prince*, Machiavelli (1469–1527) presented a conception of the ruler in which the security of the state might require the machinations of a ruthless Borgia: many readers throughout Europe found his suggestions radical and disturbing. In *The Courtier*, Baldassare Castiglione (1478–1529) proposed a new conception of the duties and opportunities of the individual in society—a conception based not on medieval monasticism or medieval chivalry but on Renaissance humanism.

A second aspect of discovering the world was the simple discovery by Renaissance people that the world, despite its trials and tribulations, was not as contemptible a place as the medieval theologians and mystics said it was. Rather, it was a scene of such winsome delight and astonishing beauty that God himself was surely present in it and could be worshiped in it. The affirmation and exuberant enjoyment of life on earth dissipated the otherworldliness that characterized some quarters of the Middle Ages. "It is good for us to be here," said the Renaissance humanists. Renaissance art was a veritable celebration of life here and now, and some of its important achievements represented the concern of artists to be faithful celebrants of the world of nature in which they lived. Nudity in art was perhaps the quintessential expression of Renaissance humanism, exulting as it did in the beauty, power, and freedom of human beings. Michelangelo's *David* is triumphantly nude. But not all Italians of the Renaissance shared this exuberance: Savonarola led a public "burning of the vanities" including nude art in Florence in 1497, and Popes Eugenius IV and Hadrian VI both condemned what they saw as licentious and pagan works of art.

The Renaissance acquired a "new" basis on which to reconstruct Western society: the civilization of ancient Greece and Rome. This basis is called classicism because it refers to the cultural archetypes of classical antiquity. If one sought the best possible model for, say, painting or architecture, philosophy or ethics, law or literature, education or town planning, one would refer to the works of the ancient Greeks and Romans. Such an attempt to retrieve classical civilization was not entirely new: to a certain extent the attempted recovery of the ancient world had begun even with the fall of the Roman Empire in A.D. 476. At certain times this retrieval became more intense, and thus historians have seen a series of earlier renaissances before the fourteenth century. However, the thinkers, writers and artists of the Renaissance proper saw themselves as better able to recover antiquity, and contrasted this new culture with the darkness of the ages that preceded their own.

The high value afforded to pagan antiquity led to a certain tension with the traditional faith of Christendom. At times the people of the Renaissance seemed to rather enjoy their idolatrous infatuation with a pagan civilization. However, this aspect of the period should not be overestimated. Individual mysticism as promoted by Joachim of Flora and St. Francis of Assisi continued to have influence through the fourteenth and fifteenth centuries. The students of the renowned humanist scholar Vittorino da Feltre studied Plutarch and the Bible, Caesar and St. Augustine. The single most important

The Legacy of Renaissance Humanism

Though much of the impetus of the Renaissance humanist movement has faded through the centuries, many of its concerns and motives live on, especially in academia. As Renaissance scholar Charles G. Nauert Jr. observes, the most important legacy of Renaissance humanism may be the unique kind of historical consciousness which leads intellectuals, both then and now, to act as critics of their societies and to seek improvement.

Aspects of humanistic studies live on in classical philology, the study of ancient literature, and historians' distinctively modern, critical way of thinking about the past. More broadly, Renaissance humanism has permanently affected the way in which modern people conceive their own identity, for humanist historical thought first taught us that we, too, are the products of an ever-changing flow of events and that within the bounds set by human physiology, all human values, ideas, and customs are contingent products of time and place. This cultural relativism, one of the distinctive characteristics that differentiate modern from traditional culture, was powerfully reinforced by the European discovery of non-Western societies, but its earliest roots are in the ideas of humanists about history, an awareness of change and contingency not achieved by any other civilization, not even those of ancient Greece and Rome. Clearly linked to question that both Italian and northern humanists asked was, Can Christianity and classicism be reconciled?. . .

Scarcely a populist movement, the Renaissance made headway in the society of intellectuals, artists, princes, and popes and among people of leisure, wealth, power, and artistic sensibility. One had to be literate even to gain access to some of its treasures. Although the invention of printing during the quattrocento greatly enlarged the scope of its influence, the Renaissance never approximated the vast popular appeal of the two more purely religious movements of the sixteenth century—the Protestant Reformation and the Catholic Counter-Reformation.

---

this historical consciousness is the reflective, critical mentality developed by those humanists who edited, translated, and interpreted ancient books.

The rank and file of humanists may have been conformist nonentities. Nevertheless, the critical potential was always there; and from Petrarch onward, the major humanists acted as critics of their own world. In modern Western civilization, often to the dismay of the authorities and even of the people, the intellectual functions as an outsider, as the critic who lays bare the prevailing evils and tries to effect remedial change. The intellectual is not necessarily a revolutionary, and sometimes he or she is a whining nag; but certainly he or she is a critic and would-be reformer of the world. This role was not typical of intellectuals in the ancient world, and certainly not in the medieval world. . . . Because of their unique new conception of history as a constantly changing succession of human cultures, humanists established themselves as critics, reformers, restorers of a better past. In differing ways and degrees, but always with the dream of creating a better future by capturing the essential qualities of Antiquity, humanists such as Petrarch, Valla, Machiavelli, and Erasmus pioneered in defining the role of the intellectual as conscience, gadfly, critic.

Charles G. Nauert Jr., *Humanism and the Culture of Renaissance Europe*, 1995, pp. 213–15.

Three Formative Elements

Three developments of the years normally assigned to the Renaissance (1300–1600) are closely related to the essential spirit of the Renaissance. All three contributed to the widely held impression that the Renaissance was an expansive era when the frontiers of the European world and mind were pushed back. All three contributed therefore to the equally prominent impression that the Renaissance was an era of special importance, to be distinguished and separated from the period of time that had preceded it.

One of the three was the appearance of printing. With the invention and manufacture of standard movable type, Johannes Gutenberg (b. between 1390 and 1400, d. 1468) began the printing industry in the Rhineland in the mid-1400s. By 1469 printing was being done in Italy, and by 1475 in England. In Italy, Venice had taken the lead in the printing industry, and among its presses was the famous Aldine Press, operated by the humanist Aldus Manutius (1450–1515), remembered among printers as the inventor of italic type. Beginning in the 1480s, his press published the Greek classics, including Plato, in pocket-sized editions—an enterprise that contributed handsomely toward making the intellectual riches of the Renaissance generally accessible. Mantua, and especially Venice, became centers of Jewish printing, where the Talmud and the Hebrew Bible were published, developments that would be of great importance for the northern humanists and Reformers as well.

The advent of printing made a wide range of material cheaply available: among the earliest printed books were the Bible, psalters and liturgies, the writings of St. Augustine, Cicero, and Boccaccio, and almanacs. No longer was the possession of written material limited to princes, scholars and wealthy noble patrons who could afford the cost of having a work copied by a scribe. Printing intensified the developments of the Renaissance by increasing the speed with which new knowledge and literature could be spread. Also, the numerous copies possible with a printed work greatly increased its chance of survival.

The greatest resistance to printed books came, understandably, from professional scribes, whose living was being seriously threatened. According to the scholar Elizabeth Eisenstein, one noted producer and seller of fine manuscript books, Vespasiano da Bisticci, suggested that printed books were second-rate and unfit for a nobleman like the duke of Urbino's library. However, the duke collected both printed and manuscript books, and even sponsored a press beginning in 1482.

New Discoveries

The voyages of discovery beginning with Columbus and Vasco da Gama were the second development that fundamentally molded the Renaissance. While Europeans certainly had traveled and explored in the time before the fifteenth century, the emphasis on conquest and eventually settlement marked a new phase of exploration. Although these were largely undertaken by Spain and Portugal, two essentially medieval nations that were relatively untouched by the Italian Renaissance, they were provoked by societal forces typical of the Renaissance—the economic impetus of capitalism, for example, and the expansive drives of new national states. While much of the technical skill needed for extensive naval exploration came out of Italy, it had been developed there over the previous centuries and cannot be attributed to the Renaissance.

A third formative development was the scientific revolution associated especially with the Italian firebrand Galileo Galilei, although it far exceeded the scope of his work. It occurred principally at the end of the sixteenth century and into the seventeenth and some scholars have argued that it was not part of the Renaissance, that its valuing of empiricism over ancient authority was antithetical to the veneration of the classical past that played such a large part in Renaissance art and philosophy. Even the scientific revolution however, depended to some extent upon the Renaissance preoccupation with recovering ancient sources—in this case, the scientific texts of the Greeks and those Arabian scholars who had kept Greek culture alive during the Middle Ages.

Standards of Excellence

"Renaissance" means rebirth—not of things in general but specifically of classicism. People of the Renaissance believed that the civilization of the Greeks and Romans was an ideal civilization, the golden age of culture, to which all subsequent culture should aspire. The writings of the ancient authors were (and still are) referred to as the classics—they are viewed as standards of excellence against which all subsequent literature and artistic expression ought to be measured. In short, Renaissance society believed that the quintessential expression of human culture—whether literature, philosophy, ethics, law, aesthetics, or architecture—was to be found in the artistic and literary remains of the ancient world. Renaissance people, however, were not antiquarians, proposing that we should live slavishly in the past. Rather than simply wanting to superimpose Greco-Roman civilization on the fifteenth century, they saw classical civilization as an exemplum that they proposed to honor in their own times by means of imitation. In this way the glory of Rome would be born anew in a *translatio imperii*, a transfer of the Empire. That Italy was itself geographically the site of the earlier culture may have given the concept great force there, but the idea of *translatio* was to be picked up later in France, England, and the German states as well.

The Renaissance in the Context of History

Margaret Aston

According to Margaret Aston, former lecturer at Cambridge University, the images of Renaissance art are more familiar than ever before due to the power of modern technology. But Aston asserts that the Renaissance must not be thought of only in terms of its accomplishments in the visual arts. In its literary and scholarly manifestations, the Renaissance involved both a looking back to the past and a looking inward. The result of so much reflection was a new kind of self-knowledge and a new way of thinking that is far more modern than medieval.

'No artifact is a work of art if it does not help to humanize us.' Bernard Berenson's words may be taken to heart today, half a century after they were written. The entire Renaissance movement was premised on a fresh awareness of the study of humanity, and what it meant to be fully human. The elevation of sight as the highest of the senses produced an enormous wealth of images whose full appreciation rests on some grasp of the philosophy that created them. Sculpting the human form and painting the human face reached new heights as a result of a fresh emphasis on all kinds of humane studies—studies which had their origin in the heritage of the ancient world and which came to influence literature, history, religious thought, political systems and social manners.

Every age has to make its own terms with the Renaissance. Our own age is so dominated by visual imagery that our iconographic vocabulary is in serious danger of getting out of step with the verbal. The problem facing anyone who offers a new survey of the Renaissance today is precisely how

Excerpted from *The Panorama of the Renaissance*, by Margaret Aston (New York: Abrams, 1996). Copyright ©1996 by Thames and Hudson, Ltd., London. Used by permission of Thames and Hudson, Ltd.

to use the pictorial resources open to us and at the same time ensure that the visual arts remain rooted in the literary and cultural soil from which they sprang.

The word 'Renaissance' began as a shorthand for the emancipation of Italian painting and sculpture from the stylized conventions of earlier Gothic and Byzantine forms, but gradually became descriptive of a wide cultural reorientation, and is now applied to an entire period of European history. Technology and historical methodology continue to change its meaning. . . .

Today the works of Botticelli, Leonardo and Dürer may be so familiar they can, like the music of Vivaldi, be subjected to the honour or indignity of popularity's final accolade: being fodder for advertising. Whether we recognize it or not, our world is full of objects whose form stems from enthusiasms kindled in 15th-century Italy. From the classical orders of Grand Central Station in New York to the allegorical carvings on the Paris Opera and the giant columns of Selfridges in London—let alone the new Mannerism of the Sainsbury Wing of London's National Gallery—we are surrounded by exercises in the architectural grammar relearnt with the renewed study of Vitruvius. It is as if the Renaissance had started an end game which is still being played out. . . .

The 'Rebirth' of Ancient Rome

We are in fact guilty of an initial distortion if our first thoughts of Renaissance are of the visual arts. The Renaissance was in its origins, and remained always at heart, a literary movement, concerned with the writings and teaching of classical Antiquity. It had begun generations before Brunelleschi's new dome took shape over the cathedral in Florence, or Masaccio completed his frescoes in the churches of S. Maria del Carmine and S. Maria Novella. There was no 1066 in this alteration of the mental and artistic climate, but we begin to breathe its heady atmosphere in the work of Petrarch. Whatever we make of Petrarch's reported climb up Mont Ventoux in Provence on 26 April 1336, the ceremony of the poet's coronation on the Capitoline in Rome on 8 April 1341 is an undeniable marker. Petrarch, faced with alternative invitations of honour from the University of Paris and the Roman Senate, chose to go south. His heart, his hopes and his ambitions lay in Rome. He anchored his longing for future fame to his Virgilian epic poem called *Africa*, for which, he wrote, if it should 'long outlive me, as my soul hopes and wishes, there is perhaps a better age in store; this slumber of forgetfulness will not last for ever. After the darkness has been dispelled, our grandsons will be able to walk back into the pure radiance of the past.'

The idea of Renaissance was itself dualistic, implying sleep and awakening, going down as well as coming up, darkness before light, losing before finding. It was necessary to excavate before it was possible to build anew, and to see again in a new light implied new eyes, or at least better vision. There was a great sense of exhilaration, and at the same time a nervousness in the challenge of living up to the past. 'Now, indeed, may every thoughtful spirit thank God that it has been permitted to him to be born in this new age.' The words of the Florentine humanist, Matteo Palmieri, in his book *On Civic Life*, written in the 1430s, were echoed by many others, inside and outside Italy. 'Oh century! Oh letters! It is a joy to be alive!'; Ulrich von Hutten, newly crowned Poet Laureate of the German Empire, shared in 1518 with Willibald Pirckheimer, patrician scholar of Nuremberg, his delight in the studies and intellects of the time. There seemed no end to the possibilities of new work in literature, in the arts, in the whole scope of human endeavour. Humanists of the 15th century, unlike those of the twelfth, did not think of themselves as sitting on the shoulders of the giants of Antiquity. But was it possible to stand on the same ground as Virgil or Cicero, to speak and write with their words in their language? Emulating the past brought its own problems, and to claim equal (or greater) achievements implied new criteria of judgment. Metamorphosis proved to be inherent in rebirth. . . .

Latin and the Vernacular Languages

The Renaissance ensured that Latin was the lingua franca of European learning, yet ironically the neo-classical Latin writings which the humanists themselves most valued are now the least read. Petrarch rested his posthumous fame on his Virgilian epic, *Africa*, his Livy-inspired history, *De viris illustribus (On Famous Men)*, and his Ciceronian *De remediis utriusque fortune (Remedies for Both Kinds of Fortune)*. But it is his Italian poetry, the *Trionfi* and *Canzoniere*, which has above all earned him the lasting laurels he so much desired. To humanists of the 15th century—and long after—the superiority of Latin as the medium of enduring literature seemed obvious. It needed a bold spirit to argue, as Leonardo Bruni, Chancellor of Florence, did in a humanist debate in 1435, that vernacular Italian was an independent language in its own right, as old as Latin, a popular equivalent of a learned tongue. Yet the Italian vernacular was advanced even in the 15th century by humanist writings. Alberti, who defended the Italian language in his *Della famiglia*, and made his book on painting popular in the 15th century by translating it into the vernacular, also composed the first Italian grammar. In the 16th century Machiavelli wrote his *Discourses on Livy* as well as his plays in Italian, despite their following of Roman models.

As national identities became more conscious and recognized across the whole of 16th-century Europe, vernacular writings rose to new heights, enriched by injections from classical learning. Familiarity with Latin (and to a lesser degree Greek) and training in Ciceronian diction fed back new styles and new words and new forms of writing, and it came to be seen that the vernaculars could claim equal rights with the classical languages. Pietro Bembo in his *Prose della volgar lingua* (1525) did for Italian what Joachim du Bellay did for French in his *Défense et illustration de la langue françoyse* (1549); modern languages, subject to the rules that ennobled Cicero's Latin, could yield illustrious works. The standard of comparison died hard in a world Erasmus did so much to educate. Through the conversational verve of Erasmus' *Colloquies* and the readable pools of classical references in his *Adagia* (themselves examples of rich new hybrid forms), generations were introduced to the commonplaces of Renaissance learning. Plautus and Terence, studied and staged anew, transmitted the heritage of Roman comedy to Machi-avelli's *Mandragola*, to Fernando de Rojas' *La Celestina* and to Shakespeare. If there was a sense in which Valla gave birth to Erasmus, and Petrarch to Montaigne, we can also say that without the humanists and without Erasmus, we would not have had Shakespeare.

Changing Perspectives

Human nature may not change over millennia, but ways of thinking and perceiving do. Our mental processes owe much to the Renaissance. It was a movement that was both born from and gave birth to an awareness of style—in literature, architecture, sculpture and painting—and though our un-derstanding of the concept may differ, it has descended to us from that period. Style, *maniera*, was central to the thesis of Vasari's *Lives*, which played so important a role in forming the idea of rebirth and renewal in the arts. Discernment of style was a necessity for artistic creation, which itself was progressive, being the process of becoming ever more com-petent in representing the most beautiful things in nature. Perfection was the goal, ultimately attainable—and attained by Michelangelo. In Vasari's eyes he surpassed all artists, liv-ing and dead 'even those most celebrated ancient artists themselves, who beyond all doubt surpassed Nature'. We may no longer subscribe to this thesis, but we cannot help being affected by it. We have ingrained in us the analytical eye that relates art to period and periods to each other, just as Vasari looked at the phases of development away from 'the old Greek style'. Our judgment is incurably time ori-ented and historical.

Renaissance refashioning helped to alter the consciousness of time. Temporal dimensions became more defined. There was a clearer understanding of how words and objects belong to their period and are dislocated by being misplaced in time, 'against time'. The concept of anachronism was growing long before the word arrived in the middle of the 17th cen-tury. Lorenzo Valla's consciousness of linguistic change en-abled him to see that the Donation of Constantine contained words that proved it could not date from the 4th century.

Stylistic judgment of another kind made it possible, a generation or so later, to identify the statue long honoured as Constantine at the Lateran Palace in Rome as that of the Emperor Marcus Aurelius. The young Michelangelo brought off a coup early in his career by carving a *Sleeping Cupid* which was sold in Rome in 1496 as an ancient work. When the buyer found out he refused to accept it, but the sculptor gained in repute. Expert judgment as well as expert skill was here on display, for implicit in the making and unmasking of fakes is a grasp of period and style. . . .

Refashioning the Classical Past

The pursuit of excellence through imitation, learning to follow ancient models of expression, promoted habits of comparison and self-awareness. Once the rules of the old grammar had been learnt and mastered (absorbed both by those using them and by the connoisseurs who appreciated and commissioned or bought the results), it became possible to break or bend them. Classical orders and Vitruvian proprieties could be adapted and twisted. The proportions of the human body, just as much as the constructions of linear perspective, could be manipulated for deliberate effect. Bramante's spiral staircase in the Belvedere Courtyard in the Vatican, and the vestibule staircase in the Laurentian Library in Florence showed that shock tactics as well as new skills formed part of stylistic development. The elements of licence and distortion that became evident in the paintings of Parmigianino and El Greco, the pursuit of inventiveness, as well as the quality of 'grace' so prized by Vasari, reveal mannerism as a logical development of *maniera*. Art was feeding on itself—as Vasari had shown it must. But that meant that the post-Michelangesque had to arrive, and if, as John Hale has put it 'Mannerism offered a holiday from the *School of Athens*', in the end it was ultimately the same process that produced pre-Raphaelites. The Renaissance established ways of seeing, as well as conventions of painting. The illusions of Escher are premised on Alberti.

There was a kind of end-process for the Renaissance self. After so much refashioning, or self-fashioning, through the imitation of classical models, it was eventually possible to discover more about both the world and the ancient past by turning inwards, taking the self as the object of study. 'I study myself more than any other subject. That is my metaphysics, that is my physics.' It was Montaigne, trying (assaying) himself in his *Essais*, who established this new department of knowledge. Here was an inescapable book to illuminate every library, 'the only book in the world of its kind'. The ancient Delphic instruction 'know thyself' now meant something further: self-ownership. 'The greatest thing in the world is to know how to belong to oneself.' It reads like Montaigne's message to posterity. And Petrarch, continuously revolving around and redefining his literary identity for transmission to his successors, had long before pointed the way.

Europe in 1600 was very different from what it had been in 1300, and it still seems fair to summarize the change by the term Renaissance. It is a period which we need to return to, since our world is rooted in it, to the extent that visiting it may involve a sense of recognition. Just as Petrarch, Machiavelli and Montaigne felt at home talking familiarly with their ancient authors, so we can feel an intimate proximity to these great figures of the Renaissance past. Distant as they are, their voices sound not unlike our own. We can recognize some of our own features in them. We can find delight in surveying their world as one that gave birth to our own, doubtful though we may be of our present's ability to live up to this inheritance. We may share their sense of the greatness of the past, even if we lack their confidence in the mission to re-create it.

Appendix of Documents

Document 1: Bruni's Promotion of Classical Studies

The Italian humanist Leonardo Bruni exerted great influence on the shape of educational reform in fifteenth-century Italy. The following excerpt, from a letter to the daughter of the count of Urbino, reveals Bruni's humanist concern for the education of women, while promoting the study of classical languages, history, moral philosophy, and literature.

What Disciplines then are properly open to her? In the first place she has before her, as a subject peculiarly her own, the whole field of religion and morals. The literature of the Church will thus claim her earnest study. Such a writer, for instance, as St. Augustine affords her the fullest scope for reverent yet learned inquiry. Her devotional instinct may lead her to value the help and consolation of holy men now living; but in this case let her not for an instant yield to the impulse to look into their writings, which, compared with those of Augustine, are utterly destitute of sound and melodious style, and seem to me to have no attraction whatever.

Moreover, the cultivated Christian lady has no need in the study of this weighty subject to confine herself to ecclesiastical writers. Morals, indeed, have been treated of by the most noblest intellects of Greece and Rome. What they have left to us upon Continence, Temperance, Modesty, Justice, Courage, Greatness of Soul, demands your sincere respect. You must enter into such questions as the sufficiency of Virtue to Happiness; or whether, if Happiness consist in Virtue, it can be destroyed by torture, imprisonment or exile; whether, admitting that these may prevent a man from being happy, they can be further said to make him miserable. Again, does Happiness consist (with Epicurus) in the presence of pleasure and the absence of pain: or (with Xenophon) in the consciousness of uprightness: or (with Aristotle) in the practice of Virtue? These inquiries are, of all others, most worthy to be pursued by men and women alike; they are fit material for formal discussion and for literary exercise. Let religion and morals, therefore, hold the first place in the education of a Christian lady.

But we must not forget that true distinction is to be gained by a wide and varied range of such studies as conduce to the profitable enjoyment of life, in which, however, we must observe due proportion in the attention and time we devote to them.

First amongst such studies I place History: a subject which must not on any account be neglected by one who aspires to true cultivation. For it is our duty to understand the origins of our own history and its development; and the achievements of Peoples and of Kings.

For the careful study of the past enlarges our foresight in contemporary affairs and affords to citizens and to monarchs lessons of incitement or warning in the ordering of public policy. From History, also, we draw our store of examples of moral precepts.

In the monuments of ancient literature which have come down to us History holds a position of great distinction. We specially prize such authors as Livy, Sallust and Curtius; and, perhaps even above these, Julius Caesar; the style of whose Commentaries, so elegant and so limpid, entitles them to our warm admiration. Such writers are fully within the comprehension of a studious lady. For, after all, History is an easy subject: there is nothing in its study subtle or complex. It consists in the narration of the simplest matters of fact which, once grasped, are readily retained in the memory.

The great Orators of antiquity must by all means be included. Nowhere do we find the virtues more warmly extolled, the vices so fiercely decried. From them we may learn, also, how to express consolation, encouragement, disuasion or advice. . . .

Familiarity with the great poets of antiquity is [also] essential to any claim to true education. For in their writings we find deep speculations upon Nature, and upon the Causes and Origins of things, which must carry weight with us both from their antiquity and from their authorship. Besides these, many important truths upon matters of daily life are suggested or illustrated. All this is expressed with such grace and dignity as demands our admiration. . . .

We know, however, that in certain quarters—where all knowledge and appreciation of Letters is wanting—this whole branch of Literature, marked as it is by something of the Divine, and fit, therefore, for the highest place, is decried as unworthy of study. But when we remember the value of the best poetry, its charm of form and the variety and interest of its subject-matter, when we consider the ease with which from our childhood up it can be committed to memory, when we recall the peculiar affinity of rhythm and metre to our emotions and our intelligence, we must conclude that Nature herself is against such headlong critics. . . . Plato and Aristotle studied the poets, and I decline to admit that in practical wisdom or in moral earnestness they yield to our modern critics. They were not Christians, indeed, but consistency of life and abhorrence of evil existed before Christianity and are independent of it.

Franklin Le Van Baumer, ed., *Main Currents of Western Thought*. New Haven: Yale University Press, 1978, pp. 136–38.

Document 2: The Power of the Latin Language

As a fifteenth-century Roman looking back at the glories of ancient Rome, Lorenzo Valla proudly asserts the power and longevity of the Latin language as the greatest legacy of Rome. He complains though of the current state of Latin studies, and he promotes one of the fundamentals of Renaissance humanism—that a return to the study of ancient Roman authors will be of great benefit to Italian society.

When I consider for myself the deeds of our ancestors and the acts of other kings and peoples, ours seems to me to have excelled all others not only in empire but even in the propagation of their language. For the Persians, the Medes, the Assyrians, the Greeks, and many other peoples have seized dominion far and wide . . . , but no people has spread its language so far as ours has done, who in a short space of time has made the Roman tongue, which is called Latin from Latium where Rome is located, well-known and almost queen . . . almost throughout the entire West and not a negligible part of both the North and Africa. Further, as far as the provinces are concerned, the Roman tongue was offered to mortals as a certain most excellent fruit for the sowing. Certainly this was a much more famous and splendid task than increasing the empire itself. For they who increase the extent of the empires are accustomed to be greatly honored and are called emperors; however, they who have conferred any benefices on men are celebrated not by human but by divine praise, especially when they further not so much the grandeur and glory of their own city but also the public utility and well-being of all men.

As our ancestors, winning high praises, surpassed other men in military affairs, so by the extension of their language they indeed surpassed themselves, as if, abandoning their dominion on earth, they attained to the fellowship of the gods in Paradise. If Ceres, Liber, and Minerva, who are considered the discoverers of grain, wine, oil, and many others have been placed among the gods for some benefaction of this kind, is it less beneficial to have spread among the nations the Latin language, the noblest and truly divine fruit, food not of the body but of the soul? For this language introduced those nations and all peoples to all the arts which are called liberal; it taught the best laws, prepared the way for all wisdom; and finally, made it possible for them no longer to be called barbarians. . . .

The Roman dominion, the peoples and nations long ago threw off as an unwelcome burden; the language of Rome they have thought sweeter than any nectar, more splendid than any silk, more precious than any gold or gems, and they have embraced it as if it were a god sent from Paradise. Great, therefore, is the sacramental power of the Latin language, truly great in its divinity, which has been preserved these many centuries with religion and holy awe, by strangers, by barbarians, by enemies, so that we Romans should not grieve but rejoice, and the whole listening earth should glory. We have lost Rome, we have lost authority, we have lost dominion, not by our own fault but by that of the times, yet we reign still, by the more splendid sovereignty, in a greater part of the world. Ours is Italy, ours Gaul, ours Spain, Germany, Panonia, Illyricum, and many other lands for wherever the Roman tongue holds sway, there is the Roman Empire. . . .

Who does not know that when the Latin language flourishes, all studies and disciplines thrive, as they are ruined when it perishes? For who have been the most profound philosophers, the best orators, the most distinguished jurisconsults, and finally the greatest writers, but those indeed who have been most zealous in speaking well? . . .

But when I wish to say more, sorrow hinders me and torments me, and forces me to weep as I contemplate the state which eloquence had once attained and the condition into which it has now fallen. Indeed, for many centuries not only has no one spoken in the Latin manner, but no one who has had read Latin has understood it. Students of philosophy have not possessed, nor do they possess, the works of the ancient philosophers; nor do rhetoricians have the orators; nor lawyers the jurisconsults; nor teachers the known works of the ancients. . . . Many, indeed, and varied are the opinions of the wise men on how this happened. I neither accept nor reject any of these, daring only to declare soberly that those arts which are most closely related to the liberal arts, the arts of painting, sculpture, modeling, and architecture, had degenerated for so long and so greatly and had almost died with letters themselves, and that in this age they have been aroused and come to life again, so greatly increased is the number of good artists and men of letters who now flourish.

But truly, as wretched as were those former times in which no learned man was found, so much the more this our age should be congratulated, in which (if we exert ourselves a little more) I am confident that the language of Rome will shortly grow stronger than the city itself, and with it all the disciplines will be restored. Therefore, because of my devotion to my native Rome and because of the importance of the matter, I shall arouse and call forth all men who are lovers of eloquence, as if from a watch tower, and give them, as they say, the signal for battle.

Donald R. Kelley, *Renaissance Humanism*. Boston: Twayne, 1991, pp. 137–39.

Document 3: Ficino Explains Platonic Love

Marsilio Ficino's philosophy of neo-Platonism influenced many Renaissance writers and artists. Probably no aspect of his writing was as influential as his description of Platonic love, which is excerpted here.

I urge and beg you all, my friends, to embrace immediately this love, a thing certainly divine, with all your strength and be not deterred by what they say Plato said about a certain lover: "That lover," he said, "is a soul dead in its own body and living in that of another." Likewise, be not dismayed by what Orpheus perchance sang about the wretched and deplorable lot of lovers, for I shall tell you next, if you please, how these grievances are to be understood, and how it is possible to remedy them, so listen carefully.

Plato calls love "something bitter," and correctly so, because whoever loves dies. Orpheus calls it "bitter-sweet" because love is voluntary death. Insofar as it is death, it is bitter, and insofar as it is voluntary, it is sweet. He who loves, dies; for his consciousness, oblivious of himself, is devoted exclusively to the loved one, and a man who is not conscious *of* himself is certainly not conscious *in* himself. Therefore, a soul that is so affected does not function in itself, because the primary function of the soul is consciousness. The soul which does not function in itself does not exist in itself, for function and existence are equivalent. There can be no existence without function, and function cannot survive existence itself; a thing cannot function when it does not exist, and whenever it does exist it functions. Therefore, the soul of a lover does not exist within the man himself, because it does not function in him. If it does not exist in him, it also does not live in him, and he who does not live is dead. Therefore, everyone who loves is dead in himself. But at least he lives in the other person, does he not? Certainly.

There are these two kinds of love: one simple, the other reciprocal. Simple love occurs when the loved one does not return his lover's affections. In this case the lover is completely dead, for he neither lives in himself, as we have already sufficiently proved, nor does he live in his loved one, since he is rejected by him. Where, then does he live? In air, water, fire, earth, or in some animal carcass? In none of these, for the human soul does not live in any but a human body. Will it perhaps eke out an existence in the body of some other person whom it does not love? No, not there either, for if it does not live in that in which it most fiercely desires to live, how can it live in any other? Therefore, the unrequited lover lives nowhere; he is completely dead. Moreover, he never comes back to life unless indignation revives him.

But when the loved one loves in return, the lover leads his life in him. Here, surely, is a remarkable circumstance that whenever two people are brought together in mutual affection, one lives in the other and the other in him. In this way they mutually exchange identities; each gives himself to the other in such a way that each receives the other in return. . . .

Likeness generates love. Similarity is a certain sameness of nature in several things. If I am like you, you are necessarily like me; therefore, the same similarity which compels me to love you, forces you to love me. Moreover, a lover withdraws from himself and gives himself to his loved one. The loved one cherishes him like a possession, for one's own possessions are very dear to him.

Moreover, a lover imprints a likeness of the loved one upon his soul, and so the soul of the lover becomes a mirror in which is reflected the image of the loved one. Thereupon, when the loved one recognizes himself in the lover, he is forced to love him.

Astrologers think that the interchange of love is truly reciprocal between those at whose birth there was an exchange of the lights, that is, of the sun and moon (if, for example, at my birth, the sun were in Aries and the Moon in Liber, and at yours the sun were in Liber and the Moon in Aries); or for whom the same sign or a similar one, or the same planet or a similar one was in the ascendant; or on whom friendly planets shone on the same angle of orient; or for whom Venus was in the same mansion and in the same angle. The Platonists add the suggestion that it is those whose lives the same daemon [or certainly a similar one] directs. The natural and moral philosophers would have it that a likeness of complexion, upbringing, education, habit, and attitude is the cause of mutual affection. Finally, where several causes occur together, the passion between the two people is most reciprocal; but where all

do, there rise up passions like those of Damon and Pythias, or
Orestes and Pylades.

Julian Mates and Eugene Cantelupe, eds., *Renaissance Culture: A New Sense of Order*. New York:
George Braziller, 1966, pp. 308–11.

Document 4: Columbus Describes the People of the New World

*Columbus was somewhat disappointed by the first natives he met, for they
did not have any gold or jewels. In the following excerpt from his logbook
diary, Columbus describes his first encounter and the trading of goods
that ensued.*

As I saw that they were very friendly to us, and perceived that they
could be much more easily converted to our holy faith by gentle
means than by force, I presented them with some red caps, and
strings of beads to wear upon the neck, and many other trifles of
small value, wherewith they were much delighted, and became
wonderfully attached to us. Afterwards they came swimming to the
boats, bringing parrots, balls of cotton thread, javelins and many
other things which they exchanged for articles we gave them, such
as glass beads, and hawk's bells; which trade was carried on with
the utmost good will. But they seemed on the whole to me, to be
a very poor people. They all go completely naked, even the
women, though I saw but one girl. All whom I saw were young, not
above thirty years of age, well made, with fine shapes and faces;
their hair short, and coarse like that of a horse's tail, combed toward the forehead, except a small portion which they suffer to
hang down behind, and never cut. Some paint themselves with
black, which makes them appear like those of the Canaries, neither
black nor white; others with white, others with red, and others
with such colours as they can find. Some paint the face, and some
the whole body; others only the eyes, and others the nose.
Weapons they have none, nor are acquainted with them, for I
showed them swords which they grasped by the blades, and cut
themselves through ignorance. They have no iron, their javelins
being without it, and nothing more than sticks, though some have
fish-bones or other things at the ends. They are all of a good size
and stature, and handsomely formed. I saw some with scars of
wounds upon their bodies, and demanded by signs the cause of
them; they answered me in the same way, that there came people
from the other islands in the neighbourhood who endeavoured to
make prisoners of them, and they defended themselves. I thought

then, and still believe, that these were from the continent. It appears to me, that the people are ingenious, and would be good servants; and I am of opinion that they would very readily become Christians, as they appear to have no religion. They very quickly learn such words as are spoken to them. If it please our Lord, I intend at my return to carry home six of them to your Highnesses, that they may learn our language. I saw no beasts in the island, nor any sort of animals except parrots.

Christopher Columbus, *Journal of First Voyage to America*. New York: Albert & Charles Boni, 1924, pp. 24–26.

Document 5: Leonardo Defends the Expressive Power of Painting

In response to some literary types who had disparaged the art of painting, Leonardo mounts a vigorous counterattack, contending that painting comes closer to depicting nature as it really is than poetry does.

If you contemn painting, which is the only imitator of all visible works of nature, you will certainly despise a subtle invention which brings philosophy and subtle speculation to the consideration of the nature of all forms—seas and plains, trees, animals, plants, and flowers—which are surrounded by shade and light. And this is true knowledge and the legitimate issue of nature; for painting is born of nature—or, to speak more correctly, we will say it is the grandchild of nature; for all visible things are produced by nature, and these her children have given birth to painting. Hence we may justly call it the grandchild of nature and related to God.

The eye, which is called the window of the soul, is the principal means by which the central sense can most completely and abundantly appreciate the infinite works of nature; and the ear is the second, which acquires dignity by hearing of the things the eye has seen. If you, historians or poets or mathematicians, had not seen things with your eyes you could not report of them in writing. And if you, O poet, tell a story with your pen, the painter with his brush can tell it more easily, with simpler completeness and less tedious to be understood. And if you call painting dumb poetry, the painter may call poetry blind painting. Now which is the worse defect? To be blind or dumb? Though the poet is as free as the painter in the invention of his fictions, they are not so satisfactory to men as paintings; for, though poetry is able to describe forms, actions, and places in words, the painter deals with the actual similitude of the forms, in order to represent them. Now tell me which is the nearer to the actual man: the name of man or the image of man? The name of man differs in different countries, but his form is never changed but by death.

And if the poet gratifies the sense by means of the ear, the painter does so by the eye—the worthier sense; but I will say no more of this but that, if a good painter represents the fury of a battle, and if a poet describes one, and they are both together put before the public, you will see where most of the spectators will stop, to which they will pay most attention, on which they will bestow most praise, and which will satisfy them best. Undoubtedly painting, being by a long way the more intelligible and beautiful, will please most. Write up the name of God [Christ] in some spot and set up His image opposite and you will see which will be most reverenced. Painting comprehends in itself all the forms of nature, while you have nothing but words which are not universal, as form is, and if you have the effects of the representation, we have the representation of the effects. Take a poet who describes the beauty of a lady to her lover and a painter who represents her and you will see to which nature guides the enamoured critic. Certainly the proof should be allowed to rest on the verdict of experience.

James Bruce Ross and Mary Martin McLaughlin, eds., *The Portable Renaissance Reader*. New York: Viking Press, 1968, pp. 532–34.

Document 6: The Most Important Discipline for a Prince

While in exile, the Italian courtier Machiavelli undertook to write a handbook for successful princes based on the way princes really behave rather than on the way they ought to. Though reviled for this apparently amoral stance on political power, his treatise reveals much about the world of the Italian Renaissance princes. In this excerpt from The Prince, *Machiavelli argues that the successful prince must diligently study the art of warfare.*

A prince, therefore, should have no other goal or thought, nor should he make anything his major concern, but war, its organization and discipline, because that is the only concern that awaits one who rules; and it is of such efficacy that not only does it sustain those who were born princes, but many times it will cause a man to rise from private life to that level; and, to the contrary, it is clear that once princes have given more thought to personal pleasures than to arms, they have lost their domain. And the first way to lose it is to neglect this art; and the way to acquire it is to be well prepared in this art.

Francesco Sforza, because he was armed, from a private citizen became duke of Milan; his successors, because they fled the inconveniences of arms, from dukes became private citizens. For, among the other bad results that being disarmed brings about, it makes you despicable: one of those infamies a prince should guard against, as will be discussed below; for there is no comparison whatsoever between an armed and an unarmed man, and it is not reasonable to expect one who is armed to obey willingly one who is unarmed, and that an unarmed person will be safe in the midst of his armed servants; for, with the latter being scornful, and the former suspicious, it is impossible for them to work well together. And so a prince who has no comprehension of military affairs, among the other misfortunes already mentioned, cannot be respected by his soldiers nor can he trust them.

Therefore, he should never lift his thought from the pursuit of war; he should pursue it even more in time of peace than in time of war, which can be done in two ways: one by action, the other by the mind. And as far as actions are concerned, besides maintaining his men well disciplined and trained, he should always be out hunting, and in so doing accustom his body to hardships; and at the same time learn the layout of the terrain, and know how mountains slope, how valleys open, how plains lie, and understand the nature of rivers and marshes; and to these things he should devote a great deal of attention. Such knowledge is useful in two ways: first, one learns to know his own country, and he can better understand how to defend it; then, with his knowledge of and experience with the terrain, he can grasp easily the layout of any other terrain he may find necessary to explore for the first time. For the hills, valleys, plains, the rivers and marshes that are, for instance, in Tuscany, have certain features in common with those of other provinces; so that, from knowing how the terrain is laid out in one province, one can easily arrive at an understanding of it in others. And that prince who lacks this skill lacks the principal quality necessary in a captain, because such skill teaches you how to locate the enemy, choose a campsite, lead the troops, set them up for battle, besiege cities to your own advantage.

Philopoemon, prince of the Achaeans, among the other praises that writers have bestowed on him, is praised because in time of peace he thought of nothing except the ways of making war; and when he was out in the country with his friends, he would often stop and debate with them: "If the enemy were on top of that hill, and we found ourselves here with an army, which of us would have the advantage? How could we advance to meet them without breaking ranks? If we wished to retreat, how would we do it? If they were to retreat, how would we go after them?" and he brought up to them, as they went along, every predicament an army may find itself in; he would listen to their opinions, he would express his own, supporting it with reasons; so that, because of this constant meditation, when leading his troops no possible incident could arise for which he did not have the solution.

But as for the exercise of the mind, the prince should read history, and in it study the actions of distinguished men; to see how they comported themselves in war; to examine the causes for their victories and defeats in order to be able to avoid the latter and imitate the former; and above all he should do as some outstanding man before him has done, who decided to imitate someone who has been praised and honored before him and always keep in mind his deeds and actions: just as it is said that Alexander the Great imitated Achilles; Caesar, Alexander; Scipio, Cyrus. And whoever reads the life of Cyrus written by Xenophon, then realizes how important in the life of Scipio that imitation was to his glory, and how much, in purity, affability, kindness, generosity, Scipio conformed to those qualities of Cyrus that Xenophon has written about.

Such methods as these a wise prince should observe, and never remain idle during peaceful times, but zealously turn them into gain that will show profit during adverse times, so that, when fortune changes, it will find him ready to resist such times.

Niccolo Machiavelli, *The Prince: A Bilingual Edition.* Trans. and ed. Mark Musa. New York: St. Martin's Press, 1964, pp. 121–25.

Document 7: The Utopians Embrace the Ancient Greeks

Sir Thomas More's Utopia *tells of the imaginary discovery of a new land and people who have attained a peaceful, harmonious society based on reason. The narrator of the story relates how the Utopians were immediately attracted to the literature and learning of ancient Greece when it was revealed to them.*

The people [of Utopia] in general are easygoing, good-tempered, ingenious, and leisure-loving. They patiently do their share of manual labor when occasion demands, though otherwise they are by no means fond of it. In their devotion to mental study they are unwearied. When they had heard from us about the literature and learning of the Greeks (for in Latin there was nothing, apart from history and poetry, which seemed likely to gain their great approval), it was wonderful to see their extreme desire for permission to master them through our instruction.

We began, therefore, to give them public lessons, more at first that we should not seem to refuse the trouble than that we expected any success. But after a little progress, their diligence made us at once feel sure that our own diligence would not be bestowed in vain. They began so easily to imitate the shapes of the letters, so readily to pronounce the words, so quickly to learn by heart, and so faithfully to reproduce what they had learned that it was a perfect wonder to us. The explanation was that most of them were scholars picked for their ability and mature in years, who undertook to learn their tasks not only fired by their own free will but acting under orders of the senate. In less than three years they were perfect in the language and able to peruse good authors without any difficulty unless the text had faulty readings. According to my conjecture, they got hold of Greek literature more easily because it was somewhat related to their own. I suspect that their race was derived from the Greek because their language, which in almost all other respects resembles the Persian, retains some traces of Greek in the names of their cities and officials.

When about to go on the fourth voyage, I put on board, in place of wares to sell, a fairly large package of books, having made up my mind never to return rather than to come back soon. They received from me most of Plato's works, several of Aristotle's, as well as Theophrastus on plants, which I regret to say was mutilated in parts. During the voyage an ape found the book, left lying carelessly about, and in wanton sport tore out and destroyed several pages in various sections. Of grammarians they have only Lascaris, for I did not take Theodore with me. They have no dictionaries except those of Hesychius and Dioscorides. They are very fond of the works of Plutarch and captivated by the wit and pleasantry of Lucian. Of the poets they have Aristophanes, Homer, and Euripides, together with Sophocles in the small Aldine type. Of the historians they possess Thucydides and Herodotus, as well as Herodian.

In medicine, moreover, my companion Tricius Apinatus had carried with him some small treatises of Hippocrates and the *Ars medica* of Galen, to which books they attribute great value. Even though there is scarcely a nation in the whole world that needs medicine less, yet nowhere is it held in greater honor—and this for the reason that they regard the knowledge of it as one of the finest and most useful branches of philosophy. When by the help of this philosophy they explore the secrets of nature, they appear to themselves not only to get great pleasure in doing so but also to win the highest approbation of the Author and Maker of nature. They presume that, like all other artificers, He has set forth the visible mechanism of the world as a spectacle for man, whom alone He has made capable of appreciating such a wonderful thing. Therefore He prefers a careful and diligent beholder and admirer of His work to one who like an unreasoning brute beast passes by so great and so wonderful a spectacle stupidly and stolidly.

Thus, trained in all learning, the minds of the Utopians are exceedingly apt in the invention of the arts which promote the advantage and convenience of life. Two, however, they owe to us, the art of printing and the manufacture of paper—though not entirely to us but to a great extent also to themselves. When we showed them the Aldine printing in paper books, we talked about the material of which paper is made and the art of printing without giving a detailed explanation, for none of us was expert in either art. With the greatest acuteness they promptly guessed how it was done. Though previously they wrote only on parchment, bark, and papyrus, from this time they tried to manufacture paper and print letters. Their first attempts were not very successful, but by frequent experiment they soon mastered both. So great was their success that if they had copies of Greek authors, they would have no lack of books. But at present they have no more than I have mentioned, but by printing books they have increased their stock by many thousands of copies.

Saint Thomas More, *Utopia*, Trans. and ed. Edward Surtz, S.J. New Haven: Yale University Press, 1964, pp. 103–107.

Document 8: The Freedom of a Christian

In his emphasis on human freedom, the Protestant Martin Luther shares the concerns of Renaissance humanists, both in Italy and elsewhere. The freedom of a Christian, though, is not the freedom to create great art, but, paradoxically, the freedom to serve others and God.

Many people have considered Christian faith an easy thing, and not a few have given it a place among the virtues. They do this because they have not experienced it and have never tasted the great strength there is in faith. It is impossible to write well about it or to understand what has been written about it unless one has at one time or another experienced the courage which faith gives a man when trials oppress him. But he who has had even a faint taste of it can never write, speak, meditate, or hear enough concerning it. . . .

To make the way smoother for the unlearned—for only them do I serve—I shall set down the following two propositions concerning the freedom and the bondage of the spirit:

A Christian is a perfectly free lord of all, subject to none.

A Christian is a perfectly dutiful servant of all, subject to all.

Those two theses seem to contradict each other. If, however, they should be found to fit together they would serve our purpose beautifully. . . . Love by its very nature is ready to serve and be subject to him who is loved. . . .

Let us start, however, with something more remote from our subject, but more obvious. Man has twofold nature, a spiritual and a bodily one. According to the spiritual nature, which men refer to as the soul, he is called a spiritual, inner, or new man. According to the bodily nature, which men refer to as flesh, he is called a carnal, outward, or old man. . . .

One thing, and only one thing, is necessary for Christian life, righteousness, and freedom. That one thing is the most holy Word of God, the gospel of Christ. . . . Let us then consider it certain and firmly established that the soul can do without anything except the Word of God and that where the Word of God is missing there is no help at all for the soul. If it has the Word of God it is rich and lacks nothing since it is the Word of life, truth, light, peace, righteousness, salvation, joy, liberty, wisdom, power, grace, glory, and of every incalculable blessing. . . . The Word is the gospel of God concerning his Son, who was made flesh, suffered, rose from the dead, and was glorified through the Spirit who sanctifies. To preach Christ means to feed the soul, make it righteous, set it free, and save it, provided it believes the preaching. Faith alone is the saving and efficacious use of the Word of God. . . . The Word of God cannot be received and cherished by any works whatever but only by faith. Therefore it is clear that, as the soul needs only the Word of God for its life and righteousness, so it is justified by faith alone and not any works; for if it could be justified by anything else, it would not need the Word, and consequently it would not need faith. . . .

Now when a man has learned through the commandments to recognize his helplessness and is distressed about how he might satisfy the law—since the law must be fulfilled so that not a jot or tittle shall be lost, otherwise man will be condemned without hope—then, being truly humbled and reduced to nothing in his own eyes, he finds in himself nothing whereby he may be justified and saved. Here the second part of Scripture comes to our aid, namely, the promises of God which declare the glory of God. . . . That which is impossible for you to accomplish by trying to fulfil all the works of the law—many and useless as they all are—you will accomplish quickly and easily through faith. God our Father has made all things depend on faith so that whoever has faith will have everything, and whoever does not have faith will have nothing. . . .

Not only are we the freest of kings, we are also priests forever, which is far more excellent than being kings, for as priests we are worthy to appear before God to pray for others and to teach one another divine things. These are the functions of priests, and they cannot be granted to any unbeliever. . . .

Now let us turn to the second part, the outer man. Here we shall answer all those who, offended by the word "faith" and by all that has been said, now ask, "If faith does all things and is alone sufficient unto righteousness, why then are good works commanded? We all take our ease and do no works and be content with faith." I answer: not so, you wicked men, not so. That would indeed be proper if we were wholly inner and perfectly spiritual men. But such we shall be only at the last day, the day of the resurrection of the dead. As long as we live in the flesh we only begin to make some progress in that which shall be perfected in the future life. . . . This is the place to assert that which was said above, namely, that a Christian is the servant of all and made subject to all. Insofar as he is free he does no works, but insofar as he is a servant he does all kinds of works. . . .

In doing these works, however, we must not think that a man is justified before God by them, for faith, which alone is righteousness before God, cannot endure that erroneous opinion. We must, however, realize that these works reduce the body to subjection and purify it of its evil lusts, and our whole purpose is to be directed only toward the driving out of lusts. Since by faith the soul is cleansed and made to love God, it desires that all things, and especially its own body, shall be purified so that all things may join with it in loving and praising God. Hence a man cannot be idle, for the need of his body drives him and he is compelled to do many good works to reduce it to subjection. Nevertheless the works themselves do not justify him before God, but he does the works out of spontaneous love in obedience to God and considers nothing except the approval of God, whom he would most scrupulously obey in all things. . . .

Karl H. Dannenfeldt, *The Church of the Renaissance and Reformation*. St. Louis, MO: Concordia Publishing House, 1970, pp. 126–29.

Document 9: The Ideal of the Renaissance Man

One of the most popular of all Renaissance books, The Courtier *by Castiglione, provides an eloquent description of the ideal nobleman, a "renaissance man" in the range of his interests and abilities. Expert in war and athletics, skilled in music, poetry, and dancing, learned in the classical languages and humanities, the ideal courtier depicted by Castiglione was a source of inspiration and object of aspiration throughout the later Renaissance.*

The Count said: "I would have our Courtier born of a noble and genteel family; because it is far less becoming for one of low birth to fail to do virtuous things than for one of noble birth. For one of noble birth, should he stray from the path of his forebears, stains the family name, and not only fails to achieve anything but loses what has been achieved already. . . .

"Besides his noble birth, I would wish the Courtier endowed by nature not only with talent and with beauty of countenance and person, but with that certain grace we call an 'air,' which shall make him at first sight pleasing and lovable to all who see him. . . .

"But to come to some particulars: I hold that the principal and true profession of the Courtier must be that of arms. . . . Therefore let the man we are seeking be exceedingly fierce, harsh, and always among the first, wherever the enemy is; and in every other place, humane, modest, reserved, avoiding ostentation above all things. . . .

"I deem it highly important, moreover, to know how to wrestle [and] to be a perfect horseman. . . . He should also know how to swim, jump, run, throw stones; for besides their usefulness in war, it is frequently necessary to show one's prowess in such things, whereby a good name is to be won."

At a sign from the Duchess and from Signora Emilia, Messer Cesare began forthwith: "If I well remember, Count, it seems to me you have repeated several times that the Courtier must accompany his every movement with grace. . . . I would wish to know by what art they can gain this grace?"

Said the Count: "I have found quite a universal rule which in this matter seems to me valid above all others: and that is to avoid affectation in every way possible as though it were some rough and dangerous reef; and to practice in all things a certain *sprezzatura* [nonchalance], so as to conceal all art and make whatever is done or said appear to be without effort and almost without any thought about it."

Then the Count said: "I would have our Courtier more than

passably learned in letters, at least in those studies which we call the humanities. Let him be conversant not only with the Latin language, but with Greek as well, because of the abundance and variety of things that are so divinely written therein. Let him be versed in the poets, as well as in the orators and historians, and let him be practiced also in writing verse and prose, especially in our own vernacular; for besides the satisfaction he will take in this, in this way he will never want for pleasant entertainment with the ladies, who are usually fond of such things."

"Nay, too much," replied Signor Lodovico Pio, "for I believe it is not possible in all the world to find a vessel large enough to contain all the things you would have be in our Courtier. . . ."

Here everyone laughed and the Count began again: "Gentlemen, you must know that I am not satisfied with our Courtier unless . . . he can play various instruments. For, no rest from toil and no medicine for ailing spirits can be found more decorous or praiseworthy in time of leisure that this; and especially in courts where . . . many things are done to please the ladies, whose tender and delicate spirits are readily penetrated with harmony and filed with sweetness."

Messer Federico laughed and went on: "There are certain other exercises that can be practiced in public and in private, such as dancing. And in this I think the Courtier should take great care; because, when dancing in a place full of people, I think he should maintain a certain dignity, though tempered with a fine and airy grace of movement; and even though he may feel himself to be most agile and a master of time and measure, let him not attempt those quick movements of foot . . . which would perhaps little befit a gentleman."

Messer Federico stated: "A man ought always to be a little more humble than his rank would require; not accepting too readily the favors and honors that are offered him, but modestly refusing them while showing that he esteems them highly, yet in such a way as to give the donor cause to press them upon him the more urgently. For the greater the resistance shown in accepting them in this way, the more will the prince who is granting them think himself to be esteemed.". . .

Then Signor Gasparo said: "Women are imperfect creatures. . . . Nevertheless, since these defects in women are the fault of nature, we ought not on that account to despise them, or fail to show them the respect which is their due. But to esteem them to be more than what they are seems a manifest error to me. . . ."

The Magnifico said: "If you compare the worth of women in every age to that of men, you will find they have never been a whit inferior. . . ."

Then Messer Cesare said: "Who does not know that without women we can take no pleasure or satisfaction in this life of ours, which, but for them, would be uncouth and devoid of all sweetness, and wilder than that of wild beasts?"

Kenneth M. Setton et al., eds., *The Renaissance: Maker of Modern Man*. Washington, DC: National Geographic Society, 1979, pp. 92–93.

Document 10: Agrippa Attacks the Persecution of Witches

Though he was mostly very critical of Renaissance magic, the humanist scholar Agrippa later gained the reputation of being a notorious adherent of magic. In the following excerpt, Agrippa attacks the injustice and hypocrisy of the Inquisition in its persecution of witches.

When they [Dominican friars] conduct an Inquisition, they demand nothing else as the mark of faith than that the offender believe in the Church of Rome. If the offender professes this belief they say straightaway that the Church of Rome condemns something he has said as either heretical, sinful, offensive to pious ears or subversive of ecclesiastical authority. And immediately they compel him to recant and revoke what he said. But if the person who is subject of Inquisition sets about defending his opinion with the evidence of Scripture or other reasons, they interrupt him with great noise and verbal abuse, saying that he was not answering before a conference of Bachelors [of Arts] or scholars but before a tribunal of judges. He must not be contentious and engage in disputation but must answer plainly, whether he will abide by the judgement of the Church of Rome and renounce his opinion. If he will not, they show him faggots and fire, saying that in the case of heretics they are not allowed to contend with arguments and appeals to Scripture but only with faggots and fire. Even where the man has not been convicted of obstinacy, they force him against his conscience to deny his opinions under oath. If he will not do it, they deliver him into the hands of the secular power to be burned, saying with the Apostle: 'Take away mischief from among you.'. . .

It is expressly provided by the Laws that the Inquisitors have no power, nor any jurisdiction, to proceed upon a case of heresy . . . except where there is explicit heresy that is obviously to be condemned. But these bloodthirsty vultures nonetheless exceed the powers of the office of Inquisition granted to them. Contrary to what is right and to the Canon Laws themselves, they meddle in the jurisdiction of the judges of the Ordinaries [local] Court, they usurp the authority of the bishops in such matters as are not heretical but only offensive to pious ears, sinful or in some other manner erroneous (without being heretical).

In this way they show their stern and extreme cruelty towards poor countrywomen who are accused of witchcraft or sorcery and condemned without first being examined by a lawful judge. They put these women to atrocious and frightful suffering, till they are forced to confess what it had never crossed their minds to believe and they ['these bloodthirsty vultures'] have the means to condemn them. They really suppose they are fulfilling the role of Inquisitors when they do not cease from their duty until the defenceless woman is burned or has put gold into the Inquisitor's hand, on account of which he takes pity on her and releases her as sufficiently purged by tortures. For often the Inquisitor can change the pain of the body into the punishment of the purse and apply it to his Inquisitorial office. Because of this they accumulate no small profit and not a few of these unfortunate women are obliged to pay them an annual fee so that they will not be punished again. . . .

In the past, when I was an advocate and counsellor of the commonwealth of Metz, I had a very troublesome case against an Inquisitor. He, being a wicked man, dragged a poor countrywoman, on the strength of certain unsupported and most unjust accusations, to his prison—the wrong place—not so much to examine as to torment her. When I had undertaken to defend her and had demonstrated that there was no evidence or proof of her having done anything that could justify her being tortured, he stoutly denied it, saying that it was sufficient proof that her mother had previously been burned as a witch. I replied and showed him that this consideration was irrelevant and that the law did not allow one person to be condemned for what was done by someone else. He promptly answered me—to prevent it seeming that what he had previously said was not thought out—by appealing to details of the *Malleus maleficarum* [a handbook on witchcraft] and to the bases of Peripatetic Theology [derived from Aristotle].

He argued that it was quite right [to arrest the daughter of a witch], since witches were accustomed to dedicate their children to the Devil as they burn. Also it often happened that they would be made pregnant by spirits that had taken the form of a man. Thus (he concluded) it comes about that the wickedness is deeprooted in the child, like an inherited disease.

Then I said to him: 'O wicked father, is this the kind of divinity you study? Are these the concocted arguments by which you get the poor innocent women to the rack? Are these the sophisms by which you judge others to be heretics? Are you with this opinion not yourself as much of a heretic as Faustus and Donatus?'. . .

At these words the cruel hypocrite was very angry and threatened that he would charge me as a supporter of heretics. But I did not stop defending that unfortunate soul and finally, through the power of the law, I delivered her safely from the mouth of that lion. In consequence that bloody monk stood rebuked and disgraced in the eyes of everyone and was forever notorious on account of his cruelty. Moreover both he and the unjust accusers who attacked the woman's reputation were fined a large sum of money by the chapter of the Church of Metz, whose subjects they were.

David Englander et al., eds., *Culture and Belief in Europe 1450–1600*. London: Basil Blackwell, 1990, pp. 209–212.

Document 11: The Education of English Nobility

Sir Thomas Elyot's The Book Named the Governor *treats the background and skills necessary to be a good ruler, and it quite naturally begins with a program of education. Elyot sets forth a thoroughly classical plan of education for aspiring public servants, and many of the suggestions he makes here were actually adopted in England in the sixteenth century.*

Now let us return to the order of learning apt for a gentleman. Wherein I am of the opinion of Quintilian that I would have him learn Greek and Latin authors both at one time; or else to begin with Greek, forasmuch as that it is hardest to come by, by reason of the diversity of tongues, which be five in number, and all must be known, or else scarcely any poet can be well understood. And if a child do begin therein at seven years of age, he may continually learn Greek authors three years, and in the meantime use the Latin tongue as a familiar language; which in a nobleman's son may well come to pass, having none other persons to serve him or keeping him company but such as can speak Latin elegantly. And what doubt is there but so may he as soon speak good Latin as he may do pure French, which now is brought into as many rules and figures and as long a grammar as is Latin or Greek. . . .

Now to follow my purpose: after a few and quick rules of grammar, immediately, or interlacing it therewith, would be read to the child Aesop's fables in Greek, in which argument children much do delight. And surely it is a much pleasant lesson and also profitable, as well for that it is elegant and brief (and notwithstanding it hath much variety in words, and therewith much helpeth to the understanding of Greek) as also in those fables is included much moral and politic wisdom. Wherefore, in the teaching of them, the master diligently must gather together those fables which may be most accommodate to the advancement of some virtue whereto he perceiveth the child inclined, or to the rebuke of some vice whereto he findeth his nature disposed. . . .

I could rehearse divers other poets which for matter and eloquence be very necessary, but I fear me to be too long from noble Homer, from whom as from a fountain proceeded all eloquence and learning. For in his books be contained and most perfectly expressed, not only the documents martial and discipline of arms, but also incomparable wisdom, and instructions for politic governance of people, with the worthy commendation and laud of noble princes; wherewith the readers shall be so all inflamed that they most fervently shall desire and covet, by the imitation of their virtues, to acquire semblable glory. For the which occasion, Aristotle, most sharpest witted and excellent learned philosopher, as soon as he had received Alexander from King Philip his father, he before any other thing taught him the most noble works of Homer; wherein Alexander found such sweetness and fruit that ever after he had Homer not only with him in all his journeys but also laid him under his pillow when he went to rest, and often times would purposely wake some hours of the night to take as it were his pastime with that most noble poet.

For by the reading of his work called *Iliad*, where the assembly of the most noble Greeks against Troy is recited with their affairs, he gathered courage and strength against his enemies, wisdom, and eloquence for consultation and persuasions to his people and army. And by the other work called *Odyssey*, which recounteth the sundry adventures of the wise Ulysses, he by the example of Ulysses apprehended many noble virtues, and also learned to escape the fraud and deceitful imaginations of sundry and subtle crafty wits. Also there shall he learn to ensearch and perceive the manners and conditions of them that be his familiars, sifting out (as I might say) the best from the worst, whereby he may surely commit his affairs, and trust to every person after his virtues. Therefore I now conclude that there is no lesson for a young gentleman to be compared with Homer, if he be plainly and substantially expounded and declared by the master.

Notwithstanding, forasmuch as the said works be very long, and do require therefore a great time to be all learned and conned, some Latin author would be therewith mixed, and specially Virgil; which, in his work called *Aeneid,* is most like to Homer and almost the same Homer in Latin. Also, by the joining together of those authors, the one shall be the better understood by the other. And verily (as I before said) no one author serveth to so divers wits as doth Virgil. For there is not that affect or desire whereto any child's fantasy is disposed, but in some of Virgil's works may be found matter thereto apt and propise [suitable]. . . .

Finally (as I have said) this noble Virgil, like to a good nurse, giveth to a child, if he will take it, everything apt for his wit and capacity; wherefore he is in the order of learning to be preferred before any other author Latin. . . .

By the time that the child do come to seventeen years of age, to the intent his courage be bridled with reason, it were needful to read unto him some works of philosophy; specially that part that may inform him unto virtuous manners, which part of philosophy is called moral. Wherefore there would be read to him, for an introduction, two the first books of the work of Aristotle called *Ethicae,* wherein is contained the definitions and proper significations of every virtue; and that to be learned in Greek; for the translations, that we yet have be but a rude and gross shadow of the eloquence and wisdom of Aristotle. Forthwith would follow the work of Cicero, called in Latin *De officiis,* whereunto yet is no official proper English word to be given; but to provide for it some manner of exposition, it may be said in this form: 'Of the duties and manners appertaining to men.' But above all other, the works of Plato would be most studiously read when the judgment of a man is come to perfection, and by the other studies is instructed in the form of speaking that philosophers used. Lord God, what incomparable sweetness of words and matter shall he find in the said works of Plato and Cicero; wherein is joined gravity with delectation, excellent wisdom with divine eloquence, absolute virtue with pleasure incredible, and every place is so enforced [filled] with profitable counsel joined with honesty, that those three *books be almost sufficient to make a perfect and excellent* governor. The proverbs of Solomon with the books of Ecclesiastes and Ecclesiasticus be very good lessons. All the historical parts of the Bible be right necessary for to be read of a nobleman, after that he is mature in years. And the residue (with the New Testament) is to be reverently touched, as a celestial jewel or relic, having the chief interpreter of those books true and constant faith. . . . It would not be forgotten

that the little book of the most excellent doctor Erasmus Rotero-
damus (which he wrote to Charles, now being Emperor and then
Prince of Castile), which book is entitled *The Institution of a Christian Prince*, would be as familiar alway with gentlemen at all times
and in every age as was Homer with the great King Alexander, or
Xenophon with Scipio; for as all men may judge that have read
that work of Erasmus, that there was never book written in Latin
that in so little a portion contained of sentence, eloquence, and virtuous exhortation, a more compendious abundance.

Sir Thomas Elyot, *The Book Named the Governor*. Ed. S.E. Lehmberg. New York: Dutton, 1962,
pp. 28–40 passim.

Document 12: A Father's Advice to His Son

*The Frenchman François Rabelais was a friar, humanist, and physician,
who, inspired by the humanist scholar Erasmus, turned to the writing of
satires. The following passage, though, contains only a trace of satire, presenting Rabelais's humanist agenda for a Renaissance education in the
form of Gargantua's letter to his son Pantragruel.*

The time then [in my youth] was not so proper and fit for learning as it is at present, neither had I plenty of such good masters as
thou hast had. For that time was darksome, obscured with clouds
of ignorance, and savouring a little of the infelicity and calamity of
the Goths, who had, wherever they set footing, destroyed all good
literature, which in my age hath by the divine goodness been restored unto its former light and dignity, and that with such amend-
ment and increase of knowledge, that now hardly should I be ad-
mitted unto the first form of the little grammar-school boys, I say,
I, who in my youthful days was, and that justly, reputed the most
learned of that age, which I do not speak in vain boasting, although
I might lawfully do it in writing unto thee,—in verification
whereof thou hast the authority of Marcus Tullius [Cicero] in his
book *Of Old Age*, and the sentence of Plutarch, in the book inti-
tled, *How a man may praise himself without envy:*—but to give thee
an emulous encouragement to strive yet further.

Now it is, that the minds of men are qualified with all manner
of discipline and the old sciences revived, which for many ages
were extinct. Now it is, that the learned languages are to their pris-
tine purity restored, *viz.*, Greek, without which a man may be
ashamed to account himself a scholar, Hebrew, Arabic, Chaldaean,
and Latin. Printing likewise is now in use, so elegant and so correct, that better cannot be imagined, although it was found out but

in my time by divine inspiration, as by a diabolical suggestion on the other side, was the invention of ordnance. All the world is full of knowing men, of most learned schoolmasters, and vast libraries; and it appears to me as a truth, that neither in Plato's time, nor Cicero's, . . . there was ever such conveniency for studying, as we see at this day there is. Nor must any adventure henceforward to come in public or present himself in company, that hath not been pretty well polished in the shop of Minerva. I see robbers, hangmen, free-booters, tapsters, ostlers, and such like, of the very rubbish of the people, more learned now than the doctors and preachers were in my time.

What shall I say? The very women and children have aspired to this praise and celestial manna of good learning. Yet so it is, that at the age I am now of, I have been constrained to learn the Greek tongue,—which I contemned not like Cato, but had not the leisure in my younger years to attend the study of it,—and I take much delight in the reading of Plutarch's *Morals*, the pleasant *Dialogues* of Plato, the *Monuments* of Pausanias, and the *Antiquities* of Athenaeus, in waiting on the hour wherein God my Creator shall call me, and command me to depart from this earth and transitory pilgrimage. Wherefore, my son, I admonish thee to employ thy youth to profit as well as thou canst, both in thy studies and in virtue. Thou art at Paris, where the laudable examples of many brave men may stir up thy mind to gallant actions, and hast likewise, for thy tutor and pedagogue the learned Epistemon, who by his lively and vocal documents may instruct thee in the arts and sciences.

I intend, and will have it so, that thou learn the languages perfectly; first of all, the Greek, as Quintilian will have it; secondly, the Latin; and then the Hebrew, for the Holy Scripture-sake; and then the Chaldee and Arabic likewise, and that thou frame thy style in Greek in imitation of Plato; and for the Latin, after Cicero. Let there be no history which thou shalt not have ready in thy memory;—unto the prosecuting of which design, books of cosmography will be very conducible, and help thee much. Of the liberal arts of geometry, arithmetic and music, I gave thee some taste when thou wert yet little, and not above five or six years old. Proceed further in them, and learn the remainder if thou canst. As for astronomy, study all the rules thereof. Let pass, nevertheless, the divining and judicial astrology, and the art of Lullius, as being nothing else but plain abuses and vanities. As for the civil law, of that I would have thee to know the texts by heart, and then to confer them with philosophy.

Now, in matter of the knowledge of the works of nature, I would have thee to study that exactly; that so there be no sea, river, nor fountain, of which thou dost not know the fishes; all the fowls of the air; all the several kinds of shrubs and trees, whether in forest or orchards; all the sorts of herbs and flowers that grow upon the ground; all the various metals that are hid within the bowels of the earth; together with all the diversity of precious stones, that are to be seen, in the orient and south parts of the world. Let nothing of all these be hidden from thee. Then fail not most carefully to peruse the books of the Greek, Arabian, and Latin physicians, not despising the Talmudists and Cabalists; and by frequent anatomies, get thee the perfect knowledge of that other world, called the microcosm, which is man. And at some of the hours of the day apply thy mind to the study of the Holy Scriptures; first, in Greek, the New Testament, with the Epistles of the Apostles; and then the Old Testament in Hebrew, in brief, let me see thee an abyss, and bottomless pit of knowledge: for from henceforward, as thou growest great and becomest a man, thou must part from this tranquillity and rest of study, thou must learn chivalry, warfare, and the exercises of the field, the better thereby to defend my house and our friends, and to succour and protect them at all their needs, against the invasion and assaults of evil doers.

Furthermore, I will that very shortly thou try how much thou hast profited, which thou canst not better do, than by maintaining publicly theses and conclusions in all arts, against all persons whatsoever, and by haunting the company of learned men, both at Paris and otherwhere.

François Rabelais, *Gargantua and Pantagruel*. Trans. Sir Thomas Urquhart and Peter Motteux. Chicago: Encyclopaedia Brittanica, 1952, pp. 81–83.

Document 13: The Spanish Conquest of Peru

Francisco de Xéres was secretary to Francisco Pizarro, the conqueror of the Inca empire in Peru. Xéres records in graphic detail how Pizarro and his troops surprised, terrorized, and massacred the Incas, as Xéres says, "[so] that all may come to a knowledge of God."

The monk told the Governor [Pizarro] what had passed between him and [the Incan leader] Atabaliba, and that he had thrown the Scriptures to the ground. Then the Governor put on a jacket of cotton, took his sword and dagger, and, with the Spaniards who were with him, entered among the Indians most valiantly; and, with only four men who were able to follow him, he came to the litter where Atabaliba was, and fearlessly seized him by the arm, crying out *Santiago*. Then the guns were fired off, the trumpets were sounded, and the troops, both horse and foot, sallied forth. On seeing the horses charge, many of the Indians who were in the open space fled, and such was the force with which they ran that they broke down part of the wall surrounding it, and many fell over each other. The horsemen rode them down, killing and wounding, and following in pursuit. The infantry made so good an assault upon those that remained that in a short time most of them were put to the sword. The Governor still held Atabaliba by the arm, not being able to pull him out of the litter because he was raised so high. Then the Spaniards made such slaughter amongst those who carried the litter that they fell to the ground, and, if the Governor had not protected Atabaliba, that proud man would there have paid for all the cruelties he had committed. The Governor, in protecting Atabaliba, received a slight wound in the hand. During the whole time no Indian raised his arms against a Spaniard. So great was the terror of the Indians at seeing the Governor force his way through them, at hearing the fire of the artillery, and beholding the charging of the horses, a thing never before heard of, that they thought more of flying to save their lives than of fighting. All those who bore the litter of Atabaliba appeared to be principal chiefs. They were all killed, as well as those who were carried in the other litters and hammocks. . . .

The Governor went to his lodging, with his prisoner Atabaliba, despoiled of his robes, which the Spaniards had torn off in pulling him out of the litter. It was a very wonderful thing to see so great a lord taken prisoner in so short a time who came in such power. The Governor presently ordered native clothes to be brought, and when Atabaliba was dressed, he made him sit near him, and soothed his rage and agitation at finding himself so quickly fallen from his high estate. Among many other things, the Governor said to him: "Do not take it as an insult that you have been defeated and taken prisoners, for with the Christians who come with me, though so few in number, I have conquered greater kingdoms than yours, and have defeated other more powerful lords than you, imposing upon them the dominion of the Emperor, whose vassal I am, and who is King of Spain and of the universal world. We come to conquer this land by his command, that all may come to a knowledge of God, and of His Holy Catholic Faith; and by reason of our good object, God, the Creator of heaven and earth and of all things in them, permits this, in order that you may know him, and come out from the bestial and diabolical life you lead. It is for this reason that we, being so few in number, subjugate that vast host. . . ."

. . . The battle lasted only about half an hour, for the sun had already set when it commenced. If the night had not come on, few out of the thirty thousand men that came would have been left. It is the opinion of some, who have seen armies in the field, that there were more than forty thousand men. In the square and on the plain there were two thousand killed, besides wounded.

G.R. Elton, ed., *Renaissance and Reformation 1300–1648*. London: Macmillan, 1970, pp. 262–64.

Document 14: The Revolution of Celestial Bodies

In the following excerpt, Nicolaus Copernicus explains in clear and direct language his revolutionary new theory of planetary movement. His new axioms included the ideas that the earth is not the center of the universe and that the planets revolve around the sun instead of the earth. These claims involved a radical break with ancient and medieval astronomy.

Our ancestors assumed, I observe, a large number of celestial spheres for this reason especially, to explain the apparent motion of the planets by the principle of regularity. For they thought it altogether absurd that a heavenly body, which is a perfect sphere, should not always move uniformly. They saw that by connecting and combining regular motions in various ways they could make any body appear to move to any position.

Callippus and Eudoxus, who endeavored to solve the problem by the use of concentric spheres, were unable to account for all the planetary movements; they had to explain not merely the apparent revolutions of the planets but also the fact that these bodies appear to us sometimes to mount higher in the heavens, sometimes to descend; and this fact is incompatible with the principle of concentricity. Therefore it seemed better to employ eccentrics and epicycles, a system which most scholars finally accepted.

Yet the planetary theories of Ptolemy and most other astronomers, although consistent with the numerical data, seemed likewise to present no small difficulty. For these theories were not adequate unless certain equants were also conceived; it then appeared that a planet moved with uniform velocity neither on its deferent nor about the center of its epicycle. Hence a system of this sort seemed neither sufficiently absolute nor sufficiently pleasing to the mind.

Having become aware of these defects, I often considered

whether there could perhaps be found a more reasonable arrangement of circles, from which every apparent inequality would be derived and in which everything would move uniformly about its proper center, as the rule of absolute motion requires. After I had addressed myself to this very difficult and most insoluble problem, the suggestion at length came to me how it could be solved with fewer and much simpler constructions than were formerly used, if some assumptions (which are called axioms) were granted me. They follow in this order.

1. There is no one center of all the celestial circles or spheres.

2. The center of the earth is not the center of the universe, but only of gravity and of the lunar sphere.

3. All the spheres revolve about the sun as their mid-point, and therefore the sun is the center of the universe.

4. The ratio of the earth's distance from the sun to the height of the firmament is so much smaller than the ratio of the earth's radius to its distance from the sun that the distance from the earth to the sun is imperceptible in comparison with the height of the firmament.

5. Whatever motion appears in the firmament arises not from any motion of the firmament, but from the earth's motion. The earth together with its circumjacent elements performs a complete rotation on its fixed poles in a daily motion, while the firmament and highest heaven abide unchanged.

6. What appear to us as motions of the sun arise not from its motion but from the motion of the earth and our sphere, with which we revolve about the sun like any other planet. The earth has, then, more than one motion.

7. The apparent retrograde and direct motion of the planets arises not from their motion but from the earth's. The motion of the earth alone, therefore, suffices to explain so many apparent inequalities in the heavens. . . .

Let no one suppose that I have gratuitously asserted, with the Pythagoreans, the motion of the earth; strong proof will be found in my exposition of the circles. For the principal arguments by which the natural philosophers attempt to establish the immobility of the earth rest for the most part on the appearances; it is particularly such arguments that collapse here, since I treat the earth's immobility as due to an appearance.

The celestial spheres are arranged in the following order. The highest is the immovable sphere of the fixed stars, which contains and gives position to all things. Beneath it is Saturn, which Jupiter follows, then Mars. Below Mars is the sphere on which we revolve;

then Venus, last is Mercury. The lunar sphere revolves about the center of the earth and moves with the earth like an epicycle. In the same order also, one planet surpasses another in speed of revolution, according as they trace greater or smaller circles. Thus Saturn completes its revolution in thirty years, Jupiter in twelve, Mars in two and one-half, and the earth in one year; Venus in nine months, Mercury in three.

Franklin Le Van Baumer, ed., *Main Currents of Western Thought*. New Haven: Yale University Press, 1978, pp. 272–73.

Document 15: The Melancholic Personality

Most people in the Renaissance believed that personality is a mixture of the four bodily humors (phlegm, melancholy, choler, blood), and that everyone is dominated by one or another of these humors. The most fascinating personality type is the melancholic, for all unusual mental conditions—ranging from genius to madness—were considered to be melancholic. In the following passage, the Spanish doctor Juan Huarte describes an extreme melancholic condition which in modern terms would probably be termed manic depression or bipolar disorder. Huarte's analysis is largely derived from Aristotle, but he uses the Christian St. Paul as his prime example of the condition.

The signs by which men of this temperature [temperament] may be known are very manifest: they have the color of their countenance a dark green or sallow; their eyes very fiery . . . ; their hair black and bald; their flesh lean, rough, and hairy; their veins big. They are of very good conversation and affable, but lecherous, proud, stately, blasphemers, wily, double, injurious, friends of ill-doing, and desirous of revenge. This is to be understood when melancholy is kindled, but if it be cooled, forthwith there grow in them the contrary virtues: chastity, humility, fear and reverence of God, charity, mercy, and great acknowledgement of their sins, with sighings and tears, for which cause they live in continual war and strife, without ever enjoying ease or rest. Sometimes vice prevaileth in them, sometimes virtue, but with all these defects, they are wittiest and most able for the function of preaching, and for all matters of wisdom which befall in the world. For they have an understanding to know the truth, and a great imagination to be able to persuade the same.

Wherethrough, we see that which God did when he would fashion a man in his mother's womb, to the end that he might be able to reveal to the world the coming of his Son, and have the way to prove and persuade that Christ was the Messiah and promised in the law. For making him [Paul] of great understanding and of much imagination, it fell out of necessity (keeping the natural order) that he should also make him melancholy. And that this is true may easily be understood by him who considereth the great fire and fury with which he persecuted the church, the grief conceived by the synagogues when they saw him converted, as they had foregone [lost] a man of high importance. . . . Yet he [Paul] had an imperfection in his tongue and was not very prompt of speech, which Aristotle affirmeth to be a property of the melancholic by adustion. The vices which he confessed himself to be subject before his conversion, show him to have been of this temperature [temperament]: he was a blasphemer, a wrongdoer, and a persecutor, all which springeth from abundance of heat. But the most evident sign which showed that he was melancholic is gathered from the battle which he confessed he had within himself, between his part superior and inferior, saying "I see another law in my members striving against the law of my mind, which leadeth me into the bondage of sin." And this self-contention have we proved (by the mind of Aristotle) to be in the melancholic by adustion.

Juan Huarte Navarro, *The Examination of Mens Wits*. London, 1594. Published in facsimile by Da Capo Press, Amsterdam, 1969. English spelling and usage modernized by the editor.

Document 16: Sidney Defends the Inspirational Power of Poetry

After reading a Puritan attack on poetry and the arts, Sir Philip Sidney undertook to write a defense of poetry as an art with a moral dimension, an art that both teaches and delights.

First, truly, to all them that professing learning inveigh against poetry may justly be objected that they go very near to ungratefulness, to seek to deface that which, in the noblest nations and languages that are known, hath been the first light-giver to ignorance, and first nurse, whose milk by little and little enabled them to feed afterwards of tougher knowledges. And will they now pay the hedgehog that, being received into the den, drove out his host, or rather the vipers, that with their birth kill their parents? Let learned Greece in any of her manifold sciences be able to show me one book before Musaeus, Homer, and Hesiod, all three nothing else but poets. Nay, let any history be brought that can say any writers were there before them, if they were not men of the same skill, as Orpheus, Linus, and some other are named, who, having been the

first of that country that made pens deliverers of their knowledge
to their posterity, may justly challenge to be called their fathers in
learning, for not only in time they had this priority (although in itself antiquity be venerable) but went before them, as causes to draw
with their charming sweetness the wild untamed wits to an admiration of knowledge, so as Amphion was said to move stones with his
poetry to build Thebes, and Orpheus to be listened to by beasts—
indeed stony and beastly people. So among the Romans were
Livius Andronicus and Ennius. So in the Italian language the first
that made it aspire to be a treasure-house of science were the poets
Dante, Boccaccio and Petrarch. So in our English were Gower and
Chaucer, after whom, encouraged and delighted with their excellent foregoing, others have followed, to beautify our mother
tongue, as well in the same kind as in other arts.

This did so notably show itself, that the philosophers of Greece
durst not a long time appear to the world but under the masks of
poets. . . . And truly, even Plato, whosoever well considereth shall
find that in the body of his work, though the inside and strength
were philosophy, the skin as it were and beauty depended most of
poetry: for all standeth upon dialogues, wherein he feigneth many
honest burgesses of Athens to speak of such matters, that if they
had been set on the rack they would never confessed them, besides
his poetical describing the circumstances of their meetings, as the
well ordering of a banquet, the delicacy of a walk, with interlacing
mere tales, as Gyges' Ring and others, which who knoweth not to
be flowers of poetry did never walk into Apollo's garden.

And even historiographers [historians] (although their lips
sound of things done, and verity be written in their foreheads)
have been glad to borrow both fashion and perchance weight of
poets. So Herodotus entitled his history by the name of the nine
Muses; and both he and all the rest that followed him either stole
or usurped of poetry their passionate describing of passions, the
many particularities of battles, which no man could affirm, or, if
that be denied me, long orations put in the mouths of great kings
and captains, which it is certain they never pronounced. So that,
truly, neither philosopher nor historiographer could at the first
have entered into the gates of popular judgments, if they had not
taken a great passport of poetry, which in all nations at this day,
where learning flourisheth not, is plain to be seen, in all which
they have some feeling of poetry.

Nature never set for the earth in so rich tapestry as divers poets
have done—neither with pleasant rivers, fruitful trees, sweet-

smelling flowers, nor whatsoever else may make the too much loved earth more lovely. Her world is brazen, the poets only deliver a golden. . . .

Neither let it be deemed too saucy a comparison to balance the highest point of man's wit with the efficacy of nature; but rather give right honour to the heavenly maker of that maker, who, having made man to his own likeness, set him beyond and over all the works of that second nature: which in nothing he showeth so much as in poetry, when with the force of a divine breath he bringeth things forth far surpassing her doings, with no small argument to the incredulous of that first accursed fall of Adam, since our erected wit maketh us know what perfection is, and yet our infected will keepeth us from reaching unto it. . . . Poesy therefore is an art imitation, for so Aristotle termeth it in his word *Mimesis*, that is to say, a representing, counterfeiting, or figuring forth—to speak metaphorically, a speaking picture; with this end, to teach and delight.

John Hollander and Frank Kermode, *The Literature of Renaissance England*. New York: Oxford University Press, 1973, pp. 137–39.

Document 17: The Connection Between Witchcraft and Mental Illness

Depictions of witchcraft and the supernatural were common in the theater of Renaissance England, and actual prosecutions of witches made occasional headlines. In the following essay from 1584, Elizabethan writer Reginald Scot argues that most women accused of witchcraft were suffering from melancholy, a state which in modern terms included such things as delusions and schizophrenia.

One sort of such as are said to be witches are women which be commonly old, lame, blear-eyed, pale, foul, and full of wrinkles; poor, sullen, superstitious, and papists, or such as know no religion, in whose drowsy minds the devil hath got a fine seat, so as what mischief, mischance, calamity or slaughter is brought to pass, they are easily persuaded the same is done by themselves, imprinting in their minds an earnest and constant imagination hereof. They are lean and deformed, showing melancholy in their faces, to the horror of all that see them. They are doting scolds, mad, devilish, and not much differing from them that are thought to be possessed with spirits. So firm and steadfast in their opinions as whosoever shall only have respect to the constancy of their words uttered would easily believe they were true indeed.

These miserable wretches are so odious unto all their neighbors and so feared as few dare offend them or deny them anything they ask, whereby they take upon them, yea and sometimes think, that they can do such things as are beyond the ability of human nature. These go from house to house and from door to door for a pot full of milk, yeast, drink, pottage, or some such relief, without the which they could hardly live. Neither obtaining for their service and pains nor by their art, nor yet at the devil's hands (with whom they are said to make a perfect and visible bargain) either beauty, money, promotion, wealth, worship, pleasure, honor, knowledge, learning, or any other benefit whatsoever.

It falleth out many times that neither their necessities nor their expectation is answered or served in those places where they beg or borrow, but rather their lewdness is by their neighbors reproved. And further, in tract of time the witch waxeth odious and tedious to her neighbors, and they again are despised and despited of her, so as sometimes she curseth one and sometimes another, and that from the master of the house, his wife, children, cattle, &c., to the little pig that lieth in the sty. Thus in process of time they have all displeased her, and she hath wished evil luck unto them all, perhaps with curses and imprecations made in form. Doubtless (at length) some of her neighbors die, or fall sick, or some of their children are visited with diseases that vex them strangely, as apoplexies, epilepsies, convulsions, hot fevers, worms, &c., which by ignorant parents are supposed to be the vengeance of witches. Yea and their opinions and conceits are confirmed and maintained by unskillful physicians, according to the common saying: *Inscitiae pallium maleficium et incantatio*, "Witchcraft and enchantment is the cloak of ignorance"—whereas indeed evil humors and not strange words, witches, or spirits are the causes of such disease. Also some of their cattle perish, either by disease or mischance. Then they, upon whom such adversities fall, weighing the fame that goeth upon this woman (her words, displeasure, and curses meeting so justly with their misfortunes) do not only conceive but also are resolved that all their mishaps are brought to pass by her only means.

The witch, on the other side, expecting her neighbor's mischances and seeing things come to pass according to her wishes, curses, and incantations (for Bodin himself confesseth that not above two in a hundred of their witchings or wishings take effect) being called before a justice, by due examination of the circumstances is driven to see her imprecations and desires and her neighbor's harms and losses to concur and as it were to take effect and so confesseth that she (as a goddess) hath brought such things to pass. Wherein, not only she but the accuser and also the justice are foully deceived and abused as being through her confession and other circumstances persuaded (to the injury of God's glory) that she hath done or can do that which is proper only to God himself.

Another sort of witches there are which be absolutely cozeners [con artists]. These take upon them either for glory, fame, or gain to do anything which God or the devil can do, either for foretelling of things to come, betraying of secrets, curing of maladies, or working of miracles. . . .

If any man advisedly mark their words, actions, cogitations, and gestures, he shall perceive that melancholy abounding in their head and occupying their brain hath deprived or rather depraved their judgments and all their senses. I mean not of cozening witches, but of poor melancholy women which are themselves deceived. For you shall understand that the force which melancholy hath and the effects that it worketh in the body of a man or rather a woman are almost incredible. For as some of these melancholic persons imagine they are witches and by witchcraft can work wonders and do what they list, so do other, troubled with this disease, imagine many strange, incredible, and impossible things.

. . . But if they may imagine that they can transform their own bodies, which nevertheless remaineth in the former shape, how much more credible is it that they may falsely suppose they can hurt and enfeeble other men's bodies, or which is less, hinder the coming of butter?

. . . If you read the executions done upon witches either in times past in other countries or lately in this land, you shall see such impossibilities confessed as none having his right wits will believe. Among other like false confessions, we read that there was a witch confessed at the time of her death or execution that she had raised all the tempests and procured all the frosts and hard weather that happened in the winter [of] 1565, and that many grave and wise men believed her.

Gerald M. Pinciss and Roger Lockyer, eds., *Shakespeare's World*. New York: Continuum, 1990, pp. 75–78.

Document 18: The Patriotic Strength of Queen Elizabeth

Queen Elizabeth ruled England for forty-five years, from 1558 to 1603, years that included much of the great English literary Renaissance. She was held in high esteem by her people, and her speech from the time of the attempted Spanish invasion of 1588 shows her skill at inspiring patriotic fervor in her subjects.

My loving people,

We have been persuaded by some that are careful of our safety, to take heed how We commit our selves to armed multitudes, for fear of treachery; but I assure you I do not desire to live to distrust my faithful and loving people. Let tyrants fear, I have always so behaved myself that, under God, I have placed my chiefest strength and safeguard in the loyal hearts and good-will of my subjects; and therefore I am come amongst you, as you see, at this time, not for my recreation and disport, but being resolved, in the midst and heat of the battle, to live or die amongst you all; to lay down for my God, and for my kingdom, and my people, my honour and my blood, even in the dust. I know I have the body but of a weak and feeble woman; but I have the heart and stomach of a king, and of a king of England too, and think foul scorn that [the duke of] Parma or [the king of] Spain, or any prince of Europe, should dare to invade the borders of my realm; to which rather than any dishonour shall grow by me, I myself will take up arms, I myself will be your general, judge, and rewarder of every one of your virtues in the field. I know already, for your forwardness you have deserved rewards and crowns; and We do assure you in the word of a prince, they shall be duly paid you. In the mean time, my lieutenant general shall be in my stead, than whom never prince commanded a more noble or worthy subject; not doubting but by your obedience to my general, by your concord in the camp, and your valour in the field, we shall shortly have a famous victory over those enemies of my God, of my kingdom, and of my people.

M.H. Abrams et al., eds., *The Norton Anthology of English Literature*. New York: W.W. Norton, 1993, p. 999.

Document 19: "To the Memory of . . . William Shakespeare."

The pervasiveness of classical culture in late Renaissance England is quite evident in Ben Jonson's eulogistic poem for Shakespeare written in 1621, five years after Shakespeare's death. As scholars have long noted, Jonson's remark about Shakespeare's "small Latin and less Greek" should be taken with a grain of salt. Shakespeare almost certainly had eight or more years of Latin study, as well as a passing acquaintance with Greek.

TO THE MEMORY OF MY BELOVED,
THE AUTHOR MR. WILLIAM SHAKESPEARE:
AND WHAT HE HATH LEFT US

To draw no envy (Shakespeare) on thy name,
Am I thus ample to thy book, and fame:

While I confess thy writings to be such,
    As neither Man, nor Muse, can praise too much.
'Tis true, and all men's suffrage. But these ways   5
    Were not the paths I meant unto thy praise:
For seeliest ignorance on these may light,
    Which, when it sounds at best, but echoes right;
Or blind affection, which doth ne'er advance
    The truth, but gropes, and urgeth all by chance;   10
Or crafty malice might pretend this praise,
    And think to ruin, where it seemed to raise.
These are, as some infamous bawd or whore,
    Should praise a matron. What could hurt her more?
But thou art proof against them, and indeed   15
    Above the ill fortune of them, or the need.
I, therefore will begin. Soul of the age!
    The applause! delight! the wonder of our stage!
My Shakespeare, rise; I will not lodge thee by
    Chaucer or Spenser, or bid Beaumont lie   20
A little further, to make thee a room:
    Thou art a monument without a tomb,
And art alive still, while thy book doth live,
    And we have wits to read, and praise to give.
That I not mix thee so, my brain excuses;   25
    I mean with great, but disproportioned muses:
For, if I thought my judgment were of years,
    I should commit thee surely with thy peers,
And tell, how far thou didst our Lyly outshine,
    Or sporting Kyd, or Marlowe's mighty line.   30
And though thou hadst small Latin and less Greek,
    From thence to honor thee, I would not seek
For names; but call forth thundering Aeschylus,
    Euripides, and Sophocles to us,
Paccuvius, Accius, him of Cordova dead,   35
    To life again, to hear thy buskin tread,
And shake a stage: Or, when thy socks were on,
    Leave thee alone, for the comparison
Of all that insolent Greece or haughty Rome
    Sent forth, or since did from their ashes come.   40
Triumph, by Britain, thou hast one to show,
    To whom all scenes of Europe homage owe.
He was not of an age, but for all time!
    And all the muses still were in their prime,

When like Apollo he came forth to warm   45
   Our ears, or like a Mercury to charm!
Nature herself was proud of his designs,
   And joyed to wear the dressing of his lines!
Which were so richly spun and woven so fit,
   As, since, she will vouchsafe no other Wit.   50
The merry Greek, tart Aristophanes,
   Neat Terence, witty Plautus, now not please;
But antiquated, and deserted lie
   As they were not of nature's family.
Yet must I not give nature all: thy art,   55
   My gentle Shakespeare, must enjoy a part,
For though the poet's matter, nature be,
   His art doth give the fashion. And, that he,
Who casts to write a living line, must sweat
   (Such as thine are), and strike the second heat   60
Upon the muses' anvil: turn the same
   (And himself with it), that he thinks to frame;
Or for the laurel, he may gain a scorn,
   For a good poet's made, as well as born.
And such wert thou. Look how the father's face   65
   Lives in his issue; even so, the race
Of Shakespeare's mind, and manners brightly shines
   In his well turned, and true-filed lines:
In each of which, he seems to shake a lance,
   As brandished at the eyes of ignorance.   70
Sweet Swan of Avon! what a sight it were
   To see thee in our waters yet appear,
And make those flights upon the banks of Thames,
   That so did take Eliza and our James!
But stay, I see thee in the hemisphere   75
   Advanced and made a constellation there!
Shine forth, thou star of poets, and with rage
   Or influence, chide, or cheer the drooping stage;
Which, since thy flight from hence, hath mourned like night,
   And despairs day, but for thy volume's light.   80

TO SHAKESPEARE

5 *suffrage:* vote. 7 *seeliest:* most foolish and naive. 20: They are buried in Westminster Abbey; Shakespeare, in Stratford. The lines refer to an epitaph by William Basse. 28 *commit:* place alongside. 29 *Lyly:* John Lyly (1554?–1606), author of such romantic come-

dies as *Endymion*. 30 *sporting:* ironically punning on "Kyd"; for he was melodramatic. *Kyd:* Thomas Kyd (1558–1594), author of *The Spanish Tragedy*. 31: An often misread line, it means only that he did not frequently imitate Roman and Greek authors as did so many of his contemporaries. Note ll. 33–36. 35 *Paccuvius, Accius:* Roman writers of tragedy. *him:* Seneca, author of revenge tragedies. 36 *buskin:* the boot signifying tragedy. 37 *shake a stage:* punning on his name; see also "shake a lance" (1. 69). *socks:* the shoes signifying comedy. 46 *Mercury:* inventor of the lyre. 57 *matter:* subject matter. 76. *constellation:* Cygnus, the Swan.

John T. Shawcross and Ronald David Emma, eds., *Seventeenth Century English Poetry*. Philadelphia: J.B. Lippincott, 1969, pp. 132–34.

Chronology

1341 Petrarch, the first great humanist, crowned poet laureate in Rome.

1353 Boccaccio, founder of Italian prose, publishes the *Decameron*.

c.1387 Chaucer writes *The Canterbury Tales*.

1397 The study of Greek literature initiated at University of Florence.

c.1400 Humanism begins to flourish in Italian city-states.

1433 Prince Henry the Navigator begins exploring the coast of Africa.

1434 Accession to power of the Medici family in Florence, Italy.

1436 Alberti writes first treatise on theory of painting.

1440 The scholar Valla writes exposé of the *Donation of Constantine*.

1453 Fall of Constantinople; many Greek scholars come to Italy.

1455 Gutenberg Bible published using movable type; printing revolution begins.

1462 The Platonic Academy founded in Florence.

1470 Ficino completes first Latin translation of Plato's *Dialogues*.

1482 Ficino, *The Platonic Theology*, formulates Neoplatonic philosophy.

1483 Leonardo da Vinci completes *Virgin of the Rocks*.

c. 1485 Botticelli completes *Birth of Venus*.

1486 Pico completes *Oration on the Dignity of Man*.

1490 The prolific Aldine press established at Venice.

1492 Christopher Columbus discovers the New World.

1498 Leonardo da Vinci completes *The Last Supper.*

1503 Art patron Julius II becomes pope.

1504 Michelangelo completes his sculpture of *David.*

1505 Leonardo da Vinci completes *The Mona Lisa.*

1507 Violent death of Cesare Borgia.

1509 Erasmus publishes *The Praise of Folly*, making him the most famous European writer; Henry VIII becomes king of England.

1511–1513 Raphael paints *The School of Athens* and *The Sistine Madonna.*

1512 Michelangelo completes the Sistine Chapel ceiling.

1513 Machiavelli publishes *The Prince* whose main character is modeled on Cesare Borgia; Leo X, son of Lorenzo de Medici, becomes pope.

1513–1514 Artist Albrecht Dürer completes *Knight, St. Jerome*, and *Melancholia I.*

1514 Copernicus publishes the first theory of the solar system.

1516 Sir Thomas More completes *Utopia*; Erasmus's Greek edition of the New Testament published.

1517 Martin Luther posts his 95 Theses to begin the Reformation.

1519 Cortez invades Mexico.

1521 Luther refuses to recant and is excommunicated; Magellan crosses the Pacific Ocean.

1524–1525 Peasants' revolts in Germany and Austria are crushed by the nobility.

1525 William Tyndale translates the New Testament into English.

1527 Rome is sacked by troops of the Holy Roman Empire.

1528 Castiglione completes *The Courtier.*

1534 Rabelais completes *Gargantua*; Luther translates the Bible into German.

1535 Sir Thomas More beheaded for treason.

1536 John Calvin completes *Institutes of the Christian Religion*; death of Erasmus; his books banned by Catholic Church.

1540 Loyola's Society of Jesus (the Jesuits) approved by Pope Paul III.

1541 Michelangelo finishes *The Last Judgment* in the Sistine Chapel.

1543 Publication of Copernicus's *On the Revolution of Celestial Spheres*; publication of Vesalius's *On the Structure of the Human Body.*

1545–1563 The Council of Trent, start of the Counter-Reformation.

1555 Peace of Augsburg divides Germany into Protestant and Catholic areas.

1558 Elizabeth I becomes Queen of England, rules until 1603; Marguerite de Navarre, *Heptameron.*

1564 Death of Calvin and Michelangelo; birth of Shakespeare and Galileo.

1580 Michel de Montaigne, *Essays.*

1580–1640 Peak period for witchcraft trials.

1588 Defeat of the Spanish Armada against England; Christopher Marlowe completes *Doctor Faustus.*

1595 Shakespeare completes *A Midsummer Night's Dream.*

1596 Sir Edmund Spenser completes *The Faerie Queene.*

1597 Sir Francis Bacon completes *Essays.*

1600 Shakespeare completes *Hamlet*.

1605 Cervantes completes *Don Quixote*; Bacon completes *Advancement of Learning*.

1610 Galileo announces his telescopic discoveries.

1611 King James translation of the Bible into English; Shakespeare completes *The Tempest*.

1616 Catholic Church declares Copernican theory "false and erroneous."

1618–1648 The Thirty Years' War.

1633 Galileo condemned by the Inquisition.

1667 John Milton, last great Renaissance poet, publishes *Paradise Lost*.

For Further Research

Collections of Original Documents of the Renaissance

Kenneth J. Atchity, ed., *The Renaissance Reader*. New York: Harper-Collins Publishers, 1996.

Kenneth R. Barlett, ed., *The Civilization of the Italian Renaissance*. Lexington, MA: D.C. Heath, 1992.

Ernst Cassirer et al., eds., *The Renaissance Philosophy of Man*. Chicago: University of Chicago Press, 1948.

G.R. Elton, ed., *Renaissance and Reformation: 1300–1648*. 3rd ed., New York: Macmillan, 1976.

David Englander et al., eds., *Culture and Belief in Europe 1450–1600: An Anthology of Sources*. Oxford: Basil Blackwell, 1990.

Paul F. Grendler, ed., *An Italian Renaissance Reader*. Toronto: University of Toronto Press, 1992.

John Hollander and Frank Kermode, eds., *The Literature of Renaissance England*. New York: Oxford University Press, 1973.

Gerald M. Pinciss and Roger Lockyer, eds., *Shakespeare's World: Background Readings in the English Renaissance*. New York: Continuum, 1990.

Surveys of Western European Civilization

Norman Davies, *Europe: A History*. New York: HarperCollins, 1998.

Robert E. Lerner et al., *Western Civilizations: Their History and Their Culture*. Vol. 1. 13th ed. New York: W.W. Norton, 1998.

J.M. Roberts, *A History of Europe*. New York: Allen Lane, 1997.

Richard Tarnas, *The Passion of the Western Mind*. New York: Harmony Books, 1991.

Studies of the European Renaissance

Margaret Aston, *The Panorama of the Renaissance*. New York: Harry N. Abrams, 1996.

Alison Brown, *The Renaissance*. New York: Addison-Wesley, 1990.

Gloria K. Fiero, *On the Threshold of Modernity: The Renaissance and the Reformation*. Dubuque, IA: Wm. C. Brown Communications, 1992.

John R. Hale, *Renaissance*. New York: Time-Life Books, 1965.

George Holmes, *Renaissance*. New York: St. Martin's Press, 1996.

Charles G. Nauert Jr., *The Age of Renaissance and Reformation*. Lanham, MD: University Press of America, 1981.

Lewis W. Spitz, *The Renaissance and Reformation Movements*. Vol. 1. Revised ed. St. Louis: Concordia Publishing House, 1987.

Bard Thompson, *Humanists and Reformers: A History of the Renaissance and Reformation*. Grand Rapids, MI: Eerdmans, 1996.

Social and Religious Contexts of the Renaissance

E.R. Chamberlin, *Everyday Life in Renaissance Times*. London: B.T. Batsford, 1965.

Karl H. Dannenfeldt, *The Church of the Renaissance and Reformation*. St. Louis: Concordia Publishing House, 1970.

A.G. Dickens, *Reformation and Society in Sixteenth-Century Europe*. New York: Harcourt, Brace & World, 1966.

Carlo Ginzburg, *The Cheese and the Worms: The Cosmos of a Sixteenth-Century Miller*. Trans. John and Anne Tedeschi. New York: Penguin, 1982.

De Lamar Jensen, *Reformation Europe: Age of Reform and Revolution*. Lexington, MA: D.C. Heath, 1981.

Margaret L. King, *Women of the Renaissance*. Chicago: University of Chicago Press, 1991.

Brian P. Levack, *The Witch-Hunt in Early Modern Europe*. 2nd ed. New York: Longman, 1995.

Charles G. Nauert Jr., *Humanism and the Culture of Renaissance Europe*. Cambridge, U.K.: Cambridge University Press, 1995.

Steven Ozment, *Protestants: The Birth of a Revolution*. New York: Doubleday, 1991.

———, *When Fathers Ruled: Family Life in Reformation Europe*. Cambridge, MA: Harvard University Press, 1983.

Eugene F. Rice Jr., *The Foundations of Early Modern Europe, 1460–1559*. New York: W.W. Norton, 1970.

Merry E. Wiesner, *Women and Gender in Early Modern Europe*. Cambridge, U.K.: Cambridge University Press, 1993.

Renaissance Science and Exploration

Marie Boas, *The Scientific Renaissance: 1450–1630*. New York: Harper & Row, 1966.

J.H. Elliott, *The Old World and the New. 1492–1650*. Cambridge, U.K.: Cambridge University Press, 1970.

J.R. Hale, *Renaissance Exploration*. New York: W.W. Norton, 1972.

Thomas S. Kuhn, *The Copernican Revolution*. Cambridge, MA: Harvard University Press, 1957.

Kirkpatrick Sale, *The Conquest of Paradise: Christopher Columbus and the Columbian Legacy*. New York: Penguin, 1991.

The Italian Renaissance

Jacob Burckhardt, *The Civilization of the Renaissance in Italy*. 3rd ed. London: Phaidon, 1995.

Peter Burke, *The Italian Renaissance: Culture and Society in Italy*. Rev. ed. Cambridge, U.K.: Polity Press, 1987.

E.R. Chamberlin, *The World of the Italian Renaissance*. London: G. Allen Unwin, 1982.

Bruce Cole, *Italian Art, 1250–1550: The Relation of Renaissance Art to Life and Society*. New York: Harper & Row, 1987.

Denys Hay, *The Italian Renaissance in Its Historical Background*. 2nd ed. Cambridge, U.K.: Cambridge University Press, 1977.

Michael Levey, *High Renaissance*. Baltimore: Penguin, 1991.

J.H. Plumb, *The Italian Renaissance*. New York: American Heritage, 1985.

The Northern Renaissance

Alexander Leggatt, *English Drama: Shakespeare to the Restoration, 1590–1660*. New York: Longman, 1988.

I.D. McFarlane, *Renaissance France, 1470–1589*. New York: Barnes & Noble, 1974.

Margaret Mann Phillips, *Erasmus and the Northern Renaissance*. Rev. ed. Totowa, NJ: Rowman & Littlefield, 1981.

James Snyder, *Northern Renaissance Art*. New York: Abrams, 1985.

Gary Waller, *English Poetry of the Sixteenth Century*. Rev. 2nd ed. New York: Longman, 1993.

Index